THE INNOVATIVE SPIRIT

CHANGE IN HIGHER EDUCATION

Algo D. Henderson

THE
INNOVATIVE
SPIRIT

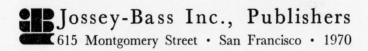

Jossey-Bass Inc., Publishers
615 Montgomery Street · San Francisco · 1970

THE INNOVATIVE SPIRIT
Change in Higher Education
Algo D. Henderson

Copyright © 1970 by Jossey-Bass, Inc., Publishers

Copyright under Pan American and
Universal Copyright Conventions

Jossey-Bass, Inc., Publishers
615 Montgomery Street
San Francisco, California 94111

Library of Congress Catalog Card Number 78-128698

International Standard Book Number ISBN 0-87589-073-3

Manufactured in the United States of America
Composed and printed by York Composition Company, Inc.
Bound by Chas. H. Bohn & Co., Inc., New York

JACKET DESIGN BY WILLI BAUM, SAN FRANCISCO

FIRST EDITION

Code 7022

THE JOSSEY-BASS SERIES IN HIGHER EDUCATION

General Editors

JOSEPH AXELROD
San Francisco State College and
University of California, Berkeley

MERVIN B. FREEDMAN
San Francisco State College and
Wright Institute, Berkeley

PREFACE

Changes in the objectives of higher education and in organization, curriculum, and teaching must be made to alleviate the stresses occurring within our technologically based society. American ideals need fresh interpretation and implementation, and our colleges and universities have a social mission to find paths toward a better life than that which has been realized amidst our affluence and our poverty. Innovation, as I use the term, has an ethical aim as well as an aim to make education effective and productive.

My concern with innovations is not new. During the twenty-two years I was at Antioch College—six as dean and thirteen as president—I was a participant in the planning of many of its adventures. As a member of the President's Commission on Higher Education in 1946–48, I joined a distinguished group of colleagues in proposing fresh goals for higher education in the United States. In New York, I helped to initiate the public community college law and the fair education practices act—the first in the nation—and to organize the state university system. This legislation reversed the historic policy of the state—which had favored elitist, private higher education —and launched a new and diversified program of public colleges and universities. I have chaired two national commissions specifically concerned with equality of opportunity in higher education. At the University of Michigan I founded the Center for the Study of Higher Education, which helped to stimulate a new movement to do research on the problems of higher education and to train fresh leadership for colleges and universities. All these experiences have colored my views.

A portion of *The Innovative Spirit* is based on studies of innovations that I have been making while a member of the staff of the Center for Research and Development in Higher Education at the University of California. Some of the chapters draw on papers and journal articles that I have published, but in such cases the content has been rewritten. The journals include *Administrative Law Review, The Antioch Review, Educational Record, Engineering Education, Journal of Higher Education, Improving College and University Teaching,* and *NASPA Journal.*

The first two chapters of the book provide a philosophical base, the next three open both problems and challenges, and the remainder discuss many facets of higher education, first concerning programs and then concerning organization and administration.

For his criticisms of the manuscript, I want to thank Joseph Axelrod. For editorial assistance on the full manuscript, I am indebted to John Warner, and for other assistance, to Natalie Gumas, Katharine Kunst, and Norman Rae. For the typing of the several drafts of the manuscript, my thanks go to Katharine Kunst, Ann Sherman, Mildred Bowman, Rosemary Moyer, and Kate Pernish. I am also much indebted to the Center for Research and Development in Higher Education of the University of California, Berkeley, for providing the opportunity to do this research and writing, and to the director, Leland L. Medsker, as well as several senior research staff, for encouragement and, in some cases, for suggestions relating to content.

I dedicate the book to Dean Jean.

ALGO D. HENDERSON

Berkeley, California
September 1970

CONTENTS

꧁꧂꧁꧂꧁꧂꧁꧂꧁꧂꧁꧂꧁꧂꧁꧂꧁꧂꧁꧂

xi

24 *Coordinating Commissions*   *281*

    Epilogue: Toward Innovation   *293*

    Index   *303*

THE
INNOVATIVE
SPIRIT

CHANGE IN
HIGHER EDUCATION

VIEWPOINT ON EDUCATIONAL PHILOSOPHY

PART **ONE**

CHAPTER 1

BASIC ASSUMPTIONS

ͷͷͷͷͷͷͷͷͷͷͷͷͷͷͷͷͷͷͷͷͷ

Almost any discussion of what is currently happening in higher education seems to hinge upon the concept of innovation. Yet innovation is not a departure from tradition in American higher education—witness the normal school for training public school teachers, the land grant college system, the elective plan for the liberal arts, the complex university, the public community college. One might also mention general education, audiovisual aids in teaching, study abroad, and a shifting focus in medical education from curing disease to keeping people well.

What, then, are the advocates of fresh innovations talking about? Why are students making vociferous demands for change? *The Innovative Spirit* answers these questions. It discusses change—first concerning objectives and programs in higher education and then concerning organization and control of higher education. Some stu-

3

dents and faculty are using the university as a platform from which to get attention for their ideas about social change. Such ideas should be heard. And, in the university, of all places, they should receive rational analysis. Some of the ideas are unquestionably good—as, for example, the need to reorient our values toward creative living and away from gross materialism. Perhaps the students' strategy of violence has served its purpose, that of starting a dialogue with those who make decisions. But now it is time for a thoroughgoing, rational examination of our society and our education. We are witnessing the first and painful stages in the emergence of postindustrial society. This book takes some account of social change, but its focus is on higher education.

I make one tacit assumption: that social change is a means of achieving the democratic ideal. As I see it, democratic ideology assumes a social organization which enables the individual and the social interests to be most nearly reconciled for the optimum advantage of both. Because freedom for the individual is found within the context of social organization, this ideal is at a midpoint between the extremes of individualism and of authoritarian domination. The midpoint is not static but shifts as the need for the balancing of interests becomes evident. Such a concept of social organization is basic to the philosophy of education which I now examine.

The function of higher education in a democracy rests on certain premises concerning the fulfillment of individual and societal needs. A basic premise is that each individual, regardless of his race, color, creed, or social class, should have the opportunity to develop to the full extent of his potentialities, to learn how to live as fully as possible. Democracy assumes the individuality and the dignity of man. A second premise is that every person should have the opportunity to prepare himself to the best of his ability to make a living. In a democracy each individual has a free choice of vocation, be it as home manager, factory worker, electrician, doctor, or scientist. Democracy is characterized by the absence of an idle or privileged class, and therefore everyone, ideally, derives his income from his work.

From the perspective of societal needs, a democratic society should develop its human resources as fully as possible. But we in the United States are far from identifying and cultivating the potential talents and abilities of our people. For the continued growth of our economy, we will have to depend more upon the development of the knowledge and skills of our people than upon any other factor—than upon our natural resources, for instance. To achieve additional productivity and distinguished achievement in the arts, in the sciences, and in social organization and administration, we must discover and nurture the best talents of all of our young people in these areas, again regardless of their social origins, and we must encourage our young people to educate themselves appropriately.

Our society must also work toward the solution of the problems which confront it and toward the realization of the good life. Looking back over any reasonable length of time—one hundred years, one thousand years, ten thousand years—one can readily see the remarkable progress that men have made in the development of civilization. It is amazing that we have come so far in so short a time. I hope that this march of progress will continue, but with the weapons now in the hands of men and the apparent lack of concern of many of our leaders about the consequences of using those weapons, civilization could easily destroy itself or at least set back its progress for many decades, if not centuries. The method of achieving a better society lies in substantial part in attacking and attempting to solve the major problems that exist today. The effort to solve these problems should be made not only by those who are on the firing line in diplomatic, administrative, and scientific posts but equally by those who are educating our students for these purposes—through intensive research and through relating the whole educational process to human beings and how they live.

This philosophy of education contrasts sharply with that based upon the monastic heritage of universities. That philosophy visualized the university as an ivy-covered tower within which finite and authoritarian dictates about the world and the good life were taught and studied. Also, only those who were considered to have the ambition and social background needed to make good were allowed into the hallowed halls. The impact of science considerably modified the effectiveness of this approach to learning, but the attitude of seclusion remained. Now, because man has sufficient intellectual tools to plan for the good society, the goals of education should be to discover and cultivate our human resources and to apply these resources to the further advance of civilization. The implications of this change in philosophy are far reaching, for the new theory involves the concept of social investment in education.

In a democratic society, the full development of human resources comes through fostering the best vocational adjustment and all-round physical, intellectual, and spiritual growth of all individuals. Likewise, the enterprise, the cooperative endeavors, and the organized planning and actions of people toward overcoming social ills and toward progressing in industrial, artistic, ethical, and other areas are means of obtaining the fullest possible life for all individuals. Under this philosophy, the welfare of individual people is the primary consideration. The state, like any other organized community of people, is a means through which to attempt to achieve the best life for the individuals who constitute it. We can see the principle working well in the planning of such projects as the Tennessee Valley Authority and our national highway system; but we have blind spots in such areas as education and medicine.

How do some of the problems of concern to the individual and society relate specifically to the problem of higher education? Consistent with the premises stated, there are two phases to the student's problem. One phase is to define the career for which he should prepare and to get good preparation for it. The other phase is to prepare himself for other aspects of his life, including his use of leisure time, his family life, his work within his community, and his responsibilities as a member of organized society. These areas are important to the individual because he derives his major satisfactions from them. He gets satisfaction from earning a good living, from being alert to and from understanding the events of the world, from developing his ability to participate with other people in productive and creative work. He derives satisfaction from his hobbies and avocational activities, from participation in his family life, and from joining with others in seeking social reforms. A wise person once said to me that a person gains happiness in activities when he is successful. Higher education must find ways to start the individual from wherever he is in motivation and knowledge and then to lead him toward higher ideals. In theory, education should help the individual to learn the best and most satisfying way of making a living, to understand the events in his environment, to appreciate artistic endeavors and scientific discoveries, to participate successfully in his family life; it should teach him how to use his free time to get the greatest personal satisfaction from it and how to perform effectively his role as a participant or leader in community, national, and international affairs.

The freedom of the individual to create a good life for himself

BASIC ASSUMPTIONS   7

depends in part upon whether his environment—the society of which
he is a member—is conducive to his effort. Higher education has a
responsibility to help create this environment—that is, the good society. While attempting to realize this general goal, however, we meet
numerous specific problems, some of which are unusually urgent today.
William James described our stream of consciousness as composed of
successive perchings and flights. Social progress is similarly made by
successive perchings and flights. At certain times problems loom so
large or opinions and emotions become so polarized that one's belief
in progress falters. But at other times we feel the exhilaration and con-
tentment that come from successfully solving great issues.

   Some of the serious and urgent problems that face us today are
all too obvious. At this point I speak of them in a comprehensive way;
in other chapters I am more specific. To begin, there are the relations
between people on the international scene. People who are dependent
upon each other for the production of necessary goods and services
must discover how to participate and work effectively together for the
good of the whole. Our social fabric is composed of people of all races,
cultures, and religions. They have their own personalities and the
dignity shared by all men. Yet prejudice and discrimination on grounds
of race, creed, and color are widespread and deeply ingrained. We
must learn to free ourselves from racism because it is a terrible blight
on society. We who are white must free ourselves from the myth of
white superiority; the only tenable relationship with the nonwhite
people of the world is one of fully mutual respect and goodwill. Thus,
we need revisions in our social order, but they should be the result of
rational analysis and decision, lest we merely create more problems.

   The last two wars and subsequent events have made it clear
that the peoples of the world are so interdependent that some overall
world organization is necessary for the general welfare of mankind.
One of the essentials for international understanding and world organization is the evolution of common ethical concepts and standards.
The ethics of the Judeo-Christian heritage and the democratic ideals
of Western Europe and America commend themselves. But other codes
of ethics and ideologies also exist, and it is necessary to work toward
a common pattern of values which recognizes and includes them. As
intelligent, wisdom-seeking people, we should also be searching all
histories and cultures for greater wisdom. The day of provincialism
in ideas and attitudes is past. It may appear forbiddingly difficult to

fuse all knowledge, but the necessity for doing so is one of the major challenges to intellectual effort today.

Atomic energy has brought to the people of the twentieth century a new power many thousands of times greater than any previously available. The nations must find an international means of controlling its use, and we must learn how to harness this great energy with economy of operation for industrial, transportation, and other constructive uses. Although the threat of the atomic bomb causes men to recoil in horror from further world wars, the prosecution of war in Vietnam has awakened the American people to the immorality of any war and to the risk to our democracy from the growing military-industrial power. We must raise the question Why at this stage of civilization is war still used in the settlement of disputes?

There are still great inequities in the economic life of our free society. We must therefore learn how to distribute our economic resources to maintain employment and purchasing power for the masses of the people and how to control the malfunctions in the economic system, such as inflation and depression, without regimentation of enterprise. An industrial machine has been developed that supplies us with goods, conveniences, and services in abundance. We are not yet at the end of our material advancement, even though great material success has already been achieved. However, managing the economy in the interests of the people remains a problem of worldwide significance.

Perhaps the most challenging problem of all—and one of special interest to higher education—is to learn how to use our material means as a base from which to create fine art, music, and literature. Because of increased leisure time, countless additional persons have the opportunity to develop their creative talents. From the social viewpoint, it is time we diverted some portion of our talents away from the production of convenience gadgets toward the creation of treasures of lasting value.

The United States cannot consider its job well done until it has found some way to make the benefits of our material well-being accessible to all people, until we value the welfare of people above materialism, until our creative and intellectual endeavors have enduring value for the future, and until we live in peaceful understanding with all people. This description may sound like an unrealistic dream, but it is the business of higher education to be visionary and to work toward ideals.

Because advances in civilization are made only as knowledge becomes available and wisdom is gained, the twofold role of education —specifically higher education—becomes clear: discovering knowledge and assisting individuals to learn. In putting it this way, I am acknowledging the traditional role of the university. The institutions of higher education have been failing in another sense, however. In part they have been failing by concentrating on the periphery of specialized knowledge, thus not advancing the general knowledge needed to resolve the comprehensive problems and issues I have been describing. They have also been failing by refusing to become involved at stress points in society where people feel most oppressed. And they have been failing by viewing the dissemination of knowledge as sufficient; unfortunately dissemination is not necessarily education.

It has frequently been stated that a basic function of a college is to transmit the cultural heritage from one generation to another. In a sense this is true because the cultural heritage is our source of wisdom. It comprises the accumulated experience of men in the past, and learning about it enables men today to start where others have left off. The essential difference between men and animals, with respect to intelligence, is that men have the capacity to learn from the experiences of other men; thus they do not have to repeat these experiences in order to possess the knowledge that comes from them. The cultural heritage, therefore, is not to be transmitted for its own sake—although admittedly esthetic and other values result from such transmission. The real use to be made of the wisdom of the past is to apply it to living in the present and to planning progress in the future. Thus, a college needs to focus on the present rather than on the past, even though it uses the accumulated knowledge of the past. For example, perspectives relating to values, good and bad, are noticeably changing. Values should be accepted not because they have survived or seem authoritative but because they relate to perceptions of the good life.

The argument for relevance can, of course, lead to extremes by giving rise to purely utilitarian courses of study. Following World War I, this argument resulted in the creation of schools and colleges with specialized curricula, the dominant characteristic of which was applied knowledge. There was a great outburst of new schools of business, of journalism, of engineering, of education, and so forth, and these schools are still developing and attracting huge enrollments. In addition, there is the growth of two-year programs following high school; most of the graduates of these schools seek jobs rather than broader education. There is a genuine need for these vocational and professional programs. Some professional schools—such as schools of law, medicine, and the ministry—have been with us a long time. It is only natural in our modern technological society, with its great increase in number and types of professions and occupations, that other schools and colleges be established to educate people for new fields of work. From the viewpoint of a democratic society, however, it is a mistake to give training that is too narrow in its purpose. It is also a mistake to have, at the same time, other schools and colleges whose faculties disclaim any vocational implications of the subject matter they teach. Individual students usually do not attend both kinds of schools, and thus they fail to get the advantages of both kinds of education. Even when they do experience both kinds, much of the value is lost because of the absence of any demonstrated relationship between the two.

Although I advocate that the liberal arts college be concerned with the vocational adjustment of students, I also believe that the primary objectives of the liberal arts college should relate to broad social purposes. Liberal education should prepare potential leaders in society, persons who have good historical perspective, who are trained to observe critically the functioning of contemporary society, and who have a broad understanding of social dynamics. Such persons, because of their education, can be helpful in planning and directing the process of social change. Theirs is essentially the intellectual and rational approach, and their intelligence and effort should be used to forward the progress of civilization.

Although we have had a rapid development of vocationalized curricula since World War I, we have been retarded in developing studies and experiences that prepare students with intellectual and social skills for fruitful planning and living. Today many youth are more interested in gaining competencies for constructive services in their communities than they are in acquiring occupational skills. Skill in social planning is an example of such a competency. Such skills for social action are a dimension that has been much neglected in education.

We have entered an era when human relationships have become complex and interdependent. Furthermore, the discoveries of science have had profound significance for education: they have released men from fetters of ignorance, superstition, and fear, and they have shown that men can, in part at least, be the masters of their own destiny. This mastery is the mark of the free man, and it becomes possible because of man's ability to analyze problems and to join with other people in making dependable plans for overcoming these problems. The rapid acceleration of civilization during recent decades has been attributable to more than the natural process of evolution; it is in some part the result of having men lift themselves by their own boot straps. That is, men have been learning how to draw upon the accumulated wisdom of the past to plan their courses of action in the future.

Men, however, are still in the infancy period with respect to their ability to plan for further social progress. I speak here essentially about intellectual development and about how we can help discover additional social skills. A horse is a horse wherever it may be, but a man has a choice: He may live in a state of bare subsistence (as do the Eskimos, we are told). Or he may design television equipment, skyscrapers, and spaceships; organize and administer corporations, community organization, and government; conquer poverty and disease; and create fine drama, poetry, and music. Men can develop the capacity and the techniques for harnessing for constructive purposes the explosive forces they have released in the twentieth century.

CHAPTER 2

EXPERIENCE AS
A FACTOR

Experience as a means of educating the individual is gaining recognition on several fronts. The cooperative work-and-study plan has been extended widely through governmental encouragement in economic-opportunity programs. Study-abroad plans are now available at hundreds of colleges. Certain law and other professional schools are providing community experiences for their students. Some medical schools are bringing clinical experience into the first year of study, where it is interrelated with basic theory. Several student groups—notably Asians, Chicanos, and blacks—are motivated to perform social services and to act as civic leaders in their own communities, partly for the purpose of making their education more relevant. College students everywhere are insisting on participation in decision making, and this too is educative.

EXPERIENCE AS A FACTOR

Some of the newer educational methods emphasize personal experience. Examples are programmed learning and individualized study, in which students can design their own study plans and forge ahead on their own. These methods are in contrast with the passive methods that dominate most college teaching.

While guiding the efforts of one institution—Antioch College —in its use of experience as an educating medium, I formulated an experience philosophy with five broad objectives: to subject the student to certain personal disciplines and to many stimulations which help mold his character, develop his personality, and accelerate his learning; to assist the student in his exploration for the best vocational choice; to give the student practical training intertwined with theory in preparation for his life's work; to cause the student to observe contemporary society, critically assess its strengths and its weaknesses, and thereby acquire a motivation for study and a basis for comprehending the wisdom of the past; and to train the student to learn better how to couple thought with action. In 1944, in the book *Vitalizing Liberal Education,* I summarized this philosophy as one which could

> use experience as one of the primary methods in developing the whole personality, which includes increasing the ability to think effectively and to couple the thinking of the individual with his acting and living. The aim is to make the learning process more genuine, more meaningful to the student, and to teach him how to make his thinking on social problems applicable to the culture in which he lives.[1]

The reason for turning to a more dynamic intellectual experience than that which commonly prevails in the colleges is that much of our education is noneducative. Passing knowledge from master to pupil sounds like a good method. But knowledge must be assimilated as a way of thinking and behaving or it will shortly be dissipated. The inadequacy of our methods is all too apparent in the living patterns of our alumni. Education does not occur unless the individual changes and grows. The graduate should have become a different person from the entering student: an individual who has gained the freedom to live by rational principles rather than by the press of his social environ-

---

[1] Algo D. Henderson, *Vitalizing Liberal Education* (New York: Harper & Row, Publishers, 1944), p. 117.

ment and who has achieved intellectual competence in problem solving. This goal is one of the factors involved in the student demands for relevance in education.

However, not all experience is educative. Experience can be either educative or miseducative. John Dewey made this distinction clear. He called miseducative those experiences which engender callousness and lack of sensitivity and responsiveness.[2] These effects inhibit the process of self-control, and self-control is a mark of the free man. I would add that experience can also be miseducative when it closes the door to exploration or is antisocial rather than social in influence. The former occurs, for example, when a group disciplines its members in obedience to a closed ideology; the latter occurs when motivations and methods are primarily egocentric rather than directed toward the good of mankind.

As an example of miseducative experience, I am reminded of my own experience in joining a legal fraternity at a state university. I was flattered by the invitation and failed to examine the group carefully before accepting. The fraternity, I soon learned, housed one of the two leading political gangs on the campus—and I use the word *gang* because the group was using all of the tricks of machine politics. This practical experience in campus politics taught the participants much more than did their courses in political science, but much of what was learned was antisocial. The skills learned were carried over into community and state action. My memory of this experience influenced my later effort at Antioch College to provide a structure for student participation in decision making that would be socially constructive and educative—the Antioch community government plan.

While presenting the rationale for experience as an educational method, I should like to make a point about the generation gap. We are now aware that a sizeable portion of our youth has become alienated—alienated from the older generation and alienated from society. Almost certainly a contributing factor, possibly a determining one, has been the segregation of youth in our society. Segregation lessens communication and polarizes goals and, hence, alienates. I am old enough to have experienced the single room school, to have worked with my father at farm chores and field work, and to have spent time

---

[2] John Dewey, *Experience and Education* (New York: The Macmillan Company, Publishers, 1950).

at meals and on weekends in youth-adult conversation and interaction. A vertical integration of the living-learning experiences between youths and older people was the dominant characteristic in those days. But this situation has changed. The family and the social pattern are now composed of horizontally separated age groups. From early childhood on, the child of today runs with his crowd, is taught in mass groups of the same age, accepts little responsibility for helping run the home, and spends his free time watching television programs, many of which are attuned to his age. Thus he progresses in growth as one of a mass, everyone having the same experiences and everyone being subjected so largely to the conditioning of his own immature social group. As a result, we have a learning situation in which the immature teaches the immature. The vertical inflow of ideas, attitudes, and skill techniques is minimal.

This situation is not entirely bad. The break in continuity between generations produces mobility and flexibility. Youth become sophisticated in their own ways and come forward with some fresh ideas. They learn to avoid authoritative types of indoctrination. Their return to a more natural way of living, for example, is the result of observing the stuffiness, lack of color, and inhibited ways of their elders. They have an opportunity to stand off and look at the competitive greed, the pollutions, the wastage of natural resources, and the inhuman sacrifices of youth to the god of war, and their observation has resulted in a confrontation that augurs well for reform. But the impatience, the demands, the resort to violence are the products of inexperience. These tactics seem very similar to those used by the spoiled child to get his own way. They fail to take account of the nature of a social organism—that it is a whole and not merely a composition of discrete and disparate parts. Social engineering is required if change is to be effected.

The essence of the social problem is communication. Youth are growing up and going through college without having genuine communication with the older generation. Colleges that teach students in mass groups, in ivy-clad seclusion, and without the benefit of out-of-class dialogue between students and professors contribute to the horizontal segregation. Learning, to be genuine, must be individual, and it must be personally experienced. The experiences must include those that build bridges of communication.

Referring again to the five objectives listed at the outset, I should like to elaborate upon each of them. The first objective that I mentioned has to do with personal growth. The vast majority of students who enter college do so in their immediately postadolescent years. They remain for a period that has high potentiality for personal growth. The educational methods of many schools—methods that treat students as children, regulate their lives, force them into curricular patterns which fail to take account of their previous achievements or for which they do not have motivation, subject them to explicative and didactic forms of teaching, and in general make decisions that are "good for them"—tend to prolong immaturity and delay the development of initiative, independent reasoning, and the ability to assume responsibility. The formation of the best qualities of character is delayed at the very time when young people have the most potential for development. College should be a period for the tempering of character, and this tempering happens best in the forge of experience. Through individualized experience the student learns how to meet and define problems, wrestles with solutions, makes decisions, and lives with those decisions as they are tested and examined by others. A person learns how to reason by practicing reasoning, to take initiative by taking initiative, and to assume responsibility through continuous practice in assuming it.

Embedded in the idea of how people develop their latent abilities is an assumption that is also basic to the concept of experience. The assumption is that men develop their capacities in relation to the number, variety, and intensity of the stimulations that they receive. To provide the optimum rate of learning, these stimulations should be applied in a sequence in which one experience builds upon another rather than a manner that overwhelms the individual. The principles of curriculum design (which I shall discuss later) apply here. In an earlier observation I have given the illustration that the difference in intellectual power between an Eskimo and the scientist can be accounted for by the stimulations they respectively have received. The purpose of college, then, should be to subject the student to many varied and intense stimulations. Intellectual stimulation is one—number one—but it is only one type. Others can be provided through experiences of the sort which I have described in the first paragraph of this chapter.

As for the second objective, assisting the student in exploring for the best vocation, I have already mentioned the interrelationship that should exist between vocational and cultural education. Horace Kallen summarized this interrelationship with a pungent phrase: "The root of culture is vocation; the fruit of vocation is culture, alike in the institutions of society and the personal life."[3] It is in the social interest to have good vocational choices made. It is equally in the individual interest, and college is the best time to do this. One of the objectives of the distribution plan in liberal arts is to require the student to sample subject matter from each of several major areas of knowledge. Clearly this is a helpful objective—providing that the student senses the purpose and value of this sampling and is sufficiently motivated to undertake it. The student, however, is not confronted with the reality of vocation until he has made tentative choices and tried them out. Through the trial-and-error process he discovers more clearly his interests and aptitudes as well as his potential for success. He should have this kind of experience not following graduation from college but early in his college career so that he can select courses of study that relate to his vocational interests. It is extremely frustrating for the individual and wasteful socially for persons to decide upon their lifetime careers only after leaving college.

There is another consideration of high importance. In choosing a vocation the student decides on a career for a lifetime, but career opportunities change as a result of technological advances and other factors. An effort should therefore be made during the college years, by the student and his counselors, to uncover fresh opportunities that appear to have potential for interesting careers and that will make more than the usual contributions to society. College programs tend to emphasize subject matter that is well established and areas of human endeavor that are well advanced. The student, however, should seek to understand the forces of change and to anticipate what the changes will bring. Experiences off the campus, wisely guided, can bring the student into intimate contact with persons who are at the exploring, changing frontier of knowledge and practice. The findings of the student while off campus may also incidentally provide a stimulation to those professors who have become too oriented to the past.

The purpose of the third objective—causing the student to interrelate theory and practice—is to make the theory more meaningful and to illuminate the practice. In some areas of the American uni-

[3] Horace M. Kallen, *The Education of Free Men* (New York: Farrar, Straus, & Giroux, Inc., 1949), p. 307.

versity, such as in engineering and in agriculture, this principle is well understood. American engineers, for example, learn how to apply theories relating to structures in building a bridge. In India, where university students memorize principles from the textbook and data from the handbooks, they sometimes build bridges that collapse. But important as this applied objective is, there is more to it than that. When the approach in education is the memorization of foundational materials to be followed later by laboratory or other experience, much of the benefit of the earlier study is lost. It is lost because the motivation to learn has been absent and because comprehension of meaning has not really been achieved. Interweaving of the theoretical and the practical should accelerate learning and make it more lasting. It should result in a higher degree of competence in the individual.

The fourth objective—causing the student to become a keen and critical observer of his environment, of contemporary society—has relevance to much of the discussion in subsequent chapters of this book. Students need to acquire firsthand knowledge as a basis for understanding the wisdom that is derived from men's past experience. In this perspective students study history not merely to give them cultural veneer but to enable them to project their learning through problem solving after taking advantage of the knowledge that has accumulated to date. History is a narration of human experience. As such, it should be lap-welded (to use one of Charles F. Kettering's happy expressions) with the student's own experience. Here I am assuming, as I noted earlier, that the well-educated man is concerned with the social consequences of his increasing knowledge as well as with the personal satisfactions derived from it.

It is typical of men that they take their environment for granted. Most of us accommodate ourselves to our environment but do not really study it. We merely perpetuate existing mores and forms of social intercourse and hence do not question the nature and quality of our living. This hardly seems the best role for an educated man. Is this really enough recompense to society for its investment in the institutions of higher learning? Ways should be found to induce students to observe factually, to analyze problems, and to apply principles to action. Students at the doctoral level learn this methodology through their research, much of which is empirical, but the training of the student in his earlier years is very deficient. Field experiences, work experiences, travel and investigations of research problems are means of bringing about the desired exposure to real problems. Here again, one of the by-products is an increased motivation to learn, and motivation has a lot to do with the rate of learning. I believe this element in its program helps account for the quality of learning achieved by students at Antioch College—a point illustrated later.

From what I have said above, the reasoning in relation to the last objective—learning how to couple thought with action—should already be clear. I should like, however, to add an important point. One of America's most influential educators, Robert Hutchins, seems to hold the view that if a person, through the study of the best wisdom of the past, came to know the difference between right and wrong, he would know how to act in the future. I do not accept this hypothesis. Man is too much a victim of habit and of social pressures for this to be true. College needs to be more than just an accumulation of knowledge. Indeed, it needs to be more than just an intellectual awakening. The student may achieve both of these and still retrogress after leaving college, because his knowledge is a veneer and has not become the basis for living. The universities of Great Britain in the nineteenth century made a great point of producing men with a cultural veneer. But these men, coming from the social elite, continued to live as cultural parasites in a society that was founded upon a hierarchy of inherited privilege. This type of education today could be the cause of revolution. But to return to my main point: Men must learn through experience the meaning of good and bad ways of living, of social and antisocial actions; they must adjust their habits of action to accord with the knowledge derived from this experience if that knowledge is to become a dynamic factor in their own lives. Unless education produces this kind of change, it is not genuine education. It is through experiencing thought in action that the change comes.

Of the several plans for student experience mentioned at the outset of this chapter, some are discussed in relation to specific topics later on in this book. Certain of them, however, need and deserve description and some limited comment at this point. The philosophy and method of cooperative work-and-study was first enunciated by Herman Schneider in 1906 at the University of Cincinnati. Thus the method is not new. What is new is the considerable spurt of interest in it. At Cincinnati, the method was first used in engineering and involved a cooperative relationship between industry and the university. The plan called for students to spend alternate periods at study in the

College of Engineering and at work on jobs. The purpose was to have students learn through apprenticeship, using industry as an extension of the laboratories at the school. The plan thus was heavily oriented toward vocational adaptation and the interweaving of theory and practice. These objectives, plus the one of helping students to earn money as a means of going to college, have continued to be important.

The work-and-study plan has been frequently identified with Antioch College, probably because Antioch gave it a broader philosophical base and used it for purposes of general education as well as for training in vocations. An original impulse of Antioch, dating from 1920, was to stimulate students to become enterprising and to learn how to create productive enterprises for their own communities. The orientation of their training was not to help them become better employees, say, of a large corporation, but rather to help them to become engaged in more broadly conceived, productive work and to make contributions toward the improvement of their communities. As time went on, and especially during the period of the Great Depression of 1933 to 1938, still broader objectives were enunciated. It should be remembered that the foundations of the economy in the United States were badly shaken at that time. There was much question about what the future of the economic system, and indeed of the society, might be. Thus the thinking of faculty and students turned toward the ills of society. The question arose: How could young people learn to diagnose the ills of contemporary society and apply to the solution of those problems the best wisdom of the past? Part of the answer was to give the other educational objectives listed above more complete definition. The work-and-study plan had been the major medium for educative experience. Now other avenues—such as a revised community government and various forms of community participation and social action —were opened. Later, study-abroad projects—not only in Europe but also in Asia, Africa, and Latin America—became a dynamic part of the program. Utilization of experience as a factor in education became a fundamental characteristic of the Antioch plan. It has remained so for fifty years, seemingly with outstanding educational results.

It was during this second period of the evolution of the concept that an extension of the work-and-study plan was made. The objective remained as already described, to cause the students to become critical observers of their environment. But the plan was implemented by asking the students, while on their jobs, to identify problems that could become the subjects of research papers to be evaluated by the academic faculty. Such a study might consider the job and the company of which it was a part, or it might focus on the community or the general geographic area in which the company was located. In some cases, comparisons of the observations and conclusions of various students became possible. For example, during the early war years the large department stores of the Midwest began to import labor from the rural South in rather large numbers. Much friction among employees and many difficulties between management and labor ensued. It was the first department store experience for those employees and, indeed, their first experience living in a metropolitan area. A large department store in St. Louis handled its problems by using disciplinary and repressive measures, while a department store in Indianapolis devised a plan to educate its new employees and help them become assimilated. The contrasting methods created different results in store morale and in employee effectiveness. Antioch had arranged for some students to work in these stores. Their reports became the basis for a fascinating analysis of human factors in personnel administration and in race relations.

A couple of other illustrations will show further how we attempted to train students to become critical observers of their job situation and of their environment. A young woman student employed as a guide at a motion picture studio in Hollywood studied the labor unions in the movie industry. She traced events through the newspapers, attended union meetings, interviewed employers, and talked with interested citizens. She brought back to the campus a thesis that gave firsthand facts and an objective analysis of all points of view. Another student was asked to write character analyses of people with whom she came in contact on her job. She was given a sequence of three jobs—in an Italian community in Connecticut, in a rural area of Tennessee, and as a psychologist's aide in a school for delinquent girls. These experiences and her study of them deepened her understanding of human beings and showed her the economic and social factors involved in the problems of depressed groups.

During the Great Depression some students entered jobs with high expectations, only to be laid off after a couple of weeks because of economic difficulties at the company. The students learned at firsthand what it means to become suddenly unemployed. This last illustration sheds some light on the mood of present disadvantaged students who come from areas where unemployment is high. Being so aware of the social problem, they become motivated to return to the ghetto for community service and potential leadership. Because they have lived in and intimately experienced the ghetto, they know the conditions and meaning of life there. They are motivated to help eradicate what they regard as a blight. This motivation leads to their demands for development of new ethnic studies programs which include field work in the community. And the students consider these demands nonnegotiable, in part because of the injustices and disadvantages still being suffered by their people.

We are witnessing a cultural revolution among our disadvantaged people which could lead to great social benefits. I believe that we should foster, rather than suppress, the educational demands of disadvantaged youth. Their feelings about studying their own people and learning at firsthand how to improve their conditions should be respected. A study-and-community experience has social justification of a high order, and the method of introducing a community experience integrated with learning has genuine educational merit.

It is an easy step from recommending experience in the local community to that of planning for experiences abroad. Americans have typically been very provincial in attitude and outlook and have cared very little about understanding the languages and cultures of other peoples. Americans are distrusted and disliked by the citizens of many countries in part as a result of our ignorance about those countries and their peoples, and of the attitudes that we exhibit toward them. Rather than being smugly content with our own ideas, we can become much better educated through the study of others. This is one of the objectives of study-abroad programs. Travel undertaken with a spirit of inquiry is definitely broadening and enriching. The gain is personal to the individual; and, in the course of time, the accumulation of individual experiences can transform the attitudes of the American people and the quality of their associations with other peoples of the world.

Experience is also an important ingredient in what transpires within the academic scene on the campus. I have mentioned that problem-solving laboratories provide this kind of experience, and I have elaborated upon the significance of training students, whether in the liberal arts or within the professions, in problem solving. Although the term *programming of instruction* seems to indicate that the student is becoming the victim of some mechanical device, the significance of programming lies in enabling the student to study in relation to well-defined objectives and expected outcomes. The procedure reduces his dependence upon the instructor and requires the student to pace himself and to evaluate his own progress. When the student participates in this kind of planning of the learning process, as he must when he undertakes independent study, the learning experience is additionally accelerated. It is for such reasons that some of the new educational methods have high significance.

Elsewhere I have advocated student participation in decisions about the formation of college policies and programs, and I have justified my advocacy on the ground that the student has a legitimate interest and a worthwhile contribution to make through such participation. I should like now to state that such participation also has educative value. From the various arguments I have given above, it should be apparent that a student learns when he is confronted with ongoing problems and discusses with peers and persons of broader knowledge and experience the facts relating to those problems and the alternatives for their solution. In so doing he learns much about problem solving and about decision making. When a student carries responsibility as a member of a policy or program council and is confronted with all kinds of human relations problems, he has an opportunity to learn much about group processes and conflict resolution. He also learns through sharing in the responsibility for the decisions that are made, and his horizons may be enlarged by reason of the complexity and magnitude of some of the problems. For example, students typically know little about the problems university administrators encounter in getting public support for their institutions. Students may be only vaguely aware that such support is needed; they can easily disregard the question of obtaining financial resources because they do not share responsibility for it. But when they assume responsibility for the institution, students learn the necessity of reconciling institutional aims with public interests in ways that facilitate institutional progress without creating the hostility that courts disaster. Administrators build hot seats for themselves on this issue by their secretive practices regarding finances.

Ours is a highly complex society involving not only huge governmental structures but many thousands of large aggregations of

24

people in institutions, corporations, and associations. If this society is to survive, a flow of qualified persons into positions of high responsibility and authority is essential—persons who have been prepared to make judgments about policies, to envision programs that can achieve the objectives, and to carry the vast administrative and leadership roles. If my thesis is correct—that college ordinarily tends to prolong immaturity rather than to develop steadily the larger potentialities of the individual—the final effect is a serious delay in preparation for these important roles. Stated more positively, one objective of the experience element in education should be to train students for the assumption of these large responsibilities. This is in part the theoretical justification for involving students in community government. The institution can be used as a laboratory in social organization and group processes. If this kind and quality of experience is gained while the student has the guidance and assistance of faculty, he also acquires an ethical outlook that is oriented to human progress.

IDEAS FOR CHANGE

PART TWO

CHAPTER 3

FRESH CONCEPTS
AND NEW TOOLS

𝕴𝖚𝕴𝖚𝕴𝖚𝕴𝖚𝕴𝖚𝕴𝖚𝕴𝖚𝕴𝖚𝕴𝖚𝕴𝖚𝕴𝖚𝕴𝖚

In making prognostications about the future of science and its applications to the needs of men, the RAND Corporation has described thirty-one breakthroughs that will doubtless be achieved in the next century and beyond.[1] One example is the discovery of how green plants use their chlorophyll and the process of photosynthesis to convert energy from the sun into starches and sugars. With events in the world moving at such a rapid pace, it is time to give more consideration to possible breakthroughs in the kinds of knowledge that affect higher education. In this connection, I discuss here three broad topics: value changes, systems concepts, and new intellectual technologies and tools. The first two topics

[1] T. J. Gordon and Olaf Helmer, *Report of a Long-Range Forecasting Study* (Santa Monica, Calif.: The RAND Corporation, 1964), p. 13.

relate to social changes that have impacts on education, while the third concerns the use of new intellectual tools to effect educational change.

The alienation of youth is spreading, and at its base is a change in values. The challenge to values appears to have come suddenly but actually is an expression of change that has been taking place for more than a quarter of a century. This change is a drift away from the individualistic moral and social concepts that dominated the nineteenth century and the Coolidge-Hoover eras of the twentieth. In the economic area, for example, the Great Depression of the 1930s jolted our thinking about the laissez-faire economic system and revealed the need for social action to control competition and the economic cycle. The change in outlook is a natural product of the increasing complexity of our society. Economic cycles—the consequence of the uncontrolled demand and supply of goods and money—are too costly to tolerate. Gross disparities between affluence and poverty shock our national conscience.

In part the youth movement is a reaction against the materialism that has come to dominate our affluent society. Bluntly stated, we have put a premium upon large monetary rewards, which have been displacing as incentives the rewards that flow from quality of product and of services. We have ignored poverty although it exists side by side with affluence. The conveniences and luxuries we can buy with money have enslaved us. Competitive living, accompanied by competition for jobs, tends to embed the prejudices and discriminations of racism. We have nonchalantly accepted the wastage and contamination of our natural resources—let future generations look out for themselves. Youth severely condemn these attitudes of contemporary society. The drift toward materialistic and mundane values is viewed as evidence of the need for change in higher education since, traditionally, the aim of higher education has been to cultivate the mind and the spirit.

Questions about value relationships are also being raised by thoughtful educators. Gordon S. Brown, dean of the School of Engineering at the Massachusetts Institute of Technology, has said that engineering must now be concerned with civilian affairs rather than with those of industry and the military. Eugene V. Rostow, former dean of the Yale School of Law, spoke in his annual report for 1966 of the changing view of his faculty and students about law. "They see law as a part of the process of social change. They use law in the interest of improving society," he said.[2] The fact that deans of professional schools express this change in view is further evidence that the cultural foundation of the education provided by certain professional schools has not been effective in infusing humanistic values.

The values expressed in the traditional provincialism of the American people have also changed. Before World War I we were well isolated from the rest of the world, concerned with the development of our own nation. Participation in two world wars has changed that. Since World War II we have become heavily involved around the world and in efforts to make the United Nations work. The universities have been especially active—educating students from abroad, training American students for service in foreign countries, and giving professional assistance to innumerable universities in developing nations. Preparation for service is only a small segment of the problem. However it is interesting that the U.S. State Department, concerned with the inadequate qualifications of personnel—even of graduates of Harvard, Yale, and Princeton—considered it necessary to set up a special institute for further training for employees who were to enter foreign service. The heart of the curriculum in this institute was cultural anthropology. Language, literature, and history as they are taught in our colleges, within the framework of Western culture, do not give the American abroad the understanding and empathy that he needs.

Why do we not have any depth of understanding for other cultures or any real appreciation of them? Why do we continue to be so provincial in our outlook toward other peoples' history, religion, philosophy, art, music, and other expressions of culture? Liberal education, regarded as the foundation of all of higher education in the United States, is based squarely upon European history, religion, philosophy, art, and culture, although our population is a mixture that includes many nonwhite and non-Western peoples. The adoption of Grecian culture as a model for study during the Renaissance was natural because of its tremendously stimulating effect in arousing people from the intellectual retrogression of the medieval period. And until recently, the utilization of Western classical materials for education in America was logical and beneficial. It was a desirable cultural heritage for us to assimilate. But now the point has been reached where

[2] Yale University, *Yale Law School Report of the Dean* (New Haven, Conn.: Yale University, 1966), p. 3.

the study of world culture can serve similar purposes and is needed
even more than it was before.

With some notable exceptions—such as in the ministry, in social
work, and to some extent in education—professional training in the
United States is oriented toward the affluent society, toward individualism, and toward the profit-motivated economic system. An example is
the fee system under which doctors practice medicine. Doctors charge
fees based on their patients' incomes, which seems justifiable at first
glance. But the system encourages physicians to serve mainly individuals with good incomes. Uncertainty about fees causes persons
with low incomes, especially those at the poverty level (which includes
about 19 per cent of American families[3]), to refrain from visiting
physicians' offices except in cases of dire necessity. The social consequences of this system are apparent in the disparate extent and quality
of medical services being given to disadvantaged groups. An affluent
society cannot permit this situation to continue.

In speaking of objectives for students of engineering, the Report
of the Committee on Goals in Engineering Education lists as the first
goal preparing the student ideologically to serve in "competitive profit-
motivated industry." This report, the result of a five-year study of
engineering education, is supposed to set the goals for schools of engineering whose students will practice for the next generation or two. I
comment further on this matter when discussing engineering education,
but the statement illustrates well a misplacement of ethical focus.

Still another value change that is affecting our way of life relates to individual behavior, notably in sex mores. I speak of attitudes
toward sex rather than sexual behavior, although that is changing too.
The principal change is that women are seeking the freedom in sex
that men have always had. Some women students contend that pre-
marital behavior should be based upon sincerity in the emotional relationships between a man and a woman. Let us hope that this is the
case. If women's sororities press toward sexual promiscuity in the manner that characterized college fraternities during their heyday, the
change in campus environment will not be healthy.

As I have said, the basic change toward sex is in attitude. The
attitude that has prevailed for many generations probably was formulated by the early Christians, who were revolted by the licentiousness

_____

[3] See the *Economic Report of the President* for the latest information.

of the Romans. Church doctrine preached of sex as something tainted, at times evil, at best sex to be limited to the conception of children. The devising of effective methods for birth control came at an opportune time, in view of the threatening population growth in the world. Birth control is now a practice accepted by most people; it is also essential in the long run to the balance between the number of mouths to be fed and the amount of available food. The subject of sex in general has been rapidly emerging from obscurity and has become the subject of rational discourse and education. In the future the school and the college, not the church, will influence individual behavior and social attitudes toward sex.

The complex conditions of modern society have also been forcing a change from concepts of individualism to concepts of systems. I do not use *system* merely in a mathematical or technical sense but to mean a complex organization directing the diverse activities of groups of people. An illustration of such a system is the Tennessee Valley Authority (TVA), concerned as it is with the production of power, flood control, erosion, transportation, recreation, and economic opportunity for the people of the Tennessee Valley. The operation of the TVA draws together specialists from many fields, such as engineering, agriculture, business administration, regional planning, public health. It was made possible by the collaboration of seven states and the initiative, sponsorship, and financing provided by the federal government. As a consultant to the TVA at its founding in 1933, I became intimately familiar with the poverty of the people, the eroded land, and the extent to which the natural resources of the region had been dissipated; I can therefore visualize the transformation that has taken place under the system. Call it socialism if you wish, the change in the happiness of the people, in the appearance of the countryside, and in the productivity of the region has been tremendous.

A system now familiar to all of us is the system of space exploration, which requires the massing of resources in money, energy, and intellectual skills and the mobilization of teams of specialists from mathematics, science, engineering, medicine, law, public administration, and business administration. Both TVA and the space exploration system are so complex and so costly as to be beyond the reach of private initiative. They require the organizing capacities of government.

Examples from the past, however, are few compared with those systems that will be necessary and occur in the near future. Again, let me give two examples from among many. The northeast corridor of the United States—lying between Boston and Washington—is growing rapidly in population, in the creation of pollutions and contaminations, and in the hazards of living and transportation. The separate communities which constitute this corridor have grown up without much regard for one another, except to be linked by the most expedient modes of communication and transportation. If growth continues without basic planning, the area will become increasingly congested and chaotic. Fortunately a beginning is being made, through the sponsorship of the federal government and the collaboration of the Massachusetts Institute of Technology, in studying the northeast corridor. The aim of the study is to devise a plan—a system—for further integration, coordination, and development of the corridor. The northeast corridor is but one of several corridors of congestion, the problems of which need attention.

My second example of a system needed for the future is also already familiar—we must develop a system to cope constructively with the growth and decay of our urban centers. The problems of urbanization are so urgent and so complex as to require a great mobilization of resources and of teams of specialists. A report on home economics education recommended that home economists now shift their attention from the rural region, where in the past they have done an excellent job in enhancing the cultural life of the rural inhabitant, to the urban centers, where the disadvantaged populations live.[4] It would be impossible, however, for the home economist, working alone, to achieve in urban centers the significant results earlier secured in the rural area. Teams attacking the problems of urbanization need to include not only the home economist but also the social worker, health officer, engineer, lawyer, businessman, architect, and environmental design expert. As things now stand, a particular urban community may have a hundred or more agencies at work, each rendering its type of services but uncoordinated with the others. Usually the services of these agencies are directed toward relief rather than toward rehabilitation. The urban problem must be approached as a problem of system. We usually think of it in this way in designing rapid transit

---

[4] Earl J. McGrath and Jack T. Johnson, *The Changing Mission of Home Economics* (New York: Teachers College, Columbia University, 1968).

facilities, but we must extend this approach to social, economic, and health problems.

The implications of systems planning for colleges and universites are these: the objectives of higher education need to be reconsidered, and the curriculum must be reorganized so that young people are prepared for understanding and attacking the broad social problems that exist today. Fortunately, the computer has been invented in time to be of use in assisting with the complex analyses necessary. The computer compresses the time required to study problems and serves also as a tool for the storage and retrieval of information. By using the Sketchpad technique, it can function as a tool for design. The computer is also transforming library methods and the processing and dissemination of information.

Education made a great leap forward when the printed book became available. Now we have some fresh intellectual concepts and tools; I refer to such things as information theory, decision theory, games, systems problems, simulations, and models. These tools make possible the use of tremendously comprehensive and integrative types of problems, often representing several disciplines in the training of students. The testing of decisions that have been made by students or groups of students is now feasible. The ability of the computer to process data, analyze variables, and store information has made these advances in intellectual training possible.

The use of games and of systems analysis has become common among progressive schools of business and engineering. For example, the School of Engineering at Stanford University used as a systems problem the designing of a satellite for educational communication between the United States and three less developed nations, Brazil, India, and Indonesia. Groups of thirty students, representing several types of engineering and certain of the social sciences, worked as teams of specialists. The solution, prepared by the students in the form of a comprehensive report, was in itself a remarkable document in composition. The report was given to experts in the field for reactions— which meant that the judgments that had been made by the students were subjected to the most meaningful type of criticism. The subsequent interactions of the students with the criticisms of these evaluators added an important dimension to education.

The development of intellectual skills must inevitably become an important aspect of present-day education. The development of quantitative, behavioral, and conceptual skills should also be stressed. Much progress has been made already in the restudy of the methods of teaching quantitative skills. I emphasize the need to acquire these skills because of the growing importance of statistical analysis—including probability theory for all students—almost irrespective of the discipline or professional area. The acquisition of behavioral skills will come through a greater recognition of the contributions to be made by the behavioral sciences. Here, understanding of interpersonal relations is important, but I refer more especially to the development of skills in relation to group organization and processes. Training in conceptualization should come from study of almost any of the disciplines, but I would suggest the need for more conscious design of the kinds of discussions and problem situations that involve the use of conceptual skills. New theories of organization, for example, have enabled us to reason more precisely than before about the interrelationships of people within groups. There is involved in this development something more than memorizing the vocabulary of the particular discipline.

Study of the skills of problem solving is undertaken to achieve two results. One, of course, is to learn the scientific method of analysis and synthesis. Long recognized as the heart of work in the sciences, it is now accepted as the method of analysis and synthesis in the social sciences and, indeed, in other disciplines and professional areas. The second result is related to the nature and extent of the knowledge that is available today. Knowledge has been accumulating at such a rate and is now available in such quantity and complexity as to render it impossible for any one person to cover satisfactorily any discipline or professional area, regardless of how small the area may be. In addition, growth and change in knowledge are occurring so rapidly that much knowledge becomes obsolete within a short period of time. Engineering educators speak now of occupational training having a halflife of five years. It is becoming clear that the old method of "filling" a student with all of the available knowledge, in order to make of him a practitioner of one of the professions, simply does not work today. Knowledge in many fields has grown to the extent that it cannot be successfully assimilated within any reasonable period of study. Whatever knowledge is memorized may not be well understood. And, in all probability, some of the content will become obsolete within the near future.

The solution seems to lie in preparing a student to continually educate and reeducate himself during his lifetime. The main objective is to teach students to learn how to learn and to motivate them to want to keep on learning. (This, of course, involves the usefulness of theory in the area of professional education and in psychology. We know a certain amount about learning theory, but we need to know a great deal more—hence the importance of continuing research in this area if we are to develop educational methods that will result in adequate preparation for the professions.) If the student becomes a problem solver while he is in school, he may continue as a problem investigator and a discoverer of fresh research findings in his professional field. He may also see the wisdom of continuing his education by returning to the colleges and universities for refresher study.

The whole of what I have said here relates to the need to put more dynamic quality into higher education. Our colleges and universities have become cluttered with discrete courses hemmed in by watertight compartments and with processes of evaluation that count course credits as achievement. Colleges and professional schools in the future must reassess their value orientations. They must conceive of specialists not primarily as successful individual practitioners but as members of teams that can attack systems problems. They must further adjust learning objectives to include skills in the use of new intellectual tools. Students now in college will be living in an era when many breakthroughs in knowledge will be achieved.

CHAPTER 4

COLLEGES AND
SOCIAL CHANGE

◗❂◖◗❂◖◗❂◖◗❂◖◗❂◖◗❂◖◗❂◖◗❂◖◗❂◖◗❂◖◗❂◖◗❂◖

Colleges and universities are by their nature instruments of social change. A college, however, can play an active role in effecting change, or it can play a passive role; it can support faculty and students, or it can exercise varying degrees of restraint on their actions. In considering policy relating to social change, we must first get some historical perspective. We note immediately that problems center on issues which at the time of consideration are controversial. That colleges and universities, in the past, have been instrumental in promoting social change on a host of noncontroversial fronts is well known. A good example is the initiation of colleges of agriculture and mechanical arts. It was clear from the beginning that the purposes of these programs were to transform agriculture and provide further momentum for the industrial revolution. Another example

36

is the assistance of universities in designing the computer. Today the impact of the computer varies from the commonplace—such as selling an airplane ticket—to the spectacular—such as placing a man on the moon. These illustrations could be multiplied, but no one questions the role of the college and university in these social changes.

What is controversial at one period of history is not controversial at another. In retrospect, therefore, actions that were the subject of heated controversy at the time become constructive contributions when viewed from a later time. The controversies over religion are a prime example. The theory of evolution, barely a century old, was attacked unmercifully when first introduced into the curriculum. The theory sharply contradicted the accepted beliefs of men. Although the Scopes Monkey Trial occurred so recently that it is still within our memory, the apprehensions about evolution have largely disappeared. Indeed, a move among the colleges to revert to the teaching of a century ago would probably meet with a storm of disapproval.

When human slavery existed in the United States, certain colleges took the then courageous position that slavery was a social evil that had to be abolished. We still have racism, but we do not have slavery. In the light of the fast moving shifts in attitude toward the Negro in the United States, if slavery were still an issue, it would be unthinkable today for the colleges and universities to stand silently by. Reflecting further upon the black-white issue, I am reminded of an informative article that appeared in *Ebony* about fifteen years ago. It described the predicaments of the presidents of leading Negro colleges and universities. Quite apart from their personal views about the Negro problem in American society, these men were locked in the vise of regulations imposed by their governing boards, most of the members of which were white. Perhaps this helps to account for the authoritarianism of the typical Negro college president, who depends for his tenure of office upon executing the will of the board. It may help explain the attitudes of Black Power students toward the establishment.

The social press existed for both white and Negro colleges. I recall a conversation, shortly before the 1954 Supreme Court decision, with the president of a college operated in the South by the Society of Friends. I asked him why this Quaker college did not admit any Negro students. He said that the board prevented him from doing so. Evidently the board sacrificed the principles of the college in order to conform to the mores of the community. This is not a very pretty picture.

Let me describe a case on another social issue. About forty years ago William Leiserson, an experienced arbitrator in the labor relations field and a professor of economics at Antioch College, was appointed by the governor of Ohio as chairman of a commission to study unemployment insurance. Antioch at that time was vulnerable on two fronts: Its endowment was less than $200,000 and so it depended heavily on annual contributions, and under its work–study program, large numbers of students were being placed in businesses and industries in the Miami Valley of Ohio. The college received an avalanche of demands that Leiserson be fired. Some of those demands were accompanied by threats to boycott the student placement. After consultations between administrators and faculty, a consensus was reached that the professor should be supported.

Some time later after the president of the college, Arthur E. Morgan, had left to become chairman of the Tennessee Valley Authority—then labeled a socialistic adventure—the president of one of the largest manufacturing companies in the Miami Valley and a former member of the Board of Trustees of the college wrote to me demanding a change in the Antioch policy of social action. To reinforce his arguments he said that Horace Mann, the first president of the college, would "turn over in his grave" if he knew what was happening at the institution. I took delight in reciting to the writer a number of the radical positions—on such things as religious beliefs, slavery, and the education of women—that Mann had taken when he was president of the college. An instance of Horace Mann's courage in countering current beliefs was demonstrated when he, a Unitarian but president of a college that was controlled by a church of trinitarian beliefs, was persuaded to join the latter church. When his membership was announced to the congregation, Mann rose in his place, said that he had reservations about the doctrines of the church, and proceeded to recite them. This incident was still being discussed by the villagers a half century later. As for the unemployment insurance, a law was enacted by the state of Ohio, and within two decades the concept became almost universally accepted.

Present students feel strongly the need for certain social changes. As a result of pressures from them, we have become highly sensitive to student activism. It has taken a form which we in America have not previously experienced, although activism is a phenomenon common in other universities of the world. We can get additional perspective about it, I think, by considering it in the light of historical events. The magazine *Daedalus* published papers given at a Conference on Students in Politics held in San Juan, Puerto Rico, March 27–April 1, 1967. Much of the discussion in this symposium was an assessment of student activism. In his summary of the discussion, Seymour M. Lipset states the following:

> Students were a key element in the revolutions of 1848 in Germany and Austria, and student activism stimulated the "professors parliament" which almost succeeded in toppling several monarchs. In czarist Russia, students spearheaded various revolutionary movements, and the university campus was a major center of revolutionary activity. In the East European countries, where education was limited to a small proportion of the population, students were often the carriers of modern ideas of liberty, socialism, industrialization, and equality of opportunity. The important role of students in the movements for national independence in the developing areas also goes back a half century or more. In imperial China, students were crucial to the imperial effort at modernization but at the same time spread republican and radical ideas throughout the society. Students helped overthrow the dynasty in 1911 and were thereafter one of the elements continually pushing China toward modernization and radical ideologies. In other Asian and African countries, students were often a central element in anticolonial struggles.[1]

Not all student-fomented movements have been good, however. At the time of the Nazi movement in Germany, students were simply caught up in the tide of nationalistic fervor. But, generally speaking, the changes that students have proposed have been constructive—at least that seemed to be the consensus of the 1967 conference.

The student activists who press for reforms today have worthwhile things to say to us. I discuss some of these things in Chapter Five, but they also have relevance for the present discussion. On the subject of educational change, student activists are pointing out the deficiencies in the multiversity and the need to personalize again the experiences of students. They are telling us that our value system is

---

[1] Seymour M. Lipset *et al.*, "Students and Politics," *Daedalus* (Winter 1968), p. 344.

warped. They are saying not only that the colleges ignore several great cultures of the world, but also that our indoctrination in Western culture leads to some evil consequences—emphasis upon materialism, white supremacy, and a disinterest in and intolerance for the ideas and contributions of other cultures.

In respect to social change, student activists point to the enormous problems of urban ghettos, to the wastage and pollution of natural resources, to the influence of large corporations on politics, and to the growing military influence on our government. Their demonstrations against the war in Vietnam have helped to influence the American public to make a major shift in viewpoint. Many students identify the administrations of the universities with the establishment, and I think rightly so. The administrations are the executive arms of the governing boards, and governing boards typically are populated by wealthy older persons from business and the professions. And of course, the activists' objection to student governments, which really do not govern anything, is understandable.

Whenever either government or industry wants anything important to be done, the universities are called upon to loan their faculties. This is what occurred in the case of the development of atomic energy. In the light of our topic, such activities of the universities as managing the government atomic laboratories is interesting. Too, university economists have been largely responsible for the extent to which macroeconomic theory has been applied to governmental operations and has replaced the laissez-faire theory that characterized the thinking of the century and a half preceding the Great Depression. Perhaps colleges and universities have never officially adopted macroeconomics as a dogma for their own institutions to follow—I shall presently argue against permitting any ideology to dominate a college or university—but the fact remains that departments of economics universally have adopted the new theory with its related statistical techniques. Business and financial leaders still talk about the older theory of supply and demand, but presidents of the United States have repeatedly appointed as chairmen of their economic advisors professors who subscribe to the new theory. However, the debt owed by society to economists, mostly university professors, for the greater stabilization of our economy is large indeed. It is difficult to argue other than that society has gained tremendously from the scholarly theories that have been carried from the professors' laboratories into applications in government, industry, and the professions.

My view about the role of institutions as initiators of social change can perhaps best be explained by the following case. When Antioch College was being reorganized in the 1920s, it had the dual problem of launching an innovative educational program, described in its catalog as "revolutionary," and of reforming the community environment of the institution in order to lessen the constricting forces that would bear upon it. The environment was distinctly provincial and reactionary, and the aim was to create an environment that would be permissive of critical inquiry and encouraging to progressive action. An attempt to reform the larger community was also deliberately undertaken on such fronts as politics, culture, economics, and health.

The local political machine was ousted from control of the community by the mobilization of public support behind a civic leader who was elected mayor. Still later, the people of the town were persuaded to reorganize the city government by adopting a city manager form. The cultural activities were the usual ones, but special effort was made to involve community members as well as college students and faculty in music, art, and drama. Some small industries were started, at first largely for the purpose of training students under the work–study program; later, certain fruits of research done at the college were plowed into these and additional enterprises. Originally the industries were sponsored and owned entirely by the college. The two largest ones originally were started in a small barn and in the basement of the science building. After a number of years of development, they were set up as separate corporations and the majority stock interest was sold to the employees and to persons in the community. Encouraged by these activities, young entrepreneurs launched several additional enterprises. As a result, the people of the region have enjoyed full employment and currently some $25 million of annual income, a large sum for a small community. The productivity of farmers in the region was also increased after the college introduced hybrid corn.

Because of its location in southern Ohio, the community had a racial problem, symbolized in the local theater by a rope behind which Negroes had to sit. Students and faculty descended on the theater with a careful plan of social action and with copies of the Ohio law that prohibited segregation. As a result, this blight on the community was removed. That particular march had full support from the president's office. The college also took the lead in transforming the medical services of the region. With the cooperation of some of the local physicians, the college medical clinic was converted into a community clinic, enlarging and tremendously improving the health services within the community. The college also acted to force a lowering and restructuring of the electric power rates. The college, with power facilities of its own, competed successfully with the established power company for the municipal franchise. In doing so, it developed a lower rate structure that stimulated the use of power. At about this time, the Hydro-Electric Power Commission of Ontario was revolutionizing the marketing philosophy in the utility field by using this same policy,[2] and the principle was shortly afterward adopted by the TVA. Within a few years the major utility companies had themselves also adopted this reform, and at that point the college withdrew from the activity.

The Antioch situation is a simple one compared with that of a large institution located in an urban area. But the college had to determine, as a matter of policy, to relate itself to its environment; it had to buck rural, provincial attitudes and educate people in order to stimulate support for its actions; and it had to withstand the usual attacks made by label pinners. We were accused of being communistic; we were investigated by the House Un-American Activities Committee; and we were threatened with the withdrawal of financial support. But the college survived and the community became a model. The changed tone within the community brought a considerable influx of people who were concerned about and interested in social action. The consideration which should be emphasized is that the college worked for the transformation of its own community.[3] It is the failure of colleges to assume this responsibility that has become the concern of so many students.

The policy I have been describing has two facets. The first facet concerns the degree of freedom and support that should be given to individuals who are members of the college when they, as

---

[2] The Ontario theory held that in an operating company where the fixed charges were high (arising, for example, from large costs from plant) and the operating costs were stable, the income would be largest when the charges for services were sufficiently low to produce greatly increased sales.

[3] Algo D. Henderson and Dorothy Hall, *Antioch College, Its Design for a Liberal Education* (New York: Harper & Row, Publishers, 1946), p. 280.

individuals, take a position on a social issue. Freedom must be provided to all individuals and to groups of individuals within the institution, to speak, write, and act in relation to social action—if they make it as clear as they can that they are expressing their own views or the views of a particular group rather than speaking for the institution. The policy toward academic freedom must be one of complete support, including the adoption of the usual procedures for hearing cases in dispute.

The second facet concerns the position taken by the institution, as such. When a college takes a position on a social issue—as it occasionally should—that position must be the result of a consensus, the position of the majority of persons and groups that form the institution. If this were not the rule, the college would be pushed into speaking with the voice of a minority. The total group must bear the risks. To avoid friction on this point, it is essential to have a mechanism by which the views of individuals and minority groups can become the subject of serious consideration and can influence the feelings of the total organization. Elsewhere I also describe the qualities and styles of leadership that are essential for obtaining the type of agreement of which I speak.

The problems which arise out of controversy are best understood if we fully appreciate the nature of the conflict. According to Kenneth Boulding, tensions between the community and the institution develop because the institution, although it grows out of the folk culture, by its very nature becomes a superculture.[4] Colleges and universities are initiated to meet the needs of the folk culture. Using historical perspective, we can see the reasoning of church groups and governmental units when they establish colleges and universities to supply religious leaders, teachers, professional services, and research findings. An elementary case perhaps best explains this mode of origin. Suomi College in the Upper Peninsula of Michigan was founded by immigrants from Finland who desired to accomplish several things: to preserve elements of Finnish culture; to give their particular church continuity, especially by providing educated ministers; and to assure their children an opportunity to assimilate American culture. The point is that the community set up an agency for the purpose of

---

[4] Kenneth E. Boulding, "The Role of the University in the Development of a World Community," in *Higher Education in Tomorrow's World*, ed. Algo D. Henderson (Ann Arbor: University of Michigan, 1968), pp. 135–41.

gradually evolving a new culture, blending with it elements of the old. The history of Suomi College is similar to the history of many other colleges, and if all situations were as simple as this, there probably would be no conflict.

However, it is the nature of a college or university to become a superculture. The goal is to seek truth, not to perpetuate the status quo. It is inconsistent with the purposes of the college to indoctrinate its students with dogma, including indoctrination in the prevailing customs and conventions. The university has a large responsibility to society not only to educate its youth but to disseminate the ideas and methodology that are the product of scholarly and research activity. The responsibility of the university is determined in part by the implementation of public policy and in part by the individual responsibilities felt by forward looking faculty.

Thus, a college or university cannot permit itself to be overwhelmed by the folk culture. It must grow into a superculture. But neither should it wrap the cloak of academic respectability around itself and withdraw behind its ivy covered walls. The basic problem is to reconcile the two cultures sufficiently to have a viable situation. Conflicts there will be, and there is no way to avoid them. But the question is whether the institution will submerge itself in the folk culture, attempting to be safe and secure, or will venture to fulfill its larger responsibility in spite of the conflict.

In this connection, I want to make a number of points. The first is that an institution becomes dynamic in relation to its policies respecting social change. Reed College, for example, was founded for the distinct purpose of supplying a cultural stimulation to the Portland area. The greatness of the University of Wisconsin has resulted from its basic concept that the campus of the university is the entire state, making the welfare of the state a principal concern. It founded, for example, the Legislative Reference Bureau, which has endeavored to improve legislation and clarify the wording of state laws. The vitality of the Antioch educational experience can be heavily attributed to the manner in which it has used the community as a laboratory. In the Reed, Wisconsin, and Antioch cases, the high quality of intellectual effort by faculty and students has been due in part to the stimulation from this feeling of mission. Although the concept of mission was articulated by educational leaders, it has permeated the institutions as a whole. The second point is that the educational leaders who have become historically significant figures are those who have provided fresh vision—related either to educational innovation or to social advance—for their institutions. Those who merely navigate a safe course are doomed to obscurity. These respective courses of action mark the difference between administrative leadership and administrative management. Third, the quality of creative work by faculty and students is considerably enhanced by their involvement in significant issues—social, scientific, or other. Fourth, the professional reputation of the individual and of the institution depends upon the publication of scholarly interpretations and findings. The purpose of those publications should be to make an impact on the development of society, rather than merely to accumulate points toward promotion in rank or increases in salary.

As I have indicated earlier, I make a distinction between critical inquiry into controversial issues and the adoption of an ideology. In Soviet Russia, the policy of adopting dogmas relating to economics, genetics, and creative work has had an inhibiting effect which has become apparent to the scholars of the rest of the world and, more recently, to the Russians themselves.[5] Scholarly efforts must be free. The institution should not impose any *ism* upon its faculty and students. The college needs to move with care and consensus when it adopts an institutional position, and it must preserve the freedom to dissent. This stipulation applies equally to radical new ideas and to the preservation of the status quo. All too often we do impose— through church controls, board resolutions, or presidential decrees— the beliefs and conventions of the folk culture. Yet, because the business of higher education is critical inquiry, we must accept the challenges to shed light on social issues and to work toward solutions of the problems. This is a primary function of higher education; it is also the direction in which educational vitality lies.[6]

I should like to add here a thought on a very sensitive matter. The ecumenical spirit that prevails now among the three branches of Western religion hopefully will spread among all of the religions of

[5] Zhores A. Medvedev, *The Rise and Fall of T. D. Lysenko,* trans. I. Michael Lerner (New York: Columbia University Press, 1969). See also the *Current Digest of the Soviet Press* for documents relating to economists, artists, composers, and writers.

[6] Algo D. Henderson, *Vitalizing Liberal Education* (New York: Harper & Row, Publishers, 1944).

the world. The people of the world must agree upon values and goals for mankind if we are to live together in peace. Among the values that youth are questioning are some of those that we hold most sacred. These values must be examined afresh and one means of doing so, I think, is through an examination of the wisdom embedded in other religions around the world. My point is, then, that within our colleges and universities we must apply the test of dogma versus critical inquiry to religious beliefs as well as to other subjects.

If a policy is to be pursued that supports academic freedom and also freedom of speech and action in the larger sense that I have been describing, it is important to organize the university in a manner which reduces tensions and conflict to the minimum and determines when institutional activism is warranted. For this purpose a good organization is one that, first, assures sufficient intercommunication among the parties of interest to obtain reasonable consensus about goals, and second, demonstrates a willingness to incur risks. In my judgment, the dangers from these risks usually do not materialize; and if they do, they do not remain for long. And the institution that makes constructive contributions toward social change attracts fresh support.

CHAPTER 5

CAMPUS
REVOLUTION

𝄢𝄢𝄢𝄢𝄢𝄢𝄢𝄢𝄢𝄢𝄢𝄢𝄢𝄢𝄢𝄢

Campus violence—the killing of students at Kent State University and at Jackson State College, rock-throwing at college buildings and at police, and prolonged student strikes—has given the public a picture of campus turmoil. The invasion of Cambodia by American forces added a new dimension. Violence did not cease, but the activities of a much larger portion of the student body turned toward political action. Some universities, or segments of them, were reconstituted by students and faculty members toward direct involvement in finding solutions to the war and to the social ills of the nation. Thus revolution has come to the campus.

Acting-out behavior is not a new phenomenon among students. Many of us can remember the days of fraternity stunts, panty raids, telephone booth stuffing, and Fort Lauderdale Easter vacation hijinks.

Sometimes homecoming activities accelerated into window smashings, town–gown fights, and even occasional physical violence done to students and police alike. In the old days, college and other authorities shrugged off such activities as typical youthful pranks. Today's student behavior is interpreted, however, as a threat to established order and a violation of academic tradition.

Political defiance of authority—manifested by the presentation of nonnegotiable demands, blockades, strikes, and the occupation of campus buildings—is relatively new in the American academic world. Not so in Europe, Latin America, and Asia, where behavior of this sort has long been part of traditional university life. Indeed, unrest among students today is worldwide, as witness the riots in Paris by students from the Sorbonne, the tearing down of the security gates at the London School of Economics, the several months long strike at the University of Chile, and the police–student battle at the University of Tokyo aimed at reopening the institution after several months of shutdown by students.

The disturbances that are appearing on so many American college campuses seem to the public to be the work of some mischievous or evil-minded radicals. Yes, the leaders are radicals. And among them, especially influential nonstudents, are some revolutionaries. But student pressure groups as a whole are not evil-minded and the situation is not as simple as the public may think. Indeed, it is both complex and critical. Turmoil follows in the wake of disruptions because the universities are vulnerable. The modus operandi of universities is characterized by rational thought and discussion, and so they are unprepared for violence. Universities are dependent upon public support, financial and otherwise, and so they are timid in the face of movements for social change. They are in need of educational reform, but the wheels of decision making grind slowly, and to students time is of the essence—they are in college now.

Militant students are motivated by a desire for change in two areas outside of the structure of the university. The more far-reaching goal is the elimination of supernationalism, war, competitive goals, and concentrations of power. The second goal, which merges with the first, is the desire for true freedom for black people and an end to racism. This goal is a rejection of the melting pot so meaningful for immigrant minorities, but from which the blacks, Chicanos, native Americans, and orientals have been excluded; in the case of the blacks, the goal is black cultural identity, black self-enhancement, and black power. The other disadvantaged minorities want similar recognition. These two goals merge at the university because the university is the intellectual base for fresh concepts and because students believe that the university should lead the way in effecting social change.

Although radical students disagree among themselves about the means of effecting social change, there is considerable agreement on two primary issues, one relating to values and the other to power. Youth are becoming discontent with some of the values that our society has taken for granted. The views of youth about concentrations of power can easily be illustrated by referring to the growth in this country of centralized government supported by a tremendously complex bureaucracy, by the huge concentrations of economic power in our gigantic corporations, and by the terribly fast growth of power in the military. The military consumes over half of the budget of the national government and a tenth of the gross national product—which means that the military gets the highest level of priorities in the allocation of resources, several times the portion devoted to higher education.

Concerns about values and about power become fused because the war in which our country is engaged is deemed by many to be immoral and so much of the money spent for military purposes appears to be a wastage of our resources. It is especially unfortunate that we spend so much money on immoral wars when the needs of our people who are hungry, ill, or uneducated could so easily be materially fulfilled with these funds. The youth see a gross disparity between traditional American ideals—especially those relating to the individual human being—and the practices in which we engage as a result of our technological revolution. Democracy seems a sham when there are gross discrepancies between affluence and poverty and when pronounced differences between first- and second-class citizens still exist.

Youth also are rebelling because they feel helpless to effect changes in any direction or to discover for themselves the good life. The war in Vietnam, more than any other single cause, has contributed to this feeling of helplessness. Youth are fed into the war with no way to resist short of outright rebellion. Black youth feel especially helpless because the black community has not been permitted to organize and run its own affairs. Indeed, blacks in the ghettos feel that they are living within a police state because their principal contact with white society has been through the police who patrol the streets of their communities. The police have been there for legitimate purposes, but it has seemed to the blacks that they are there primarily to keep the community intimidated and suppressed, and blacks view the situation as a form of colonialism.

In this conflict over goals and values, the issue of students versus the establishment stands out most clearly. The organizations and institutions of a society are highly protective of the status quo. Most people do not like to be disturbed in their enjoyment of things as they are. But students believe that change is necessary and that colleges and universities must have an impact in effecting change. To the student, the establishment includes the university, the most obvious symbol of all those forces making decisions about his life without listening to his voice. He feels far removed from any meaningful communication with the university administration, and especially with the president; indeed, he may not even recognize the president walking across the campus. And the president—as the student knows all too well—spends his time speaking before luncheon clubs, negotiating with government bureau chiefs whose decisions control significant portions of the university's budget, and conferring with corporation executives whose investment advice and contributions pay for what the government does not. Suggestions for change, sometimes the result of intensive student effort, typically disappear into a labyrinth of faculty committees, emerging only months later in emasculated form.

Let us now consider some of these criticisms in greater depth. The most familiar one is that the university, because of its growth in size, has become impersonal. Students say that they feel as if they have become a computer number. The objection here is not so much to the mechanization of registration—which after all is aimed at simplifying procedures and making them less time-wasting for the students—but rather to the tendency of faculty to withdraw from teaching. The more vital members of the faculty get wrapped up in their research and lessen considerably the time they devote to meeting with students informally and in the classroom. Inducements to faculty to go into research are considerable. They are offered carrots in the form of research grants that provide funds for more adequate facilities, research assistants, travel, and other perquisites. But more than that, the reward system for professors in universities is based on publication.

Thus the road to professional advancement lies through research rather than through teaching.

A university commonly is pressured by its governing board to be more businesslike, but this concern with greater efficiency also results in larger classes and laboratories and the use of graduate students as teachers to reduce the unit cost of operation. So the students, notably the lower division students, find themselves in large classes, often with instructors who are little better qualified to teach than they are themselves. In such an impersonal system there is a tendency not to recognize individual differences in motivations, cultural backgrounds, secondary school achievements, and creative potential. The judgments made about the quality of an individual's performance are determined by standards that pertain to a field of scholarly knowledge, whereas it is the individual's growth—his learning in relation to his intellectual and vocational progress—that should be measured.

Paralleling students' criticisms of our technologically dominated society are criticisms directed specifically against the humanities. The humanities are in a cultural cocoon, students claim, and the cocoon is Western culture—history, art, thought, religion. We are resistant to other forms of political and economic organization because of our intense belief that the capitalistic system is superior and the only system to be tolerated. We also believe that Christianity is infallible and hence the only true religion. The values instilled in us impel us to attempt to police the nations of the world that differ from us. The questions being raised by students about technology and about the failure of the colleges to draw also upon non-Western cultural knowledge and wisdom suggest the need for a thoroughgoing examination of the objectives and the programs of our institutions.

The criticisms extend to the professional schools. In medicine they pertain to the social consequences of the entrenched power of the American Medical Association. A sprinkling of medical students and younger physicians are launching attacks on the citadel. Such an attack occurred at a meeting of medical school deans in February, 1969. Medical students interrupted the meeting and read a statement that said, in part:

> We are informing you that we refuse to be dehumanized by an education which either ignores or denies basic human dignities and which graduates generation after generation of physicians more con-

cerned with their own economic well-being than with basic human needs.[1]

Students have little or no voice in the matters that really count. They feel that the need for change is urgent, but the actions of the institution are deliberate. The decision-making process is very complex, and this means that adoption of new ideas is quite slow. Some of the proposals for change are radical, and they arouse public opinion and political clamor. Among the public institutions, interference by political leaders in the state is almost certain to occur.

The university has become, in the minds of the more militant students, a symbol of the need for change. They perceive the colleges and universities as agents for funneling graduates into the impersonal corporations and the government, both of which are central to the power complex. The schools direct the students toward materialistic gains and away from the communities that most need their services and leadership. And the faculty concern themselves with specializations, studying the trees rather than the forest, while the forest is dissipated and humanity is threatened. The faculty, so the students say, will explore any topic and do any research, social or antisocial, if it is sufficiently subsidized. The colleges and universities run with the tide.

Our students—and often the most intelligent and discerning ones—feel frustrated. Let me cite an example which shows how such frustration develops. Because San Francisco State College is an institution to which most students commute, there is an urgent need for a student union building on the campus. A plan to construct such a building was devised; the costs were to be amortized through the payment of student fees. Students devoted themselves with enthusiasm to developing the plans. They employed a world-famous architect, Moshe Safdie, to prepare a design. When the plan went before the Board of Trustees for approval it was voted down, largely on esthetic grounds. Two appeals, one in the form of a petition with six thousand signatures, failed to break a tie vote of the Board. Many persons believe that the highly imaginative architectural design would have given some sparkle to the otherwise staid appearance of the campus, but the Board's vote defeated the plan. A possible interpretation is that

[1] Philip W. Semas, "Students in Medicine, Law, and Architecture Challenge Their Professions on Social Aims," *The Chronicle of Higher Education,* October 20, 1969, p. 3.

the vote of one man (to break the tie), probably only remotely familiar with the campus, prevailed over the opinion of six thousand students and faculty.

Taking into account both the student criticisms and those I have described in preceding chapters, we can now see the underlying bases for student unrest. Students who are aware bring with them to the university ideals, not of a society based on war and competition but rather of a society in which each individual, regardless of color or race, is able to pursue and find his own happiness. These students realize that the university can be, and actually is, an intellectual base for fresh concepts. Yet, they realize that the fresh concepts now coming out of the university exacerbate the sickness of our society and do little to solve major human problems. Students observe that in many ways the university, like the society, is based on the support of the military–industrial complex, that it maintains an inequality of admissions standards, that it is bureaucratic and inflexible. They demand change.

Not all of the students' demands are as appealing or make as much sense as the union design at San Francisco State College, or as ethnic studies degree programs, or, as at Columbia University, the cessation of construction of a gymnasium located without regard to the feelings and rights of the people of Harlem. A few student leaders in this country, and perhaps many more abroad, have become committed to an *ism* that supposedly solves all problems. Their disruptive tactics are designed to give them a platform from which to influence people in the community. Some of these leaders are determined to destroy the establishment because it represents entrenched values and the power that supports them. Unfortunately such student leaders do not hesitate to injure the university in the process.

Still, these social–economic–political problems need attention, hopefully using an evolutionary rather than a revolutionary approach. Of all forms of social organization, the democratic form is the one that endeavors to reconcile individual and social needs in a manner consistent with the statement of philosophy offered in Chapter One. The task of education now is to refine the concept and improve its application to the contemporary scene.

One basic question is central to almost all major issues raised by students: Should the university be—or can it be—an agent of social change? The negative view of this question is taken by educators, perhaps a majority, who feel that a college should be a sanctuary for debate and scholarship, uninterrupted by secular problems. The alternative view—the positive one—is the one I presented in the preceding chapter. As the students express it, the institution must devote itself to the concerns that are relevant in its environment. Yet it is the negative view that dominates our college campuses at present.

Traditionally, college is a place for the intellectual development of youth and the systematic training of professionals. A college degree has meaning in terms of intellectual achievement. But to follow tradition may not be the action of greatest social value. In 1948 when the President's Commission on Higher Education recommended that the nation greatly enlarge college enrollments, there was much opposition from leading university presidents. But the enrollments did increase. When San Francisco State College raised its admission standards after the California Master Plan was enacted into law in 1960, the action appeared to blacks to be the erection of a wall to exclude them.

When black students, convinced that the university must be an agent of social change, demand the admission of all minority applicants, they bump up against this kind of established admission standards. On many campuses the demand of black students for complete autonomy for departments of black studies also raises this issue. The blacks look at other such programs and observe that an academic department has considerable power over its own affairs. An example is the Jewish Studies Program at Roosevelt University, which is staffed by qualified Jewish faculty who are given the primary decision-making authority over the program and the students.[2] Departmentalization (as I shall demonstrate) fragments the university in an undesirable way, but it is a precedent for autonomy.

Another consideration is that when students set their own goals, they are motivated to learn to a degree never achieved when the goals are imposed by others. An opposing view is that a university possesses unity and has standards that control the appointment of professors and the content of curricula. How then can the control over one particular program be given to a group of black students? Within the black community itself there are deep differences in basic philosophy (e.g., black educators versus black militants)' and also rivalries for power (as demonstrated by the gunfight between the Black Panthers

[2] Charles V. Hamilton, "Relevance of Black Studies," in *Agony and Promise: Current Issues in Higher Education 1969,* ed. G. Kerry Smith (San Francisco: Jossey-Bass, 1969), p. 70.

and the US group at UCLA and by the assassinations that have occurred between the two Muslim orders)'. What then should the program be, and who should run it? An answer has not been found; but
it evidently lies in reconciling the concept of black power with the
concepts underlying higher education. The solution at several institutions is to give blacks a significant voice in the planning, but not a veto
power.

My plea, as will be clear from later chapters, is for participation
in decision making relating to policy and program. Control by any
single vested interest—a student group or an ideological group or an
administrator in charge of teaching or research—is a violation of academic freedom and undermines the larger purposes and the integrity
of the college. The black man feels that the white man has cheated
him out of an education and believes that these structures and standards are barriers imposed by the white man to control and restrict admission into college and into practice in a profession. The reply that
blacks have been the victims of social prejudice and must take additional time to catch up is not acceptable to the black student. He is
preparing for his life's work right now.

One solution is the creation of community learning centers to
complement the colleges. However, like his white counterpart, the
black student wants to go to college, not a substitute for it. College is
the magic that brings entree into jobs and licensing exams. The community learning center, therefore, must include a college program (the
public community college has this potential)'. In this type of institution,
the establishment of standards will need to be governed by a recognition of the achievements of individuals in relation to their past and
to what they can be trained to do. Another solution is a revision of
admissions criteria in the regionally placed four-year colleges and professional schools. It would be a distinct social loss if some colleges did
not serve the intellectual elite, if some graduate schools did not base
their programs on theoretical research, and if some professional schools
did not concentrate on advancing knowledge and techniques. But in
our egalitarian society greater diversification of institutions is needed.
The criterion of intellectual ability may be valid for some colleges, but
it must not be the central criterion for all of them.

The black students have been shocking us with their demands.
They are trying to say to the colleges, "You have been completely overlooking a cultural stream that has great relevance to our particular

identity." They also point to an obvious fact—that white people are the minority pigment group in the world and will presently be a minority in resources and power. Thus, for its own good, the white, Anglo-Saxon, Protestant segment of American society which dominates our activities today—the so-called WASPs—must reconsider the goals, content, and outcomes of all of American education.

Colleges to some extent have identified roles for themselves, and thus individual institutions operate at differing levels of intellectual effort. Under certain of the state systems, as in California, the functions of the respective groups of institutions are controlled by state coordinating councils on higher education. In California, the university limits its enrollments to those students who stand a good chance of doing distinguished work at the graduate and professional level; the state college system takes those who show good promise for specialization in the academic disciplines; and the public junior colleges can accept all students who have high school diplomas. From the viewpoint of planning a state system based on program hierarchies, this functional differentiation is valid. From another viewpoint, that of having regionally placed colleges serve the needs of their communities, the plan is deficient.

There are two reasons why state colleges have not been responsive to local needs. First, placing state colleges under a single board and chancellor has had the effect of standardizing the college by centralizing management, establishing uniform rules and regulations, and using state-controlled line-item budgets. The result has been a tendency to inhibit innovation at the local college level. America needs a highly diversified system to meet all of the needs beyond the high school. Second, four-year colleges have been ambitious to emulate and eventually become universities. A pecking order exists that impels individual colleges and universities toward imitation of such institutions as Harvard, Stanford, Michigan, and the University of California, Berkeley. These distinguished universities have a tremendous drawing power for faculty and students. Thus, regionally placed colleges copy the university reward systems for scholarly publication, as well as the usual departmental structures which pressure for graduate instruction and faculty research. The university psychology often pervades a college faculty and has a detrimental effect because the objectives really cannot be achieved: The institution cannot become—is in fact not permitted, by the total system of American higher education, to become—

another Harvard or Berkeley, and so the faculty is frustrated. They attribute much of their frustration to insufficient appropriations of funds to do research with a stable of graduate students. At the same time they refuse to recognize that the most fruitful role of the regional college lies in teaching, counseling, and public service.

This conflict in educational philosophy creates divisiveness within the college. It was an important element in the strife at San Francisco State College. The militant students and a portion of the faculty want to create an urban-focused institution responsive to the local community. (That such a goal is feasible is illustrated in Chapter Eight, devoted to the urban-related college.) Unfortunately for the achievement of this goal, however, disruptions and violence sway public opinion in favor of "law and order," centralizing authority and inhibiting innovations. But one way for those who propose change to get a hearing is through confrontations, disruptions, and violence. The strategy has produced some results: the initiation of Afro-American studies at Yale and Harvard, a liberalization of the rules and practices in free speech at Berekeley, the resignation of an ivy-bound president at Columbia, and the separation of the Stanford Research Institute from Stanford University, among others. Of most importance, the turmoil has induced fresh dialogue on many educational issues, and the students are participating. Indeed, in many colleges students are being added to the policy-forming committees. Beyond the campus, it is clear that students have had profound impact on American public opinion relating to the war in Vietnam.

Still, with the good developments have come some bad ones. The resort to violence has turned public opinion into hostility, polarized the campuses into factions, caused property damage, and converted many reluctant administrators to the view that use of police is necessary. The sequel to continuing violence will probably be legislation increasing the authority of government to intervene. In Japan, where disruptions have exceeded those in the United States, such a law became effective in 1969. We need less rather than more intrusion by the state, and in the interest of making further progress in reform, militant students should weigh the fruits of their actions. Having awakened the educators to the need for reforms, the students must now work for progress through constructive participation. The theory and method of such participation will be discussed in Chapter Twenty-One.

Actions taken during emergencies still have not resolved many of the basic issues, especially those relating to the values that underlie the whole of American society and to the concentrations of power. This is a long-run task. But at today's turning point in civilization, it is the colleges and universities that must point out the new directions. It is heartening to find students around the world attacking militarism, materialism, and provincialism. Perhaps through the concerted effort of youth a world of fresh values and interrelationships will be formed.

CRITIQUE OF
THE COLLEGES

PART THREE

CHAPTER 6

COMMUNITY COLLEGES

𝄢𝄢𝄢𝄢𝄢𝄢𝄢𝄢𝄢𝄢𝄢𝄢𝄢𝄢𝄢𝄢𝄢𝄢𝄢

The public community college is a relatively young institution. Its role has yet to be well defined, and it is experiencing growing pains. It offers, however, tremendous promise as a community-related institution.

Higher education is in a critical period facing crucial problems of large magnitude. Many sources make this apparent—the numerous nationwide and state studies that have been made, the nature of the debates about federal aid for higher education, the animated and sometimes heated arguments in state legislatures about higher education, the numerous instances in which local communities or regions have begun to plan for public community colleges. More recently students have added their voices, especially in the urban-located colleges. Much of this nationwide debate centers upon the dilemma that is

61

caused on the one hand by the rapidly increasing interest of young people in education beyond high school, and on the other hand by the absence of sufficient clarification of state and national policy relating to higher education.

This crisis is confronting us because of the coincidence in time of four factors: the postwar birth rate as it has affected college attendance, the steadily increasing rate of attendance, the progressively higher costs of operations and of providing plants and equipment, and the stringency of finances. This last factor is caused by a combination of many factors, but mainly by the inadequacy of local and state tax systems. It is also a commentary on the public relations skills of our college administrators that, during the two decades in which we have had available extensive data about the future needs of higher education, we have made so little progress in informing the public about the magnitude of these needs.

Another phase of the crisis applies particularly to the community college. The public community college has been advocated by many as the institution best equipped to serve students at low cost to them and to provide study opportunity of relevance to the local community. Some community colleges obviously have large enrollments of blacks and other disadvantaged youth, and some have designed programs to meet employment conditions and other community needs. But students in many of these colleges are demanding a different focus for these efforts, a focus centered upon cultural differences and upon ghetto needs rather than upon industrial opportunities. This phase of the subject will be discussed at greater length in Chapter Eight in connection with the urban-related college.

Educators, generally, are well aware that current trends are creating bottlenecks of gigantic proportions in college facilities and in the supply of faculty members. In addition to problems caused by growth, there are other problems. First, an increasing heterogeneity of interests among college youth has been a result, in part, of the tendency for more young people from the lower socioeconomic classes to attend college. Second, an increasing heterogeneity of abilities has been revealed by the opening of college doors to all students with high school diplomas. Third, the advancing technology of American industry and the increasing practice of group work in the professions has created opportunities for persons with a new type of education, one that lies between the trade–vocational level of high school and the professional school of the university. Fourth, there is an ever-widening scope of issues with which the average citizen in our democratic society must deal, issues that have expanded in concentric circles until now the citizen must deal with problems in all parts of the world and, indeed, in outer space. And fifth, an increasing number of older persons in our society are unemployed; some require occupational retraining, some require development of avocational and intellectual interests, and almost all need to make psychological and social adjustments for old age. These trends influence materially the nature and development of the public community college.[1] They also influence current national policy relating to education beyond high school, and the present administration is giving high priority to the promotion of community colleges as a solution to the problem. At least six questions have relevance for this subject.

The first question is: What is the role of the community junior college in the scheme of higher education? Originally, junior colleges were dedicated to giving the first two years of the liberal arts curriculum; many of them prided themselves on preparing students exceptionally well to pursue the junior and senior years of college at other institutions. But this concept of the two-year college has now changed. When Leonard Koos pleaded for a people's college, he envisioned a four-year institution composed of the upper two years of high school and the first two years of college.[2] The principal idea was to integrate these four years, to eliminate much of the duplication within them, and to complete the job of secondary education. A number of colleges based on this idea were founded, but most of them have already disappeared. The work of Koos and others, however, did free the junior college of some of its dependency upon the senior institutions. The term *community college* became widely adopted because it represented the concept of an institution that met a variety of community needs. In addition to educating students who desire to transfer to senior colleges, the newer programs include terminal courses in both general education and occupational training: they play a large role in provid-

---

[1] Lamar B. Johnson, *Islands of Innovation Expanding: Changes in the Community College* (Los Angeles: Glencoe Press, 1969).

[2] Leonard V. Koos, *Integrating High School and College* (New York: Harper & Row, Publishers, 1946).

ing continuing education for adults and also emphasize student counseling. Thus the community college is really a people's college. It has been very dynamic in growth.

The problem for the near future is that the community colleges will have to take on a much larger share of the education of freshmen and sophomores than they have in the past. In the nation as a whole, the numbers of these students still represent a small percentage, but in a few states the proportion approaches three-fourths of the total number of underclass students being educated at public institutions. The state with the largest development is California, but the movement is national in scope. The reason for the phenomenal development in California is that the community colleges there are meeting a genuine need. They have attained prestige in the community and they attract huge numbers of commuting students, some traveling to the campuses by college buses. By living at home, attending a free or low-cost institution, and working part-time and in the summer, students can virtually earn their own way through college. The colleges also offer further education to students who possess high school diplomas but do not qualify at other colleges and universities; they engage heavily in continuing education for part-time students and adults; and in some instances they provide an additional center of culture for the community.

If the community colleges are to carry so substantial a portion of the collegiate load, they must think of themselves—and they must be recognized by others—as colleges. This does not mean that a community college can not engage in secondary instruction or in diploma programs (as distinguished from degree-qualifying programs). There is a good argument for serving the needs of all persons beyond high school age. These somewhat different programs need to be identified as such and awards given accordingly. Even the universities of highest reputation provide noncredit courses to serve adult needs. The University of Michigan, for example, has a course for fire fighters and one for real estate agents, and a number of prestigious universities now offer encounter group work and sensitivity training. These services, however, are recognized as unique, and a systematic program in such fields as real estate is suitable for the award of certificates of completion. The presence of such programs on a campus does not in any way call into question the standards of the degree programs at that university.

The second question is: Should the community college emulate the senior college in program, faculty, and the selection of students? The community college concept has great value in that it frees the institution from the inhibitions that pertain to the designation *junior college*. The community college is a free agent. It renders optimum service to its community by building its program on data collected through intensive community or occupational surveys. In meeting these community needs, it plays a genuinely creative role. It would be an unfortunate backward step if the junior college of today were once again to become a shadow of the neighboring university to which many of its students will transfer. A community college can surely carry out its services to the community—indeed be a creative force within the community—and also provide an entirely satisfactory educational program that meets all of the needs of students who plan to transfer to a four-year institution. Several studies at major institutions have demonstrated that transferees from junior colleges compete well with students who began as freshmen within those institutions.

In spite of the apparent enthusiasm with which many teachers in community colleges have accepted the broader concept for the program, I sense among these faculty members a widespread feeling of inferiority in their relationships with the faculties of senior institutions. Feelings of inferiority lead to envy and emulation. Ways must therefore be found to give the faculty members in community colleges a feeling of validity about their own work. Several administrative policies can help to accomplish this. One is to see to it that all new faculty members have an adequate orientation to the community college concept. The teacher who is fresh from a graduate school needs this badly. Second, continuous attention must be given to the problem of group morale. Clarity of objectives is essential to good morale. Third, the contributions that teachers can make as teachers must be emphasized. Often it is necessary to stress how important continuing scholarship is to their improvement as teachers; junior college teachers need to shake off some of the indoctrination they have received about research as a professional career. Still another way of giving community college faculty members a feeling of validity is to use objective means of defining the job that the institution should do. I have briefly mentioned the utilization of community and occupational surveys as a foundation for the creation of courses; the data collected can provide convincing evidence about the needs of the community. As a follow-up, specific objective criteria can be developed by which proposals for courses of instruction are evaluated.

This plan, used successfully by New York in planning its technical institutes, involved three steps: a sampling of employment opportunities, an analysis of the knowledge and skill requirements for each category, and a marshalling of similar types of categories into clusters used as the basis for the design of courses of study.[3] The survey technique—followed by an analysis of objectives, possible content, and methods—is equally applicable when devising cultural and other courses to meet community needs.[4] The use of objective criteria and of systematic analysis provides a rational basis for making judgments about the validity of proposed curricula. This fresh approach avoids the copying of courses merely because they belong to a prestige hierarchy, and reassures the faculty of the merits of novel or experimental programs.

I have already stated that it is the job of the public community college to serve the widespread needs of both young people and adults in the community. The greatest of all opportunities today lies in education. In the United States, I see no justification for telling any student who possesses a high school diploma that he may not attempt to get some education beyond high school. It is important, however, to counsel him wisely so that he will undertake studies that are consistent with his abilities and motivation. The community college must open its doors wide and provide a multipurpose program. Students with talents other than the intellectual one must also be served.[5] In the preparation of transfer students, the community college can render an important screening service by identifying those students who have the intellectual potential to continue.

The third question is: Should the community college be part of a state system of colleges? This question is asked because the trend today is strongly toward establishing systems of higher education. Two principles formerly of lesser importance have become operative today— decentralization and coordination. Decentralization means bringing college physically within the reach of students where they live. The trends

---

[3] Bulletin 1332, 1947, the State Education Department of New York.
[4] See Chapter Fourteen.
[5] Burton Clark, *The Open Door College* (New York: McGraw-Hill Book Company, 1960).

COMMUNITY COLLEGES   67

toward the decentralization of higher education are very obvious: rapid growth in the number and sizes of public two-year colleges, growth of urban universities, transformation of regionally placed teachers' colleges into multipurpose colleges and universities, conversion of state agricultural colleges into multipurpose universities, and establishment by many institutions of branches and extension centers. All of these moves are aimed at providing more programs of certain common types—such as programs in liberal arts, teacher education, and business administration—and at achieving wider geographic distribution of the programs to bring them nearer to the homes of the students. To some extent, these moves also increase the diversity of programs and of institutions.

Some cities have created community colleges that are regionally placed throughout the metropolitan area. States have been working out patterns for future development of their public community colleges. The eventual aim is to provide colleges within commuting reach of virtually all young people, a policy recommended by the President's Commission on Higher Education in 1948.[6] The reasons for planning are clear. The demand for college is becoming universal; the state is subject to pressures to contribute substantial financial aid; and the state, in turn, wants to be sure that each college has an adequate population and economic base, that duplication and competition are prevented, and that the planning eliminates pockets of isolated communities. Statewide coordinating commissions render the essential planning and coordinating services. The role of the state, however, must be limited to planning and coordinating for statewide coverage. The public community college must not become a state institution. It is and must remain a community college.

The fourth question is: What counseling services are needed? The community college caters to the needs that arise from its environment, and it enrolls a heterogeneous student group. The student body is complex, with varying ranges of age, many interests, substantial differences in aptitudes, and tremendous spreads in high school achievement. To meet all of the individual needs would require each institution to do everything for everybody, and that is impossible. A more sensible answer lies in diversifying the institutions to such a degree that

[6] President's Commission on Higher Education, *Report*, Vol. I (Washington, D.C.: Government Printing Office, 1947–48).

the exceptional needs of particular students are catered to through the provision of nonduplicative programs at certain places. Herein lies one of the values of thinking of a group of community colleges as representing a system, with each of the parts having distinctive features. Arrangements can be made for the interchange of students. The allocation of distinctive roles and arrangements for the interchange of students can be facilitated through a planning agency of the state.

The heterogeneity of the student body, however, strongly suggests that the counseling services must be comprehensive. Individual differences need to be identified and students advised about the availability of programs to meet their particular interests and abilities. Innumerable examples of the opportunities for good counseling can be described—the boy from the lower socioeconomic class whose environment has caused him to put too much emphasis upon vocational training, the student with talents other than high intelligence who must be advised carefully about fields in which he can achieve success, the student of unusual interests who should be accommodated in another institution, the student with exceptional ability who should be given every opportunity to progress in relation to his capacity, the adult who desires to be wisely guided into courses that will be genuinely helpful to him. The more complex the situation in higher education becomes, the greater is the demand for counseling services. The community colleges have a key role to play. They are at the threshold of the post-high school opportunity; they are dealing with the emerging adult; they have educational services to render; and they perform a highly important screening function. Wise counseling can help the student utilize his best talents in pursuit of a career and the good life.

The fifth question is about one of the most intriguing opportunities of the community college: How can new curricula be devised to meet present-day needs? The subject raises further questions about the programs of the community college. Curricula need to be considered under the respective heads of general education, technical terminal education, and continuing education. In general education the need for broad cultural courses, integrative in character, has been well stated many times, but there is little evidence that an adequate solution has been found. It is difficult for the liberal arts college to do this job because faculty members respond to the pressures to become highly discipline-oriented. The faculty members of the junior college, on the other hand, ought to respond to another set of pressures—those that urge them to give highest priority to their teaching. They teach the students at the point where horizons can be broadened and an integration of ideas can be provided. They have the opportunity and challenge to develop integrative general education courses.

The junior college must also face the necessity of providing breadth of education both for the potential transferee and for the student who will shortly terminate his formal education. Are there identifiable needs that are commonly shared by these two groups? Another problem emerges because students who transfer from the junior college go to diversified types of institutions. What are the essential elements in the foundation that these students should acquire during their freshman and sophomore years? A third set of problems is found among the enrollments from disadvantaged populations who warrant special ethnic studies programs. To what extent should these programs be tailored to meet the felt needs of these students? All these questions lead me to believe that the two-year college has a unique opportunity to make a contribution in determining the objectives and the nature of general education courses.

The opportunity is even more challenging in the area of technical terminal education. Technologically American industry has been changing so rapidly as to require an ever increasing flow of young persons trained at the semiprofessional level. As the professions have moved toward group practice, their opportunity to use ancillary personnel—that is, technicians of various sorts—has multiplied. Much of the work that has been done at the junior college level in the technical terminal field has been either in emulation of the professional school on a watered down basis or in imitation of high school vocational courses with some attempt at upgrading the content. Many courses that have been established have not been sufficiently founded upon data collected through occupational analysis. Often inadequate provisions are made for laboratory or other experiences. Nearly all institutions have experienced a dearth of well trained instructors to teach the specializations. Still another handicap has been that many of the senior colleges and universities have not had a good understanding of what the two-year colleges are endeavoring to do in this area and so have not given them encouragement and support. They have judged the programs primarily by the difficulties confronting the occasional student who desires to transfer into some specialized field, such as engineering or business administration.

These problems are difficult to resolve, but they also present live challenges to the faculty. In response, some of the community junior colleges have been highly innovative in devising new programs in technical education. Those that best fit the needs of the community have resulted from surveys of community needs. (I shall offer illustrations of some of these curricula in Chapter Eight when I discuss urban-related education.) This creative effort is highly valuable because in the United States there is a strong trend away from unskilled occupations toward middle manpower.[7]

Somewhat related has been the experience of discovering that, after recessions in industry, large numbers of adults are not rehired as business activity is resumed. The reason is that these persons no longer have skills of current interest to the employing companies. Industry, business, the professions, and government are all moving more and more toward the utilization of persons with some college education. The large enrollments of colleges and universities today forecast the graduation of increasingly larger numbers of students. These individuals, freshly educated, presumably will have priority for many kinds of placement. To the extent that they displace persons whose education has been inadequate, or whose skills have become obsolete, a problem of tremendous consequence to our society is being created. I submit that this is an additional area of service for the community college, especially in metropolitan communities that are heavily weighted with industrial and business activity; new ways need to be found to provide additional education for these older persons.

Occupational displacement is only one of the problems facing older people. This is not a new observation. What is new is the tremendous increase in the number of older people due to the greatly improved rate of survival to old age. Increased numbers also mean an increased variety of individual problems. Leaders in adult education have long sensed the opportunity of providing courses which cater to avocational interests or which endeavor to develop new interests for leisure time. Although this is a job that may be shared by many institutions and agencies, surely the public community college has a responsibility of the first order.

Still another problem is to develop curricula of service to the

---

[7] Norman C. Harris, *Technical Education in the Junior College* (Washington, D.C.: American Association of Junior Colleges, 1964).

people of the community in a cultural sense. An example is the need of people to become informed about political issues so that they can discuss them with objectivity and vote intelligently. Or they need to understand cultural differences. The essential difficulty is that the whole world has become a neighborhood. Yet the American people have been inadequately prepared to understand the cultural differences among the peoples of the world or to deal intelligently with the tremendous problems which exist in other parts of the world. Too, the concept of plurality of cultures in the United States is a fresh way of looking at American society, and we now know that we have an intercultural problem of our own. It seems apparent that a great transformation in attitudes, outlooks, and understandings must be achieved. There are, of course, many additional ways in which courses of cultural content can be given. Here, then, is another challenge and task for the community college, which is inherently a primary center of culture and of cultural learning for the community.

My sixth and final question is: What qualifications should community college teachers have? The traditional idea has been that a college teacher—any college teacher—should have the doctor's degree, a standard valid for senior work. But our image of the college teacher at the undergraduate level needs to be revised. The community colleges in particular should cease emulating the universities and define for themselves more clearly the qualifications needed for undergraduate teaching.

The prevailing mood, however, is to compete with senior institutions for persons with doctoral degrees. Admittedly, these degrees provide more luster for the institution; a faculty that includes numerous doctorates may get more recognition from its neighboring university. But the role of the teacher in a community college is one of counseling, teaching, and public service. The training at the doctoral level—as doctor's degrees are presently structured—may misdirect the aims and the energies of the teacher. In any event, granting the requirement of subject-matter competence—the master's degree and, for some, the in-depth knowledge provided by practical experience—the more genuine needs are for teaching and counseling skills, empathy for youth, and an understanding of the roles and the goals of the institution. Since the community college is a different type of college, the faculty chosen for it should possess qualifications consistent with its purposes.

It is apparent from some of my preceding remarks that the attitudes toward the community colleges held by faculty at the senior institutions seriously handicap the public community colleges. One community college president recently exclaimed on this point:

> Educational problems and failures are like city problems and failures: we have curricular slums and pockets of intellectual poverty. The best minds of our nation live in the fashionable academic neighborhoods. But we in the community colleges live and work in the other America. We are trying to bring something of value to those not rich enough, or able enough, or motivated enough, or ready enough for the other institutions. We are trying to find ways of reaching and teaching those who are not moved or touched by the versions of learning offered elsewhere. At this moment, we need help more than we need satire and metaphors. If only our friends in the senior colleges and universities would drop the rhetoric of "rigor" and "standards" and "discipline" for a little while and work with us! We need their help to multiply the options we offer, to create a dense and pluralist urban milieu for all the citizens of our communities. If we work together toward the ideal we all share, we can change the future.[8]

Let me propose some criteria for clarification of what constitutes a community college. A community college is one that is community centered and for which the community assumes major responsibility. It is one that studies the needs of the community for education beyond the high school and builds its program on the basis of such needs. It is one that serves the needs of all persons who desire its services and to whom it can offer appropriate services—including college age youth and others beyond that age. It provides college parallel courses and many other kinds of courses and educative experiences. It serves both full-time and part-time students, persons with intellectual talents and those with other talents as well. The American community junior college meets this concept of a college.[9] Among institutions of higher education, none has the youth and the vigor, nor the complexity of assignment, that the community junior college has.

[8] Seymour Eskow, "Community College," in *Agony and Promise: Current Issues in Higher Education 1969*, ed. G. Kerry Smith (San Francisco: Jossey-Bass, 1969), p. 53.

[9] Leland L. Medsker, *The Junior College: Progress and Prospect* (New York: McGraw-Hill Book Company, 1960).

CHAPTER 7

LIBERAL ARTS
COLLEGES

ʃ✽ʃ✽ʃ✽ʃ✽ʃ✽ʃ✽ʃ✽ʃ✽ʃ✽ʃ✽ʃ✽ʃ✽ʃ✽ʃ✽ʃ✽ʃ✽ʃ✽ʃ✽ʃ

The liberal arts college, heretofore the ideal unit of American higher education, is under fresh scrutiny. There are educators who think that it is passing out, that its program has become so fragmented and specialized that it no longer represents a true unit of education, that the American undergraduate college is in effect merely subordinate to graduate education. There are also educators who are alarmed at the growing size of many colleges of liberal arts, especially those that are part of a university structure. Size, these educators say, leads to impersonality in relationships and to the building of walls between departments; the liberal arts college purports to be devoted to the undergraduate, but the faculty in it are indifferent about undergraduate teaching.

Students themselves are raising many questions about these

73

very issues. Although students are concerned principally with value orientation, cultural stream exclusions, and teaching-learning methodologies, they are also critical of educational objectives as usually stated —whether the rhetoric stresses rounded men or in-depth specialists. Rounded for what—to become well adjusted? Specialist for what—to earn more money? Students are saying, in effect, that purposes, orientations, and teaching all need overhauling.

Educators in professional schools are also concerned about the colleges of liberal arts.[1] The professional schools have leaned heavily upon the faculties in liberal arts to provide a foundation for specialized study at the professional school. But often preparation is inadequate and must be repeated in the professional school. This means that the total time required of the student for the preprofessional and the professional study, especially in medicine and law, is more than it would be if the time were used efficiently. In addition, the typical courses that students take in liberal arts colleges are not really designed to be a liberalizing influence on professional study. Instead, much of the student's time is devoted to courses that are designed solely to be introductory to future specializations. For those who are preparing to teach in elementary or secondary schools where they will need breadth of knowledge, very few courses are interdisciplinary or integrative in scope. We are witnessing, too, a shift in interest from the smaller liberal arts colleges to those of the large university. Historically, it has been certain of the independent colleges that have stood out in reputation and have been pointed to as the institutions of highest quality. There have been two principal causes for the shift. The first grew out of the conditions which existed during the period immediately following World War II. Colleges suddenly absorbed large numbers of students studying under GI scholarships—veterans matured by experience. The GI Bill enabled many of them, especially those from the lower socioeconomic classes, to attend college; and a prevailing concern in their minds was to acquire preparation for jobs and a rise in status to the blue-collar and white-collar classes. The existing emotional situation caused the colleges to make every effort to meet these expressed needs. One result was a mushrooming of the liberal arts curriculum to include many courses modeled after those in undergraduate professional

[1] Aura E. Severinghaus, Harry J. Carman, and William E. Cadbury, Jr., *Preparation for Medical Education: A Restudy* (New York: McGraw-Hill Book Company, 1961).

schools.[2] To attract GI students, the smaller colleges began to emulate the larger universities in the scope of their offerings. The dilution of general education and the disturbance to the unity and integrity of liberal education were considerable.

Barely had this period passed when the launching of the first Sputnik gave rise to the second cause for the shift in interest. The flurry of activity among American educators and government officials is well known. The challenge of the day was to catch up with Soviet Russia in science and technology. Through agencies such as the National Science Foundation and the National Institute of Health, huge additional sums of money were allocated to support programs in science. The great bulk of this money went to leading universities, because it was there that the greatest research potential lay and the largest productivity was apt to ensue. Thus, these institutions were able to add much strength in faculty and in equipment rapidly, while the smaller, independent colleges gradually fell behind in the several science areas. Newly recruited faculty easily sense where the best opportunity lay both in salary and in personal advancement. Students were also stimulated by the competitive atmosphere and began to apply in larger numbers to institutions that had stronger programs in science. These developments left the independent colleges at a substantial disadvantage. Strenuous efforts were made to increase the salaries of their faculties, and some progress was made; but the increased costs had to be accompanied by large increases in tuition charges, and these in turn caused students of high ability from low-income families to go to public universities.

When the fresh objectives of today and the intellectual tools now available are kept in mind, the inadequacies of the two older concepts of liberal education become more apparent. These concepts are that liberal education is the means of passing down the cultural heritage and that general education consists of that body of knowledge that should be common to all men. The passing of the cultural heritage, as John Dewey once said, is a "wonderful mouth-filling phrase."[3] The

2 Earl J. McGrath and Charles H. Russell, *Are Liberal Arts Colleges Becoming Professional Schools?* (New York: Teachers College, Columbia University, 1958).

3 Quoted from a symposium published in Algo D. Henderson, ed., *Educating for Democracy: A Symposium* (Yellow Springs, Ohio: The Antioch Press, 1937), p. 139.

heritage is a residue of what has been screened from the experiences of men in the past and selected by scholars as useful and good to know. Possession of this cultural heritage can be a cultural veneer and, as such, it formerly served well the purposes of the social elite. The heritage concept is also congenial to those who want to educate by inculcation. To such people, certain of the neo-Thomists, for example, or certain groups professing democracy, the wisdom of the past is defined to coincide with specific ideological or religious beliefs deemed essential to the development of the good man. Such indoctrinations, if dominating, slow the process of evolutionary development.

If one grants that values become values because of the experiences of men in the past, the role of the college and university is to subject these values to rational analysis. Some of them should be supported, some discarded, and some modified. Within the halls of higher learning, values should not be imposed on students merely because they have been previously accepted as good or because it is deemed that human nature does not change.[4] Another weakness in the cultural heritage concept should be obvious: In making selections of man's heritage, nearly exclusive attention has been given to European events and ideas. This practice has led to gross biases in curriculum, as advocates of Asian and black culture studies programs now point out.

Still another concern of this view of liberal education is that it results in a passive experience for the student. He is in college for the purpose of being filled with selected knowledge. Often a teacher has not himself assimilated or internalized the knowledge about which he is lecturing. He merely repeats what he acquired in graduate school and thus falls short of being a creative, stimulating thinker who is constantly challenging his students to think. His efforts are bent on understanding the past in some one-dimensional way, and he does not keep sufficiently abreast of the rapidly expanding knowledge of today. I suggest as an alternative that faculty and students change their roles in the classroom and work together in a search for knowledge. The knowledge accumulated from the past is, of course, the product of creative men and women who themselves were genuine students in their search for wisdom. They did not rely upon dogma. They succeeded in freeing themselves from the constricting influences of tradi-

---

[4] Algo D. Henderson, "What Constitutes a Liberating Education?" in *Authoritarian Attempt to Capture Education,* ed. Jerome Nathanson (New York: King's Crown Press, 1945), Chap. 6.

tion and precedent; and they were able to learn effective modes of inquiry. Our knowledge should be an expansion of their knowledge. The act of discovery is stimulating, and students respond to the excitement of the search.

I do not mean to condemn the study of man's past experience. Animals repeat the lives of their ancestors, except for adaptations that come through the slow process of evolution. Man can begin where his predecessors left off. After Priestley discovered oxygen, the new knowledge led to further discoveries of the atomic table and presently to atomic power. Our concept of civil liberties began with the Magna Carta and was developed through dozens of enactments by the British Parliament that encompassed hundreds of years of experience. In this sense, the cultural heritage has high significance and relevance. But the difference between this concept and a simple transmission of historical fact lies in the dynamic use of the wisdom. In other words, the knowledge of the past should not be handed down as a package to be accepted in toto. Rather, it should be the basis for further study and evaluation. Our ultimate concern is with the nature and quality of living today and with planning for the future.

I believe that man can be a planner of his activities and his destiny. Man does not need merely to follow tradition and precedent. He can cultivate expertness in research and development; he can evaluate past experience and make projections from it. Although he has long had such tools as the scientific method for problem solving, today—following the developments in cybernetics, including especially the computer—man has available new technologies. These provide additional tools that facilitate his planning, particularly in matters that involve social complexities. Man does not, therefore, need to rely wholly upon authority for his decision making. The modern educated man is a planning man.

The second of the two older concepts of liberal education concerns the movement known as general education. It was an attempt to construct learning experiences from the viewpoint of the student instead of building a hierarchy of subject matter. Influenced by the philosophy of the rounded man, the purpose of general education was to prepare the student for all phases of his living: intellectual, personal, physical, social and civil. The approach was broad and was a counteraction to the view which held liberal education to be the transmission of a body of cultural knowledge. The interests of the student and his learning, rather than this body of knowledge, were central. Knowledge was drawn upon as a means to the end of educating the student. A broader view of curriculum was taken than merely the teaching of courses; the objectives permitted the inclusion of experiences outside the classroom. This movement was undoubtedly influenced by Dewey's statement of principle that the way to learn to live effectively in the future is to engage now in living experiences that produce desirable change and growth.

Earlier attempts to design curricula for the purposes of general education were commendable in their aim to produce courses that were both comprehensive and integrative. The product, however, was highly generalized and oftentimes superficial. Because students differ so much in the achievements that they bring from their high schools and from their cultural environments, these survey courses were repetitive for many of them. A problem also arose in finding faculty who were dedicated to the ideal of general education. The type of teaching required tended to remove them from their disciplines, and it was in their disciplines that the college placed incentives of salary and professional advancement.

In spite of these critical remarks, and in spite of the mediocre showing made by programs in general education, the ideal of educating the individual rather than merely disseminating a body of knowledge is sound. The motivations of the students can be built upon, and motivation is highly important in the process of learning. The subject matter can be given a degree of relevancy to living—a fact which could answer one of the complaints of students about the sterility of the education they have been receiving. During its heyday, many interesting experiments in general education were conducted.

One of the most thoughtful reexaminations of general education was made by Daniel Bell.[5] Almost simultaneously, Columbia, Harvard, and the University of Chicago—all noted for earlier experimentations with general education—have been revising their programs. Bell provided a critical review of the events at all three institutions, although his book is essentially a proposal for the future development of general education at Columbia.

I think that each of the three institutions had highly commend-

5 Daniel Bell, *The Reforming of General Education* (New York: Columbia University Press, 1966).

able features in their earlier programs of general education. The course in contemporary civilization at Columbia, for example, was initiated to cope with the world orientation of the United States following World War I. It was staffed at the outset by exceptionally broad-gauged and competent men. It was, in effect, a drastic revision of the approach to teaching history. The frame of reference was world history, not merely European and American history. An aim was to teach in a comprehensive manner the historical events that have influenced the evolutionary progress of civilization, stressing those events most significant for man and attempting to highlight and evaluate the major turning points in history. The concept still seems good, and it is relevant to the needs of today. Indeed, the issue of relevancy is one of those being raised by present-day students because they have become so conscious of America's involvement in world affairs.

At Harvard, James Conant's course in science for nonscience students was admirable in its basic philosophy.[6] It was intended to reveal to the student how ideas are initiated by one man and then developed and expanded by other men, as well as to show how the scientific method has been generated and perfected. Conant was also interested in acquainting students with the streams of scientific discovery that have most influenced our lives today. He developed a series of case studies and thus also involved the student in problem solving, the techniques of which are essential to intellectual growth. One case study, for instance, described the problem that confronted Lavoisier during a laboratory experiment when he detected an additional substance, derived from mercury oxide, that he thought was common air. The case study presented the subsequent work by Priestley. In 1774 he discovered that the substance was something new. Lavoisier then named it oxygen. Thus was launched the development of our knowledge of the atomic table. The nonscience student, motivated to understand atomic energy because of its explosive force, derived through the case study an understanding of the chemical and physical principles that underlie the atomic structure. But he also learned a lot about the scientific method. Surely this is meaningful study of historical subject matter that is highly relevant to the problems of today.

The University of Chicago's experiment with an undergraduate

[6] "The Overthrow of the Phlogiston Theory," in *Harvard Case Histories in Experimental Science* (Cambridge, Mass.: Harvard University Press, 1950).

college also had its point of merit.[7] It represented the careful design of a total curriculum that unified knowledge. It therefore had an aim similar to that of the trivium and quadrivium or of the Grecian and Roman classics. The unity was achieved in contemporary subject matter composed of three-year sequences in each of the major areas of knowledge: the humanities, the social sciences, and the natural sciences. By devising course sequences covering three years of study, the faculty was able to overcome the weaknesses of the university's earlier venture with survey courses and to utilize the educational principles of continuity, sequence, and integration in curriculum construction. Today many liberal arts programs are hodgepodges, the result of faculty logrolling rather than the product of design based on educational principles, as at Chicago. Unfortunately for its future, the Chicago College also included an endeavor to reform a portion of the high school curriculum, and this part of the plan did not succeed. The College was also attacked by many of the faculty who held appointments in the graduate divisions; they felt that the students coming into their areas should have had more specialized courses in a single field of concentration during the undergraduate years. These faculty finally prevailed after Robert M. Hutchins left the chancellorship; and thus, another liberal arts college model of considerable merit was emasculated. In retrospect, I have found the graduates of the Chicago College to be exciting and creative persons.

But to return to the findings and recommendations of Daniel Bell's book: Bell favors having a student devote the two middle years of his four-year liberal arts program to acquiring the intellectual tools of a specific discipline. Training in the ability to conceptualize, explore and observe, search recorded knowledge, analyze and synthesize, and communicate findings in the technical language of the discipline are tools and skills of major importance to future specialists. A tool such as the ability to conceptualize is broadly applicable and is therefore essential in educating the problem solver and the free man. While agreeing with the importance of this intellectual training, I contend that it should be only one of the objectives at the undergraduate level. To overstress the disciplines for three years within the undergraduate college means vitiating the concept of rounded education.

[7] F. Champion Ward, et al., The Idea and Practice of General Education: An Accounting of the College of the University of Chicage (Chicago: University of Chicago Press, 1950).

I believe in differentiation among colleges, including liberal arts colleges. The stress laid upon the disciplines is more appropriate to a college, such as Columbia College—which is in gear with a graduate school and therefore heavily preparatory for advanced study— than it would be in a college where most of the students terminate their education. In applying the principles advocated by Bell, will the colleges retain the admirable features of the three earlier plans—the fusing of the cultures of the world, the study of history to shed light on the present, the unifying of the humanities, social sciences, and natural sciences by the student? These features are among those that should be central to general education today, and they would go far to meet the criticisms that are currently being raised.

In attempting to implement an integrated curriculum in liberal arts colleges, administrators encounter two major structural problems: the two-and-two or breadth–depth concept, and the departmental system. In the traditional liberal arts college, the student used to progress through a sequence of courses which, at the end of four years, made an integrated whole. In the classics, for example, he acquired an understanding of Grecian and Roman civilizations from which our own culture has arisen. But now, with the proliferation of course offerings and the elective system, the student has available to him a wide range of subject areas. Left to his own devices, he might end his four years with specialization in a single field—for example, French language and literature—and with a smattering of knowledge in biophysics, U.S. history, and cultural anthropology. The college, to encourage him to direct his studies, has set up the objectives of breadth— a spread of courses from various areas of knowledge, and depth—the intensive study of one particular discipline. In the standard pattern adopted by all but the experimental colleges, the first two years of study constitute the program in general education, including courses prerequisite to the major, and the last two years consist largely of the departmental major together with related elective courses. This system has the great advantage of facilitating the transfer of students between two-year and four-year colleges. The stratification by levels, however, violates the principle of integration of general studies and specialized studies. For cultural knowledge to have an impact on the manner in which the student later practices his specialization, the study must be intertwined during the entire four-year period and even beyond.

There are often disadvantages in this standard pattern. The

domination of the liberal arts program by specialized interests and study in the form of departments has disrupted the unity of the faculty in its organization. The departments erect walls that militate strongly against intercommunication, both on college business and in discussions of knowledge with the faculty of other departments. For the student this means that interdisciplinary study is inhibited.

During the upper two years of college study—and often in the very first semester of the freshman year—the department captures the student. He is required to major, and the major sequence is determined by the faculty of the department. At large universities the interests of the professors, especially in research, tend to prevail and those of the student tend to be neglected.

By defining the fields of concentration offered to students differently from the way departmental units are defined, we can overcome this difficulty. Departmental organization can exist for the purpose of carrying on the business of the department, but the student's work, using the principle of study in some depth, can be a concentration that meets his own objectives. The student with appropriate guidance would select his courses—which might be from two or more departments—and evaluation of the student's program would be based on criteria set up by a faculty interdisciplinary committee rather than on course requirements as determined by a single department. We used this plan at Antioch College, and we thought that it provided the flexibility for individualizing the programs desired by a portion of the students.[8] It is in the interests of the department, for purposes of obtaining good budgets and maintaining as large a faculty as possible, to display a large enrollment of students and to graduate many majors, and the faculty strongly believe in their ability to define a specialization. But even within this given framework, the departments could innovate. If a faculty is unwilling to go this far, it can at least follow the lead of the University of Washington, which in 1969 established a Division of General and Disciplinary Studies. The aim of the division is to create a mechanism through which the critical problems of our culture can be studied.

If I was designing a liberal arts college from scratch, having in mind the considerations discussed above, I would probably not use

[8] Algo D. Henderson and Dorothy Hall, *Antioch College: Its Design for Liberal Education* (New York: Harper & Row, Publishers, 1946).

narrow departments. The appropriate organization at the undergraduate level is a broad divisional one rather than one fractionated by departments. It is in the graduate school that the study of specializations becomes important; it is here that the greatest emphasis upon the disciplines should occur.[9]

But there is another important reason why departmental walls need to be breached. The explosion of knowledge has not been occurring wholly within such walls. The spontaneous development of institutes and centers at many large universities is evidence of the interdisciplinary nature of knowledge. The institute is a device which brings together talent from two or more disciplines and focuses attention on a common problem. One difficulty with the institute or center, however, is that it creates an additional complexity within the organizational pattern of the institution. Yet if students were allowed the kind of flexibility that is obtained through the creation of institutes, they, too, might jump over departmental walls in large numbers.

My discussion of this subject is directed at raising the question of whether the organization of the faculty within the vast majority of liberal arts colleges today is the appropriate one. Embedded though the departmental structure is, I suspect that in the course of time it will have to give way to some new and more flexible structure.[10] I shall refrain from giving a pat solution to the problem of structure, but I will commend the University of California at Santa Cruz for experimenting with a plan that organizes the faculty in a twofold way. At Santa Cruz the faculty is grouped by congenial subject interests and for graduate instruction, and organized also by small college units that are integrative of the liberal arts. The Santa Cruz plan, incidentally, also suggests a model for the organization of faculty at the graduate level that achieves a more definite and comprehensive graduate operation.

I suspect that an influence that will become increasingly great in effecting structural change is the new type of program planning and budgeting. Under this new system, a program may be either for student learning or for investigation of a research problem, and the

[9] For a critique of graduate education, see Ann M. Heiss, *Challenges to Graduate Schools: The Ph.D. Program in Ten Universities* (San Francisco: Jossey-Bass, 1970).

[10] Paul L. Dressel, F. Craig Johnson, Philip M. Marcus, "Departmental Operations: The Confidence Game," *Educational Record,* Vol. 50, No. 3 (Summer, 1969), pp. 274–78. The full study by Dressel and his associates on departmental organization appears in *The Confidence Crisis* (Jossey-Bass Series, 1970).

84 THE INNOVATIVE SPIRIT

budget calls for the allocation of resources—faculty time, equipment, space, and so forth. These are the inputs. The outputs of the program may be judged by whatever results, in education or in research findings, can be measured. Institutes are now programmed on this basis, and I see no reason why the idea cannot be carried into the educational program. The faculty, then, can be organized into groups appropriate to broadly conceived interests. Through this organization, the allocations of time of each faculty member can be made, accountability secured, and opportunity afforded for maintaining congenial relations with academic colleagues. The Santa Cruz plan is based upon principles such as these.

One of the student criticisms of the liberal arts college is that it has become too large and impersonal. In an effort to remedy this weakness, a few institutions have developed the cluster idea.[11] A cluster is a group of colleges which have some reason for wanting to be interrelated, but each of which has an entity of its own. If we free ourselves from the inhibitions relating to departmental organization, we discover that there is no reason why an undergraduate liberal arts college must be large and unwieldy. It need not be dominated by professors whose interests are largely if not wholly at the advanced level of research. A university might have two or many liberal arts faculties; each might be organized around the principle of unity of knowledge, liberal in character, or around an assumption about the optimum size that permits the best interaction between faculty and students.

Another possibility is to organize the college along the lines typified by the present college divisions: the humanities, the social sciences, the natural and physical sciences. A more attractive idea, though, is to organize each faculty so that it and the students concern themselves with some focal theme. To some extent the University of California at Santa Cruz is organizing its several colleges in this way, a recent theme being human relations. One of the cluster colleges of the University of the Pacific gives all instruction in Spanish, and the most recent of the cluster colleges on that campus concerns itself with international and intercultural relations. Some of the colleges in the Claremont group have special interests such as the sciences and the administration of business and public affairs. The University of Wis-

11 Warren Bryan Martin, *Conformity: Standards and Change in Higher Education* (San Francisco: Jossey-Bass, 1969). Also, Jerry G. Gaff and associates, *The Cluster College* (San Francisco: Jossey-Bass, 1970).

consin at Green Bay has initiated four liberal arts colleges, each with a primary focus: creative communication, community sciences, environmental sciences, and human biology. These foci were identified by study of the needs of the surrounding community and through consultations with lay advisory committees. For example, the study of conservation as a problem in environmental science, around which to mobilize both breadth and intensity of knowledge, would seem to be a natural for the Wisconsin region.

In Chapters Ten through Thirteen, which discuss educating for the professions, I raise the question of whether study at the preprofessional level might best be undertaken in a university through organizing a college that has this special focus. This college, too, would be a liberal arts type of institution with a core of subject matter devoted to general education, but the subject matter would lie within the frame of reference of educating men for the professions. It would, of course, be necessary to vary the studies in depth, because each of the professions has its own preprofessional needs. The cluster college plan of organization especially lends itself to the inclusion of a college that would be devoted principally to preparing students to go on to study at some professional school.

At the outset of the present chapter, I spoke of the shift of interest from smaller colleges to larger universities. Since it is likely that this trend will continue, the cluster plan is especially germane, for it enables large institutions to operate small colleges. Thus the advantage of size in both respects can be had: on the one hand, a unified education characterized as a faculty–student shared search for knowledge, and on the other hand, access to superior equipment, library, and faculty resources.

Although the church-related and independent colleges are receiving a lessening percentage of the total college enrollments, individually most of them are not declining in size. They are by no means condemned to retire from the scene. Insofar as finances are a factor, in some states—New York and Illinois, for example—moves have been made to give them some state aid. The federal government also has made certain public money available. The future missions of these small colleges and their chances of success, however, lie in redefining their goals to meet individual and social needs. They should not emulate the universities, but instead should develop distinctive programs. They can achieve unity by building around a concept of liberal education or some other innovation in program. Such goals are more possible of achievement in a unitary college than in a large university, where pressures tend to adulterate the goals. Emphasis should be placed upon quality of counseling and teaching, taking full advantage of the possible direct relationships between senior faculty and students. In spite of the advantages of large institutions, a portion of students—some of them with the support of their parents—will be motivated to attend smaller, private institutions. Some able teachers, attracted by the goals and the environment, prefer the cooperative relationships among faculty at a small college to the competitive ones of the research-oriented university. They will choose to teach in the smaller college.

Whereas the liberal arts colleges were closely similar in objectives and curriculum a century and more ago, today they vary from one another rather widely. A recent study of a group of liberal arts colleges confirms the differences.[12] I once collected, from books on liberal and general education, twenty rather different perceptions of purposes; the current trend is obviously toward an acceleration of this differentiation. Faculty today can establish criteria based upon a frame of objectives, and thus free themselves from the domination of a curriculum hierarchy.

I do not agree with the pessimistic views about liberal arts colleges. Neither do I think that they should fall victim to the notion, prevalent among continental universities, that the gymnasium or lycee should complete the general education of the student and that higher education should mean specialized study. Our concept of liberal education is unique and it is good. It is appropriate to the nature and aims of a democratic society. The liberal arts college is the means for implementing the objectives.

[12] Morris Keeton and Conrad Hilberry, *Struggle and Promise: A Future for Colleges,* The Carnegie Series in American Education (New York: McGraw-Hill Book Company, 1969).

CHAPTER 8

URBAN-RELATED
COLLEGES

𝄞𝄞𝄞𝄞𝄞𝄞𝄞𝄞𝄞𝄞𝄞𝄞𝄞𝄞𝄞𝄞𝄞𝄞

The evolution of a predomi-
nantly urban society in America is creating a new environment. Of
our population, 85 per cent now live in urban areas, making new
demands at all levels of our educational structure. The decay of central
cities, with the attendant social, economic, and physical–environmental
problems, is creating a situation that is new to traditional educators
and educational programs. The fundamental problem is that of
educating new generations to cope with the new pressures of urban
living and to train all citizens—urban, suburban, and rural—in the
responsibilities of this new way of life. To attack the problems arising
from this situation is the responsibility of all educational institutions.
At the higher level of education, all phases of educational programs—
instruction, research, and public service—can become involved. Many

87

colleges and universities are already concerned, and literally hundreds of projects have been launched.

The traditionally structured colleges and universities are handicapped in responding as fully as needed to the new roles demanded of them; their approaches are piecemeal. New innovative programs need to be devised, with the designs changing as the needs of the community change—the designs should be fluid and flexible. In this chapter I suggest several features that might be incorporated into these new designs, and in doing so, I draw upon programs that already exist and present a model for consideration.

One of the biggest problems of the urban center is the large number of persons who are unemployed and unemployable because they lack the education and skill to hold any type of job. The first two institutions described below are confronting this problem by training persons for occupations needed specifically by the community in which they are located, as well as for occupations necessary to a technological society.

In New York City, during the 1920s it became apparent to leaders in the textile industry, both management and labor, that the supply of skilled labor for the industry was being exhausted. The members of the International Ladies Garment Workers Union, most of whom had learned skills in the needle trades in Europe, wanted to train their own sons and daughters for the industry, the second largest in the city. Immigration from Europe had been greatly curtailed. The industry needed a new generation of employees, and union members were motivated to pass on their skills to their own children. Through the joint efforts of labor and management, The Educational Foundation of the Apparel Industry was organized and financed. In 1944, it contracted with the Board of Education of the City of New York for the development of a program that became the Fashion Institute of Technology, and in 1951 the State of New York recognized the school as a public community college and incorporated it into the system of community colleges that were in part subsidized by the state. At that time, the scope of the program was considerably extended to include the whole field of fashion design and clothing manufacture. Here, then, was a college that grew out of the felt needs of the people in an industry and the willingness of the state university system in New York to incorporate it as a unit. The college, now housed in a several-storied new building in the heart of Manhattan—near many manufacturing plants, distribution and merchandising centers, and executive offices of the fashion industry—has been having outstanding success.

Laney College, a public community college in Oakland, California, has a particularly interesting program for training students to work in the Oakland community. It may shock tradition-minded college educators to contemplate what Laney offers. The Associate in Arts degree is granted to students who major in such trade–technical fields as cosmetology, dry cleaning, fashion arts, graphic arts, shoe rebuilding, and upholstery. For the Associate in Science degree, the majors include aeronautics (such as aircraft flight operations), air conditioning and refrigeration technology, automotive occupations, building and construction trades, business equipment technology, electrical–industrial control technology, electronic communication technology, industrial engineering technology, machine and metals technology, manufacturing technology, medical assisting, photography, quality control, construction technology, culinary arts, dental assisting, drafting technology, and vocational nursing.[1] In several instances the faculty have secured the cooperation of unions to assure the entrance of graduates into the occupations for which they are trained. A visit to the campus of Laney College quickly reveals it to be a dynamic place. It is crowded day and night with students, many of whom obviously are from lower socioeconomic backgrounds, including college age as well as older persons, some full-time, some part-time. The laboratories teem with motivated activity.

These two illustrations—the Fashion Institute of Technology in New York and Laney College in Oakland—are models of originality in attacking unemployment through middle manpower training. Both are public community colleges and both reveal the potential that exists in this type of post-high school institution for providing training programs (a subject I have discussed in Chapter Six along with other community-related functions of the public community college). The offering of occupationally oriented courses by colleges and universities for both day and evening students is, of course, a common occurrence in our cities. Usually, however, they are fringe activities. What is different about the two colleges I have described is the planning of programs that are innovative both in meeting community needs and in offering them as the main thrust of the educational program.

[1] For further descriptive detail, see the Laney College Bulletin.

Another major problem of the large city is the lack of adequate health and legal services for the poor. Moves by professional schools, such as law and medicine, to recruit more students from minority groups and to render services that are needed in the urban ghettos, are of major significance. In Chapter Ten I offer some illustrations of this kind of training relating to educating for the professions. It is sufficient here to mention only one example, the program called "CLEO" conducted by a number of law schools, which makes a fresh approach in evaluating the qualifications of disadvantaged applicants for admission. These special efforts are still experimental, but they are a welcome change. Many black students today are motivated to serve their own communities. If, while studying law, these students are not diverted from this motivation, they will be able to provide more adequately the legal services that are needed.

In Illinois the problem of medical education was exhaustively studied recently by the Board of Higher Education. After analyzing the inadequacies of services caused by deficiencies in personnel, a long list of professional and paramedical roles was prepared. It included the following types of health personnel: pediatricians (including nurse pediatricians and pediatric nurse clinicians), physicians assistants, midwives and nurse midwives, physical therapists, occupational therapists, radiologic technologists capable of diagnosis and therapy, dental associates who can prepare caries for treatment, nutrition experts, blood bank technologists, hospital administrators, industrial hygienists, nurses, psychiatric social workers, speech pathologists, orthologists, and addiction therapists.[2] Many of these technicians and specialists are already being trained in a variety of institutions. However, the list illustrates the possibilities that exist for a new type of school within the health personnel field. Such an institution would turn out persons with training of considerable relevance to the health needs of ghetto and other populations.

A principal need of the urban center is for health service practitioners to supplement specialists in the medical profession. An illustration is the nurse pediatrics practitioner, such as is being trained at the University of Colorado. But I explore this subject more fully in Chapter Eleven.

Elementary and secondary education is sadly neglected in the

[2] *Education in the Health Fields by State of Illinois*, State of Illinois, Board of Higher Education, Vol. I, pp. 51–59, and Appendix II.

urban center. The university has special competence for assisting with curriculum planning and the training of teachers who are motivated to teach in the ghetto. Minority groups need to learn to initiate economic ventures of their own. Since capital is lacking, launching a business is difficult. The school of business administration of the University of California at Berkeley is exploring the possibilities in franchise operation. By owning a franchise for a small business, the small investor can make a start and, with supervision, manage his own enterprise. But this program offers only a partial solution to a difficult problem. Title I of the Higher Education Act has stimulated many projects for helping small businesses, but the whole matter needs further help from the urban-related schools of business which have been, until now, strongly oriented toward big business.

The design of programs to supply vocational and professional needs is only part of the problem of urban education. Serving the cultural needs of the people of the community is just as important. A major principle of education is that a student must take the next step in learning from wherever he is. Persons who are culturally deprived must relate fresh knowledge and insights to what they already know— and what they already know is sure to be very different from what is already known by other kinds of students. Here again, we get down to that baffling problem, the orientation of the teacher. I recall an instance of a middle-aged high school teacher who had specialized in English literature at the university. In his earlier career as a faculty member in a community of high prestige within the boundaries of a large city, he had derived personal satisfaction from teaching the kinds of courses that he himself had studied, including one on Chaucer. The students who had come to his classes were from cultured and sophisticated families. But with the passage of some fifteen years, people of wealth and even of modest means moved to the suburbs. The houses in the community were occupied by blacks who had migrated from the South to obtain positions in the industries of the area. This teacher was confronted with a wholly new kind of student body. Chaucer did not go over at all, and this teacher's career was so badly upset that he left teaching. There is, however, another interpretation of his failure: He had been teaching subject matter, but it became necessary for him to teach students. He failed to understand that he had a most worthwhile opportunity to bring genuine cultural knowledge to students who had limited amounts of it. His skills in evaluating and teaching literature might well have been applied to the discovery of poetry, novels, and fiction by black authors or to a portrayal of the African cultural stream. Some of this material may be primitive, but so also is Chaucer.

Through individuals, the community can also be reached. It should be part of the mission of an urban-related college to raise the cultural level of the community. Many colleges, for instance, include nursery schools as practice laboratories for prospective nursery school teachers. The objectives of the project, however, should go beyond the teaching of college students. With the children come the mothers, and through the mothers the homes can be reached. The larger aim should be to improve the home environments and lives of the children and their families. Tradition-bound educators may question this aim. This was, however, the purpose of the home demonstration programs of the land-grant colleges, and the rural homes as a consequence were tremendously improved.

In this connection, the history of Berea College is instructive.[3] Berea influenced the development of the hill regions of Kentucky and Tennessee. In doing so, it provided a first-rate college education for the youth; but it also developed model cabins, gave instruction in interior design and decoration, designed and made pottery, furniture, and fabrics, and taught good dairy and farming practices. These college projects served the dual purposes of educating students in the practical aspects of cultural advance and of providing jobs for students without money.

When discussing colleges and social change in Chapter Four, I described some of the activities at Antioch College that were aimed at changing a provincial environment into a progressive one. There is no doubt that it was the influence of the college that brought about the community reform. Recently Antioch has begun to operate a field study center in the new town of Columbia, Maryland, focusing on urban development, education by problem solving, concurrent work and study, the environment as a learning resource, integration with the community, and programs of social impact and service. Implementation is made through several institutes which study documentary arts,

[3] Elisabeth S. Peck, *Berea's First Century, 1855–1955* (Lexington: University of Kentucky Press, 1955).

contemporary human problems, and environmental science and which include a community education center.

There exists within our society the grave problem of racism and prejudice. Blacks, Chicanos, and Asians living within our cities experience discrimination on a daily basis: they cannot get jobs; they cannot read; their children do not have adequate schools. Minority students, when they demand ethnic studies programs, hope to confront the racist concept of superiority–inferiority and replace it with the concept of race identity and pride.

Although black studies programs are the most widely sought, other programs include Asian–American studies, Chicano studies, and Native American Studies. Programs of these kinds have been established recently at a number of campuses. But regarding black studies programs, two approaches are being used by colleges to meet demands. One approach is to offer a limited number of courses in such areas as African history, African art, and Afro–American culture. In the fall term of 1969 Harvard was offering seven such courses and had identified thirteen interdisciplinary courses acceptable for concentration in Afro–American studies. Yale was teaching a long list of courses that have relevance to the needs of the blacks in America. The justification for these courses is based on a statement repeated by many prominent Negro educators: The black man has been in America as long as the white man and is inevitably a part of our pluralistic society, but his search for identity leads him also to his African origins. Many of these courses use the traditional subject matter approach and they have a contribution to make to the campus as a whole. The introduction of any cultural stream, additional to that of the Western white one, into the curriculum is a step forward. The plan has been widely implemented.

The second approach is that of a unified curriculum for general education, through which a major concentration may be studied. In substance, the plan would resemble similar studies devoted to Western European culture.[4] Although many colleges have expressed interest in this new idea, as of the spring of 1970 few had actually established

[4] Charles V. Hamilton, "Relevance of Black Studies," in *Agony and Promise: Current Issues in Higher Education,* ed. G. Kerry Smith (San Francisco: Jossey-Bass, 1969), pp. 69–73; also *Black Studies in the University, a Symposium* (New Haven: Yale University Press, 1969).

such a general education major concentration.[5] One example, apparently the oldest in the United States, is the one adopted at Merritt College, a junior college in Oakland, California. Merritt offers twenty-three separate courses in black studies. The curriculum includes four courses in Swahili, one each in Afro–American education, sociology, psychology, and history, and three each in Afro–American theater, art, and writing, a three-course sequence concentrating on the black man in America, and one course each in African history and the political science of emerging nations. Other credits may be earned through individual studies. Beginning in the fall of 1969, Merritt established departmental majors in Afro–American studies and in Latin– and Mexican–American studies.

It will be interesting to watch the development of curriculum at the new Federal City College in Washington, a federally sponsored institution that is urban-centered and primarily black. From its beginning the institution has been plagued with internal turmoil because of cleavages within the faculty over the two philosophical approaches to a black studies curriculum. As of this writing, the more traditional view has gained ascendancy.

The objective of a black studies program is to elevate an entire people through education. If such a program could have the effect of giving to black people in America a new sense of identity, a fresh unity as a community, and the feeling that their culture is one of a plurality of cultures appropriate to the American scene, it would be tremendously worthwhile. If, on the other hand, it results in a polarization of goals between whites and blacks, or even within the black group, the longer-run product might be conflict built on separatism. The concept of plurality of cultures is appealing; that of apartheid is repugnant to democratic ideals. The end result may depend upon whether a separated program develops understanding or promotes hatreds. But one good reason for trying the black studies idea is to take advantage of black motivation to learn.

Malcolm X[6] went through the complete emotional cycle: frus-

[5] Several dozen institutions have initiated plans, many of which have appeared in mimeographed outline. It is not always easy to tell from the rhetoric what is actually happening.

[6] Malcolm X, *The Autobiography of Malcom X* (New York: Grove Press, Inc., 1964; paperback edition, 1966).

tration, fear, hatred, and then goodwill. Near the end of his life, following his journey to Mecca, he was beginning a course of action that was socially oriented. Among other experiences, he came to know that there are whites who are not prejudiced against blacks. The basic problem for both black and white in ridding our emotions of racism is how to educate ourselves.

Judgments about the worth of ethnic studies should be made on the basis of criteria of contribution, rather than on the basis of hierarchical views of the subject matter. Asian studies have rich materials available; African studies need much development. Both contribute to the objectives of liberal education. The objectives suggested by Theodore Greene,[7] though stated in a different context, have high applicability: increasing the ability to be literate and articulate; increasing knowledge about oneself, one's physical world and one's social environment; increasing one's sense of values—moral, esthetic, religious, and social; and widening the horizons of a student through understanding the relationship of the parts to the whole. For the black student with his present concerns and motivations, more learning might occur through black studies than through traditional ones.

Thus far I have been discussing programs that can be accommodated within existing colleges and universities, and institutions to deal with the problems of society on a fairly sophisticated level. But I also envision programs which speak to the present needs of the entire community on a less sophisticated level. An experiment of this sort is the store front education center, such as the Cooperative Urban Extension Center in Buffalo. Through the participation of the colleges and universities of the area, the Center, located in ghetto neighborhoods, has offered programs in "the provision of information on education; the conduct of special education programs; the referral of requests to other agencies where feasible; and the provision of social services where other agencies are inactive or inaccessible."[8] The enrollees include both children and adults, and the only qualifications for admission are need and motivation. The tutoring and the courses

---

[7] Theodore M. Greene, *Liberal Education Reexamined: Its Role in a Democracy* (New York: Harper & Row, Publishers, 1943).

[8] C. T. M. Hawden, "Evaluation, Education Information Centers" (Buffalo, New York: Cooperative Urban Extension Center, December, 1967), p. 22.

range from remedial reading through an array of academic and vocational subjects.

Another illustration is the Indian Community Development Program sponsored by the federal government. With guidance from the University of New Mexico, the tribes and pueblos of New Mexico and southern Colorado are enhancing tribal life to preserve its integrity and to make it more attractive for the youth to remain or return after college. One of the tribes, the Mescalaroes, has standardized the quality of their herd of cattle, improved their agricultural practices, built a large sawmill, promoted hunting and fishing, and put into operation an excellent ski lodge with two ski tows. They have also recently erected a community center for arts, crafts, and recreation and are experimenting with new housing. Both the morale of the tribe and their achievements are impressive.

One way to reach the people of a community on a practical level is through continuing education. The land-grant colleges, with federal aid, devised programs which made deep and lasting impressions on rural culture and rural economic life, while questions of academic prestige were ignored. The home demonstration programs have been mentioned. The county farm agents of the schools of agriculture worked directly with farmers on their problems, and the faculties of the schools produced bulletins by the thousands to provide information to farmers. Continuing education programs with similar focus for the urban center are needed. What is being done is too piecemeal to have enough impact.

In the education of persons whose level of culture and vocational pursuits needs to be raised, we are dealing with deep-seated social problems. The programs should be addressed to the larger problems, not only to the education of individuals. The land-grant college program was magnificent and fruitful in its achievement of this aim. An impressive example of similar achievement in Europe can be found in the Danish Folk Schools. By concentrating on improving the quality of their butter and their bacon, the Danes developed a thriving trade with Great Britain. Nevertheless, the focus of the school was not on butter and bacon, but on cultural advance. From the motivation of the people for a better life came the fresh inspiration and energy to strive for a superior vocation.[9]

[9] Peter Manniche, *Denmark, A Social Laboratory* (Copenhagen: G.E.C. Gad, 1939).

I should now like to present a new model for an urban-related undergraduate college which differs in many ways from those discussed above. The model is based on the concept that the college should be involved with the community, and it offers a design of programs based upon the needs of the community. A field survey, as already noted, is a useful technique for exploring the needs of the community. In the model I emphasize the undergraduate level, partly because this is where the enrollment potential is and partly because the urban universities can probably do the needed job of education and research at the graduate and professional level. If the universities do not achieve this goal, the undergraduate colleges may, in time, grow into the more complex type of institution. An alternative may develop in the form of a federally sponsored system of urban-related universities. If this eventuates, the model to be described here may be used at the undergraduate level. I leave open the question of whether the model college should be private or muncipal or colleges within a system of state colleges, as I do the question of whether it should be launched as a unitary institution or created as a new college within a cluster group. One other preliminary comment: The public community college still has unused potential in serving the urban needs. I mean to complement it and not to displace it. The model, therefore, could be used as a senior college which would be composed of the upper two years of a program to which junior college graduates would transfer. I believe, however, it would gain the best prestige to attract students and support if it offered a four- or five-year integrated curriculum.

I conceive of the model urban college as one where cultural and vocational aims are blended, where students and faculty together study the problems of urban society, and where students prepare for careers of relevance to the solution of these problems. The specific problems to be considered are those within the community of which the college is a part. For purposes of forming a program of studies and experiences, the environment, though studied as a whole, would be conceived of as having a number of facets. Each facet—cultural, esthetic, civic, economic, health, and physical—would be a focus for study and research by students and faculty. The college would be composed of broad divisions, each division representing a phase of the environment—such as a division of economic environment or a division of health environment. The best unity for learning purposes in this undergraduate program could be achieved by thinking of these divisions as interdisciplinary.

The program should be problem-centered rather than focusing on a hierarchy of subject matter. By this I mean the problem-solving method would be used; the principal thrust of the concentration as an intensive study and experience would be study associated with field experience. In the division of economic environment, for example, a study of the community would reveal more clearly the problems that are economic or have economic implications. Data would be gathered relating to these problems, and methods of analysis would be developed. Factors that promote or inhibit economic viability and the interrelationship of economic with other environmental influences would be identified. The literature would be studied to find comparable situations, applicable concepts, and models for action. The environmental focus would help determine the types of formal courses that should be offered—for example, consumer economics, labor relations, public finance, and the accretion and uses of capital. Skills that would prepare for both individual careers and community action would be developed. Problems for other divisions of the college would be constructed in a similar way.

Students' major studies should be concentrations built individually for each student, and the student should participate in the planning process. The problem-solving method is a flexible one and permits a degree of individualization of studies. One student might focuse his study on credit unions, another on insurance, another on real estate, another on welfare programs, and so forth. Each student's concentration should be evaluated by criteria relating to depth of knowledge and not to faculty-dictated lists of courses. This type of program would not be a handicap to the person who wished to go on for further study, especially in the professions. The study of the physical environment, for example, would lead naturally into many avenues of engineering. Studies of the economic environment might lead either to advanced studies of the social phenomena involved or to preparation for business and franchise operations—on a scale appropriate to community needs. Knowledge of the health environment could provide a good foundation for later study of one of the professions in the area of health; indeed, the environmental impacts, the behavioral influences, and the biological factors in good and bad health could provide a better foundation for medical study than is commonly achieved.

A core of general education could be assured through courses that relate history, culture, and science to the environment. General education for disadvantaged ethnic groups, however, should have basic objectives and should not be simply the passing on of the white cultural heritage. It should not be organized by the notion that a general education course includes the knowledge that should be possessed in common by all men, although this concept has some validity for ethnic groups; instead, the objectives should be directed toward cultural identity, the meaning of cultural plurality, rational self-discipline, and preparation for roles in a democratic society. In short, the program should be relevant to the problems of the people.

Because I believe strongly in the interrelationship between the cultural and the vocational, I think the program should also have vocational objectives and appropriate courses offering preparation for vocational competence. Because vocations in the United States are changing rapidly, I suggest that the college maintain an open-end search for vocational opportunities. Programs should do more than merely prepare specifically for existing jobs. They should be developed by defining types of services that will contribute to the long-run development of the community.

The work-and-study principle should be followed. This plan would facilitate the study of the environment, help locate and create career opportunities, define the problems of contemporary society, and interweave theory and practice. It would also prepare the individual best for continuing service within the community, and as an incidental benefit, the work would provide income which would enable many more students to attend college.

I would like to see two-year programs, such as those offered at community colleges, and four-year integrated general–vocational programs developed. Ordinarily it does not work well to combine in one college two and four-year programs, because the four-year faculty consider two-year programs to be inferior. I assume, however, that the role of the new college, being revolutionary, would be clear. Moreover, it would attract faculty who understood its mission—service to the community as the basis for defining objectives and for designing educational curriculums and experiences. The faculty should themselves constitute a workshop to determine objectives, plan the program, and devise learning experiences.

Youth who come to college from families where the customary

employment is in unskilled labor or the skilled trades usually want to give early attention to occupational training. In any event, such a high portion of these students withdraw before completing the bachelor's degree that they need to reach certain vocational competence prior to the end of the senior year. In this connection there is another problem, that of successfully transferring from a lower level technician training program to a higher level major in the same broad area. For example, an electronics technician graduate finds it difficult to pursue studies to be an electrical engineer without considerable backtracking in course work. The problem stems from the philosophy of the faculty about the need of foundational courses. As a result, a student in a technician training program studies apple tree spraying in his first year, whereas in a school of agriculture he does it in his fourth year. Thus the programs are not synchronized. This is an unfortunate situation for two reasons: The American concept of opportunity favors career ladders rather than jobs that are boxed in, and many youth from unsophisticated backgrounds begin to aspire for a professional career when they have progressed only part way through a semiprofessional area.

This problem could be overcome in the model urban-related college by use of the "upside-down" curriculum, a plan which has been successfully used at California Polytechnic College and at the Milwaukee School of Engineering. It begins instruction at the practical level and progressively adds increments of theory as the study progresses. Thus at the end of a few months, a student might be competent to become an electrician; after two years, an electrical technician; and after four years, an electrical engineer.

In these illustrations, I have used vocations that are standard. But the model college might not be prepared to offer a whole array of major or undergraduate professional fields, and for some students the transfer problem would not be solved. However, the focus of the model is upon the problems of the community, and the vocations that are offered should be relevant. Educators must stop thinking in stereotypes if they are to become innovative in meeting the needs within the urban core. The colleges which I have earlier described, the Fashion Institute of Technology and Laney College, each found fresh answers to the problem.

We must also reflect upon my earlier comments about systems types of problems and the need for team approaches in resolving them.

If, as a result of a few years of operation by the college, the community had gained some educated personnel with understanding of the several facets of the community environment and with some skills appropriate for dealing with them, the community would have gained a new leavening spirit.

It is difficult to predict how many youth would attend the model college. We know that large numbers of students are seeking a new orientation to their communities and want educational programs that are relevant to life in these communities. We also know that many blacks, Chicanos, Asians, and Native Americans are motivated for service in their own communities. How do we dare pass up the opportunity to help them achieve these goals?

Thus far, I have discussed mainly the curriculum of urban-related colleges. The physical plant is also important. William Birenbaum has characterized the campus of the typical urban college or university as a superblock campus with monastic walls; it is insular, monolithic, exclusive, and representative of monopoly. He contends that the college should disperse and diffuse its resources in order to become an integral part of the community and influence the lives of the people there. And he advocates that these people should have control over it.[10] Birenbaum's ideas, as well as those of others, have been incorporated into a design for a model college plant to be located in the Bedford-Stuyvesant community in New York City.[11] The plan was prepared by the Educational Facilities Laboratory of New York. It is very different from the usual college campus and represents goals that are different from those commonly sought by administrators and their governing boards.

This new concept of physical planning is based on two principles: that the facility should be located in a spot most convenient to the people using it, and that the facility should be located in an existing building—unused or nearly so—rather than a new one built at the expense of homes and stores. Thus the library would be located where the public transportation system would make it most convenient for the

[10] William M. Birenbaum, *Overlive: Power, Poverty, and the University* (New York: The Delacorte Press, 1968). See also his essay "Lost Academic Souls" in *Agony and Promise: Current Issues in Higher Education 1969*, ed. G. Kerry Smith (San Francisco: Jossey-Bass, 1969).

[11] Another study under Birenbaum's direction developed a model for the college itself. See Arthur Tobier, "A Political Education," *The Urban Review* (September, 1969), pp. 21, 33–38.

people of the area. The recreational units would be self-contained and located in another part of the community, and they, too, would be shared with the community. The cultural activities would be focused in a cultural center, while a place somewhat central to most of these basic buildings would be found for a grouping of classroom and laboratory buildings. The other social facilities would be decentralized depending upon where the students needed them.[12]

It is difficult to get over the universal expectation in this country that a college should have ivy clad walls and be located on the hill overlooking a city or university town. I confess that in visiting universities in a number of foreign countries where the units are well scattered throughout the city—having just grown up there—I felt that the American plan of a hilltop college with a consolidated campus is the more attractive one. However, for purposes of involving and being involved in the community and of reaching the people who most need reaching today, it makes sense to locate the units where they will serve the greatest needs and where they will be most convenient for people who must walk or use public transportation.

In this chapter I have discussed possible roles and structures of the urban-related college. Many public community colleges sense that the community is their area of service and have adopted programs accordingly. There is now the need for regionally placed urban-related senior institutions, and there is an opportunity to innovate with a new type of institution that would serve the purpose. Why not? The land-grant type of college became a huge success, focusing its efforts primarily upon the rural scene. But America is now an urban-centered country. It is in need of urban-related colleges, perhaps even of a system of urban-related colleges and universities.

---

[12] Educational Facilities Laboratories, *A College in the City: An Alternative* (New York: Educational Facilities Laboratories, 1969).

CHAPTER 9

FOREIGN UNIVERSITIES

In nearly every country of the world, interest in higher education has been mounting. This is true in Asia, Africa, and Latin America, and also throughout Europe. Enrollments are huge; resources are scarce; faculties, libraries, and equipment are inadequate. Youth from the lower socioeconomic classes are finding a university education to be a means of escalating rapidly to a higher level of recognition.

In Latin America great tensions exist in the universities because many of them have failed to adjust to current needs. The older universities cling to a romantic model, with emphasis on the humanities and the prestige professions. Students have a large measure of participation but encounter frustrations in attempting to move the faculty, nearly all of whom are part-time and unable to function as a group. Student riots are common.

The universities of Africa have missions that stagger the imagination: to educate leadership, scientific, and professional personnel; to research African history and culture and make the findings available in published form; and to develop the resources of each nation. In Africa, the universities must inevitably be instruments of social change.

The new tasks before the universities of Eastern and Southern Asia seem clear. Their roles distinctly relate to the fresh goals of the several peoples: to retrieve the riches of their cultures, some aspects of which have become tainted with ingrown social customs and prejudices; to sift the best wisdom from the experiences of all cultures; to adapt for their own use the best available means of raising their standards of living; to prepare their young people for occupations that will synthesize the earning of bread with the building of a new social order; and to prepare their youth to fulfill the responsibilities of their newly oriented citizenship. To assist in understanding what is happening among the universities of the world, especially those in non-European countries, I examine in greater depth some of those in Asia. The Asian universities, founded for one purpose, now have a different job to do, and the transition is not being easily achieved.

At the campus of an Asian university, you find imposing buildings, spacious areas, and friendly hospitality. First impressions are of substantial plant and able academic leadership. Then you discover that this is only part of the story. The older of these Asian universities were established under British, German, or French influences. The Japanese, for example, following the Meiji restoration, found that the German curriculum for training specialists served their most urgent needs. In India, the British made a clear-cut decision: Education was to serve the purpose of promoting Western culture; the universities were to accomplish this purpose and prepare clerks for the subordinate levels of governmental service. Thailand, Burma, and Ceylon were also under this British influence.

Along with these patterns came several characteristics of higher education that are also part of European tradition: (1) a policy of admitting students only in limited numbers; (2) a system of examinations to determine who receives degrees and at what level of recognition; (3) a curriculum emphasizing classical and theoretical materials and ignoring or segregating the applied arts and sciences; and (4) a method of teaching that sets the professor up as the authority who lectures on his subject without participation by the students.

In Japan, the seven Imperial and ten national universities were highly centralized, with the Ministry of Education in charge. Doshisha, with its Amherst ties, Keiogijuku (commonly called Keio), which looked to Harvard for its inspiration, and Waseda became substantial private institutions; but because of the supervision of the Ministry and the prestige accorded the Imperial universities, their programs were colored by the philosophy that evolved in the Imperial universities.

In India, the plan was more nearly that of the University of London; that is, each university was an affiliating institution for various colleges, with powers to examine and to grant degrees. The colleges varied in type and in sponsorship, and each had certain autonomy in operation. Such colleges of arts and sciences as Pachaiyappa's (Hindu), Presidency (governmental), Loyola (Catholic), and Madras Christian (Protestant)—all of them constituent or affiliated colleges of the University of Madras—have heritages of which each is proud and programs with some individuality of character and of quality. Yet the overall structure permitted British influence and control to permeate the system. More recently the universities have added teaching programs of their own.

The British imprint on India, Ceylon, and Burma is deep and lasting. Professors are articulate and cultured in personal terms, though not as professional men. Efforts to replace English as the medium of instruction have not had much success. The aim of the student is still that of getting a prestige job—a position with the government. The term "clark" is permanently embedded in the vocabulary; and with socialist-minded governments rapidly enlarging the bureaucracy, the pressure to qualify as a government clark becomes greater rather than less. Many of the professors one meets speak with nostalgia of Oxford, although others are now convinced that the American pattern of education is what is needed.

The policies of limited enrollments and restricted curricula, as well as the British colonial policy with both its strengths and its weaknesses, can be seen in perspective by examining the situation in Hong Kong. The British university in this colony is the University of Hong Kong. In the scope of its services, it has the best financing, the most adequate facilities, and possibly the ablest faculty of any university in the East. I suspect that the quality of its academic work is very good. One hears among the Chinese charges that admission quotas favoring selected families have been used by the university. Though Hong Kong is one of the greatest commercial, banking, and insurance centers in the Orient, the university provides little instruction in this broad area of knowledge. Hong Kong is pitifully short of schools for children, yet the university leaves largely to other institutions the training of school personnel. To fill this void the Chinese University of Hong Kong was recently created. Its original nucleus was a group of colleges founded by refugee scholars from The Peoples Republic of China. (It makes an interesting sidelight to note that the graduates of the several refugee colleges initially had to turn to the National Taiwan University, a non-British institution, for their degrees.) The new university seems to be meeting some of the demands of the people of Hong Kong for a college education.

The examination system prevails throughout the East, and the direct relationship of college education and examinations to civil service has operated to deepen its roots. The examination supposedly provides a standard measure of achievement. Granting this assumption, the entrance to civil service is democratic. Since the results of the examinations are graded into classes and Class I graduates get the preference for specific jobs, the presumption is that merit wins. All this reasoning is logical, of course, and there is general faith in the validity of the examination as a single measure of achievement. What happens, naturally, is that textbooks are correlated with the examinations, professors lecture to secure a high percentage of passes, and students loaf during the terms and "bug up" at examination time. Some colleges give preliminary examinations to weed out those students whose performances are apt to reflect against the institution. Libraries become text-book libraries. The intellectual skill developed is that of recalling facts at the examination. Students who fail to pass are labeled as failures, and those who get the lower marks go without jobs.

Entrance examinations also determine the fates of candidates for admission to the universities and colleges. There is a justification for this practice because the preparation given by the secondary schools varies widely in type and quality. In India and Burma this preparation is seriously deficient, generally being no more than the equivalent of our tenth grade work. The examination is also a means of maintaining the enrollment at a desired number. The universities do not have the money or faculties to permit the admission of unlimited numbers of students.

In Japan, the entrance examination has a further impact on

the life of the student. There the universities are pyramided in prestige. Everybody knows without question that Tokyo University is the top university and that Kyoto ranks second. The aim of the graduate, hardly without exception, is a job with a big business centered in Tokyo or with the government. These employers extend first favor to the graduates of Tokyo, then to Kyoto, and next to Kyushu, and so on. Hence the urgency of getting admitted to the University of Tokyo is terrific. Rather than accept a lesser institution, men will try the Tokyo examinations year after year, all the while studying for the exams. Large private universities of uncertain standards feed upon this suspended and suspense-burdened student population, doing a financially profitable business—as do other coaching agencies—in preparing students for these examinations. Student unrest seems to be general throughout Japan—over one hundred universities had disturbances within the year 1968–69.

The bane of the university system in the East, especially in the less developed nations, is the failure of many graduates to get jobs. The rate of unemployment of college educated personnel in India has been terribly high; a prominent educator in India recently estimated that thirty to forty thousand trained engineers have been unable to get jobs. The Kotschnig theory that the frustrated intellectual will turn against society is partially substantiated here.[1] Certainly the proportion of college men who turn to communism for its promise to cure the ills of society is large. The stock answer of the educators has been to limit the number of students admitted to the universities, as is done in Europe. But the dilemma persists because the demand for education persists, and the institutions, sometimes grudgingly, respond—as the enrollments in all the countries testify. The admission of more students without corresponding increases in the number of faculty creates a very high student–faculty ratio.

The situation is puzzling because it would seem that these rapidly developing countries need all the educated persons they can produce. Education does not increase the number of people to be employed; rather it should increase their individual productivity and broaden considerably the range of jobs for which each can qualify. In Japan, where the employment rate is good, the problem stems from

[1] Walter Kotschnig, *Slaves Need No Leaders* (London: Oxford University Press, 1943).

108   THE INNOVATIVE SPIRIT

attitudes that create a hierarchy of jobs and locations. The graduates
of Okayama University, for example, prefer prestige positions in
Tokyo, not appreciating how green is the pasture at hand. The
Okayama prefecture is interesting in many ways. It is one of the better
agricultural regions, and some experimentation has been done in
mechanized farming. Industry is diversified and includes both large-
scale (for example, nylon) production and small enterprise. The principal cities appear to be prospering. A substantial expansion of the
harbor was made, considerably enlarging the area for factory sites. The
plan includes the creation of an artificial lake converted to fresh water
and a recreation area. The university includes a medical school—and
the need for expanded health services is obvious. Museums of art, folk
arts, and commercial products add cultural interest and stimulation.
Here, then, is a province that would seem to have job potentials for
educated people of many types. And the opportunity should be wide
open for young people to make cultural and civic contributions and to
build desirable home and community lives. Yet the graduates of Okayama University have their eyes on jobs in Tokyo; and the professors,
trying desperately to help, make trips to Tokyo to recruit such jobs.
Something clearly is out of focus.

In India, I asked many groups this question: With the obvious
need everywhere for advances in health, education, and economic well-
being, and with India's ambitious plans for social, economic, and community development, why does anyone who possesses knowledge and
skills sit idle? The answer constantly surprises me—it surprises me because of the bland assumption on the part of all Indians that Americans are materialistic while Indians are concerned with matters cultural
and spiritual. The answer is that the student must have a job that
gives him not only a living but also an appropriate position in life.
I made suggestions: one thing India needs is plows, a simple plow can
be made by intelligent men working in a shed to start with; the literacy
rate is very low and there must be a need for teachers, who would sit
under a tree as a classroom if need be; the red tape that is so prevalent
needs the skilled trimming that young men trained in administration
could give it. And I was told that the student cannot be trained for a
job that does not exist. In fairness, however, I must note that the statistics quoted on pay rates for jobs such as teaching are decidedly low.

It is the arts students who have the greatest difficulty in finding
jobs. This situation reveals, again, a weakness in the system inherited

from Europe. An educational program relevant to the needs of the society has again been sabotaged by the persistent dichotomies between arts and science and between theory and practice. The faculty of arts teaches history, literature, and philosophy; the faculty of science teaches science; the social sciences and the technologies have been left out, or left to find their places in separate schools that are regarded as substandard. Students do not get a balanced education, and those in the arts are educated with neither orientation nor preparation for jobs. The consequences of this nineteenth-century curricular pattern are apparent.

Another weakness of the Eastern university, from the American point of view, is the almost exclusive use of the lecture system in teaching. In both India and Japan the lecture system is generally used without any follow-through with the student, such as is provided in England by the tutorial plan or in the United States by discussion sections. Thus, the advantages of the lecture technique are not fully achieved and the faults are maximized. Psychologists agree that intercommunication between teacher and student is a cardinal principle of learning, but in the East there is little of this. The professer lives in a world of his own specialty; the students discuss the problems of the world in bull sessions with their peers or in the coffee houses where the radicals hold forth. This situation is most serious in India and Burma, where the students have entered the university at the age of sixteen with a poorly grounded secondary foundation. They have been sheltered at home, are immature and gullible, and thus ripe for the ventursome life of student politics.

Student government, as we know it, does not exist in these countries. Administrative officers do not trust the students and will not repose responsibilities in them, and so there is little opportunity for the students, under guidance from university officials, to learn to carry responsibility.

Not only among the students do the blind lead the blind, however. The teachers function within a highly departmentalized hierarchy where the head of the department sits on a pedestal. This department head has come to his position after years of patient waiting, diplomatic maneuvering, and skillful acquiescence to the views of his predecessor. Finally he, too, is in a position to lord it over his subordinates. The extreme of this sequence is found in Japan where every field of knowledge or activity, from archaeology to wrestling, is divided into schools of thought. Within a department the lowly instructor or assistant professor, to hope for advancement, generally speaking must subscribe to the school of thought of his superior. Knowledge becomes dogmatism and dogmatism may as easily perpetuate error as truth.

This pattern of specialization and departmentalization leaves no room for general education. True, in Japan the reforms introduced during the American administration following World War II called for a four-year college course of which the equivalent of one and one-half years should be devoted to general education. What usually happened was that the teachers in the former university preparatory schools were brought into the universities, and these faculties, working in their former plants, were assigned the job of general education. The university faculties, looking askance at the new development and their new colleagues, continued with their specialties as before on the university campus. But with this difference: now they were supposed to prepare the specialists in two and one-half years instead of three, and many of them felt strongly that this could not be done. The plan was essentially an American graft onto a basically German system.

Officially, India is in favor of general education. Several committees of educators have devised plans for enlarging the program. This interest and these views stem from the genuine commitments of the governmental leaders to democratic ideals and practices. They seem to see clearly the connection between education for good living in the good society and education for achieving the goals of a democratic nation. In this respect India differs from Japan because in India the underlying philosophy is being evolved by the leaders in public life, whereas in Japan conservative-minded governments consciously permit a retrogression from the reforms of the American period.

Given the will to introduce a program, it would seem that the government and the institutions of a new and unfettered political unit such as India, following in the British tradition, would find general (cultural) education distinctly congenial. And some individual colleges do have a balanced curriculum of arts and sciences and require students to take a distribution of courses. But as the registrar of one of the older universities—himself a firm advocate of general education—put it, there are many obstacles and difficulties. He mentioned several of these: the prevailing division of the faculties into narrowly conceived subject areas, each college having considerable voice in protecting its vested area; the tradition of teaching by lecture, although general education requires much use of dialogue and discussion; the unavailability of graduate assistants and the lack of financial provision for them; the inadequacy of the libraries; and the absence of suitable teaching materials. I would add to this list the difficulty that the Indians experience in making up their group mind. The habit of protecting self-interest is very deeply ingrained. The maze of procedures for checking and counter-checking all proposals and actions is astonishing to any American; and the tendency in group meetings for everyone to want to decide everything inhibits progress. In essence, India is lacking in cultural unity and in overall loyalties, especially in domestic affairs. Because of this, the integrating force of general education is badly needed; but, ironically, it is because of this lack of cultural unity that progress will be so difficult.

The Asian universities, due to their historical roots, find it easier to add specialized studies. Thus, the creation of new colleges in the applied arts and sciences is possible. In considerable part these new schools date from the end of World War II. The University of Delhi, for example, had faculties of arts, science, law, and medicine previous to 1947. Since that date the university has organized faculties of education, technology, and social science. In Japan, through the reforms of the American period, many former *semmon gakko* (vocational schools in agriculture, teacher training, and technical fields)— to which admission was gained from the middle schools—were incorporated into the new university pattern. The University of Kyoto, with possibly the most conservative-minded faculty in Japan, added a school of education and erected a modest new building for it. These are but a few examples of a widespread movement.

The American influence in this direction has been strong. In many cases the models for change were the land-grant university and the American type of teacher-training program. Certain of the educational leaders have been trained in American universities—many of those in Thailand, for example. To parallel the more traditional program of the University of Chulalongkorn, the government initiated some new institutions. One of these, the University of Thammasat, has as its principal function the training of persons for the public service. Operating primarily as a late afternoon and evening school, it quickly became a lusty infant with mostly part-time enrollees. The College of Education now has several campuses, the oldest of which has been in operation for about twenty years. In both cases young persons from

Thailand with doctor's degrees from such universities as Michigan and Ohio State have provided creative leadership.

The universities of Asia, Africa, and Latin America are undergoing change—in the developing countries, rapid change. It is here that the social role of the university can most clearly be seen. The creation and support of programs in higher education is a genuine social investment. With increasing complaints in our own country (from politicians and some of the wealthier tax payers) about the high cost of higher education, it might not be amiss to keep a sharp lookout on what is happening in foreign lands—especially the relationship between the costs and patterns of higher education, on the one hand, and the country's productivity on the other.[2]

---

[2] An original view on the relationship between educational productivity and the productivity of the surrounding society is expounded in James I. Doi, "Educational Productivity," in *Pressures and Priorities: Current Issues in Higher Education 1965*, ed. G. Kerry Smith (Washington, D.C.: American Association for Higher Education, 1965), pp. 112–15.

CRITIQUE OF
PROFESSIONAL SCHOOLS

∿∿∿∿∿∿∿∿∿∿∿∿∿∿∿∿∿∿∿∿∿

PART **FOUR**

CHAPTER 10

EDUCATING FOR
THE PROFESSIONS

Ⴕ·ᔕᲢᔕ·ᔕᲢᔕ·ᔕᲢᔕ·ᔕᲢᔕ·ᔕᲢᔕ·ᔕᲢᔕ·ᔕᲢᔕ·ᔕᲢᔕ·ᔕᲢᔕ·ᔕᲢᔕ·ᔕᲢᔕ·ᔕᲢᔕ·ᔕᲢᔕ

A̲s American society has grown
from a survival culture to one of affluence, the needs for professional
services have changed. It is the role of professional men to provide
expert knowledge and skills in the respective fields in which they have
been educated. From their various approaches they supply services
which, viewed as a whole, attack the problems and conflicts among
men. They provide leadership in technology through the application
of scientific knowledge, and in human relations through the art of community and institutional organization. Without professional men, there
would be little advance in health, education, industry, agriculture,
transportation, communication, and the organization of people for
large-scale enterprises and cultural and civic activities. In a period of
rapid social change, the education of professional men takes on added

115

significance. I shall analyze the reasons why certain changes should take place—and are taking place—in professional schools.

The innovative professional schools are defining for themselves larger frames of reference, and their aim is to do more than merely prepare men for niches in the professions. Central to many of the new programs is a concern for the health and well-being of man, and these programs are relating to communities as well as to individuals. Thus medicine, instead of educating merely to treat disease, is shifting to the more comprehensive aim expressed in the charter of the World Health Organization—"to promote the physical, mental, and social health of people." As Dean George T. Harrell of the Milton S. Hershey Medical Center has said, "The student must understand normal growth, development, and variability from childhood through senescence."[1] Both agriculture and medicine are concerned with the nutrition of man. And together with architecture, law, and engineering, they are becoming sensitive to the environmental problems that affect man's general well-being.

Professonial schools, then, are becoming concerned with all segments of society rather than merely with the more elite. Law relates to the impoverished victim as well as to the affluent client. Medicine is concerned with people who live under conditions that breed disease and mental illness and cause high infant mortality. An affluent society cannot tolerate the differential that has existed in medical services between high and low income groups. Agriculture now includes the problems of the urban dweller as well as those of the rural resident. Home economics has done a marvelous job of raising the value appreciations of the rural family; it must now turn to a similar mission with other disadvantaged groups.[2] In their admission of students, the professional schools need to search for talent in all socioeconomic classes. The admissions policies of the professions are still too much influenced by the guild system.

The weaknesses in American society have suddenly become visible, and the professional schools have both a special competence

[1] George T. Harrell, "The Pennsylvania State University, The Milton S. Hershey Medical Center," *Clinical Research*, Vol. 13, No. 4 (1965), pp. 494–99.
[2] Earl J. McGrath and Jack T. Johnson, *The Changing Mission of Home Economics* (New York: Teachers College, Columbia University, 1968).

and a special obligation to deal with certain of these weaknesses. An obligation of agriculture, for example, is to find out what happens to the residue from pesticides. The more alert of the professional schools are preparing their graduates to contribute toward the solution of these kinds of problems. Eugene V. Rostow whose report for the Yale School of Law was quoted in Chapter Three, added to that report the comment that the faculty and students "envision law as a means of resolving social conflicts in ways which express the considered values of the law itself, and of the democratic society it is intended to serve.[3]

In the past, the programs of professional schools have tended to be career directed or, as in agriculture, commodity based. In engineering, a student has studied to become an electrical, mechanical, civil, chemical, or aeronautical engineer. In business administration, the graduates have been pointed toward accounting, marketing, production, industrial relations, and so forth. Programs such as these are often composed of subject matter that is too specific and narrow in content.

In some instances, there has been a single route to prepare for professional practice—schools of architecture have trained architects; schools of medicine, physicians; schools of law, lawyers. The traditional goal of medical schools and of other professional programs has been to pour into the student all of the available knowledge, so that he can graduate in possession of the knowledge and skills requisite to practice successfully. But this goal is now an impossible one and methods of training must necessarily change. The older view that "a physician is a physician is a physician" is no longer valid.

Knowledge significant to each professional area has grown so tremendously in recent years that it is not possible to acquaint the student with all of it. Technological advances cause the training for a specific occupation to become obsolete. The more innovative institutions are becoming aware that, instead of producing finished practitioners, they must now prepare students as unfinished practitioners —professionals deeply committed to continuing their training on their own after graduation. If the graduate knows how to identify a problem, research the knowledge relating to it, and make decisions about solutions, he will be better able to keep abreast of new ideas and techniques and to master novel cases. The professional degree

[3] Yale University, *Yale Law School Report of the Dean* (New Haven, Conn.: Yale University, 1966), p. 3.

must come to signify this kind of capability and not merely knowledge of present practice.

Another goal of the forward looking professional school is to provide for flexibility in career objectives. At Minnesota, the majority of graduates in agriculture now go into business, and 30 per cent go on to graduate school. In medicine, preparation for academic medicine, community medicine, or a research career require somewhat different emphases in study than that for a general or specialized practitioner. Also, there are new areas of health concern such as radiation safety, environmental pollution prevention, and population control. In architecture, environmental design is becoming a major program and has many aspects that differ from the study of the design of a building. In engineering, there are not six or ten but more than one hundred possible specializations. The shifting demands can be seen in the want ads in *The New York Times*.

Programs of the various professional schools, when they implement objectives such as these, draw more closely together. In relating to man and society, the behavioral and biological sciences become essential as foundations for other fields of study. Design permeates many programs. Data processing and developmental procedures become common to all. Many opportunities occur for close collaboration among faculties in seemingly quite separate fields.

As outlook and objectives change, so also does the educational program. The revisions of curriculum are of four general types: liberalization of job-oriented programs to include greater emphasis on theory and on the basic sciences; interweaving of basic courses and professional experiences; interdisciplinary seminars and options; and new courses, seminars, and areas of concentration for students. Professional ethics takes on fresh perspective—for example, a study of professional responsibility is currently the most important study being undertaken by the Association of American Law Schools.

Formerly, the prerequisites for entering the professional school were rather strictly prescribed—a practice that limited the eligible talent—but in recent years such requirements have been modified in emphasis and made more flexible. Furthermore, needs and priorities change, as is shown in medicine by the rising importance of the behavioral sciences, in business administration by the impact of macroeconomics, and in many fields by the increased need for mathematics.

A liberal foundation makes good sense, partly for the cultural advantage it provides, and partly for its contributions to the ethical and social orientation of the practitioners. But as professional schools have increased their requirements in the liberal arts, a problem of time has arisen. In some professions the period of training has become too long, and various methods to shorten it are being used. One is to adjust the college requirements to take account of the greatly improved learning in the high school. Another is to secure a better integration between the liberal education content and the professional, by harmonizing them and arranging a better sequence of studies. Cooperative planning between the liberal arts faculty and the professional school should enable the latter to avoid repeating some foundational content.

The elimination of unnecessary duplications also would improve motivations and morale. Many students have found the first year at professional school dull and grinding, instead of inviting and challenging. Then too, this type of program is designed to force memorization of facts, the relevance of which is not wholly apparent to the student and most of which are lost to him by the time he needs them. The courses taken by preprofessional students are not an appropriate liberal foundation for a profession because they too are specialized and are treatments designed for the respective departmental majors; hence, they are deficient in cultural perspective for students heading toward professional schools. Yet the liberal arts courses, as taught within the professional schools, become adjuncts to that specialization—witness the technician-oriented courses in English. So the problem of liberalizing the professional curriculum has not really been resolved. A minor but potent factor in creating an urgent situation is the increasingly prevalent pattern at large, expanding universities of moving some of the professional schools to campuses located at some distance from the liberal arts college. Due to this logistics problem, they begin to offer courses of their own, often merely emulative of the traditional ones.

Students going into the professions need a foundation that is more than a vaguely diffused liberal education. For example, one of the acute needs is training in problem solving, and an attempt to produce a problem solving graduate carries fresh implications. Problems are used to teach thinking—analysis and synthesis. They are a basis for searching for knowledge and a means of achieving competence in decision making. This philosophy of learning does not imply that cases and problems should be used exclusively, as was formerly so common in law schools. Systematic inquiry into a division of knowledge is also necessary; both theory and application—systematic generalization and attention to particulars—must play their roles in the learning process. And even where the forms of presentation today resemble those of the past, educators must take into account that the psychology of today's student is quite different. He wants to become an active participant in his learning and not remain merely a passive recipient of knowledge.

Foundational knowledge must aim for unity and also prepare for versatility in its application. A means of helping to achieve this result lies in developing a core of subject matter which all students in the professional school take, regardless of their career expectations. For example, a study of engineering education at the University of California at Los Angeles has identified design as the basic element in its subject matter core; presumably, materials and energy would be ingredients in it. The strength of the Bauhaus school of architecture was its emphasis on materials and their qualities, followed by a program that synthesized technology, craftsmanship, and design esthetics. In business administration, logical components of knowledge for everyone above the technician level are quantitative techniques, behavioral skills, systems design, operations analysis, and sensitivity to social responsibilities.

The subject matter core should occupy only a portion of the student's time, however. Beyond this the curriculum in innovative schools must possess a high degree of flexibility, producing versatility as the student moves toward decisions about his future career. The aim of flexibility is twofold: to permit the development of a concentration of study around the student's interests and potential, and to permit a considerable range of choice among electives. The latter phase of the problem solving emphasis should include the pursuit of research problems of the student's own planning, subject to faculty approval.

Students in professional schools have traditionally been so heavily loaded with courses that they are deprived of all free time, and faculties in some of the innovative schools have tried to reverse this situation. The School of Medicine at Case Western Reserve University controls the number of formal courses for which a student may register, so that he has time for independent study. It is hoped that, if he is not gorged with course work, he will find time to think. In order to implement such a new program, the faculty are compelled to reconsider their teaching habits.

A solution to another aspect of curriculum problems is found in attempts to interweave theory and practice to better advantage. The most common method is to have the student enter the clinical part of the program early in his course of study. In the School of Medicine at Duke University, the student is introduced to the patient in the middle of his first year of study and to the hospital during the second year—a decided change from past methods. At many schools ways are found to involve the student with a practitioner, to engage him in community activity, or to alternate study and work. Another device is to have the student begin to simulate practice early in his career as a student; in business administration, this takes the form of business games assisted by computers. In some medical schools, a small group of students make use of a physicians' type of laboratory to which they bring various laboratory experiences; closely adjacent to the laboratory the student has a physician's desk. Community experiences take various forms. In law, for example, students at the University of Chicago are offered summer clerkships in legal aid offices, public defenders' offices, and legislators' offices. In medicine, students may undergo an internship in community medicine as well as in a hospital. Such examples imply a broader objective than mere exposure to professional practice; the objective, in part, is to sensitize the student to the social problems that confront the profession.

A different type of interchange with the community occurs through the location of private research laboratories on or near campuses—evidence of the assumption of leadership in research that is being taken in industry and the professions. There are many advantages to this kind of arrangement, including opportunities for collaboration, for the intellectual stimulation that comes from an interplay of the pure and the applied aspects of research, and for faculty and students to become partially involved on the frontiers of such areas as engineering, pharmaceutical manufacturing, business administration. It is interesting to note that the progenitor of the first computer (the Mark I Calculator) was designed through the collaboration of professors at Harvard and the research staff of IBM.

Among the new trends is one toward interdisciplinary teaching. The sciences increasingly provide the intellectual foundations for such areas as medicine, agriculture, and engineering; the social sciences for law, business administration, and architecture. In view of broadening objectives, no professional school can function today without recourse to other disciplines and fields. There must be interdisciplinary exchanges and interprofessional collaboration. Instances of the latter occur in the legal, mechanical, and electronic aspects of medicine. Today, 50 per cent of the law schools have medico-legal courses, and 90 per cent of the medical schools offer legal medicine. Collaboration is also required between medicine and engineering (bioengineering) to perfect devices that supplement the activity of the heart or use high-frequency sound in surgery. Much of the training for agriculture today is training for large-scale management similar to business administration. The term "environmental" is now used to suggest interrelationships. Note the shift in name from "sanitary engineering" to "environmental engineering," or the revised name "College of Agriculture and Environmental Science" at Rutgers, or the inclusion of architecture in the College of Environmental Design at Berkeley.

Certain faculty at innovative schools, such as those for business administration at Carnegie-Mellon and Massachusetts Institute of Technology, are endeavoring to make a definite shift from discrete courses and the study of practical details toward broader experiences that stimulate imagination, induce comprehension, and require the student to provide a synthesis. Thus, the student is engaged in conceptualizing, designing, model building and criticism, systems analysis and operations, behavioral aspects of organization, and information processing and utilization. Time and motion studies have been displaced by systems studies. The student visualizes systems, studies models, prepares plans, and devises means of control. He is concerned with networks, linkages, interactions, feedback, system adjustment, survival and growth, and the weaving of the elements and the activities into the whole.

Data processing becomes highly important to achieve fresh objectives such as these, and is something more than accounting as it has been taught in the past. The data needed for management today involve more than those secured through accounts, from statistics, or used in budgeting; also needed are exogenous data, such as those involving social and economic phenomena. For managerial purposes, these data should not be prepared in discrete reports, because a synthesis of them is needed. An evaluation of all the data is required because they influence future planning. Such evaluation has become possible through the computer's ability to process variables. Accounting is becoming an information development process, and courses at Carnegie-Mellon and MIT recognize this change.

The availability of the computer for data processing is all important. Within the statement of profit and loss of a business enterprise, there will be thousands of possible combinations of variables. To discover the most viable operation requires operations analysis, processed through the computer. In agriculture, data processing enables the student to find the most rewarding combinations of resources, labor, and management. Data processing becomes important also in the study of design, as in architecture or in engineering. In urban design, for example, the variables in skylines, in traffic patterns, and in population are so great that they can only be handled through the computer. The computer makes feasible the devising of study problems at a level of intricacy that formerly was impossible. A few professors have begun to experiment with such problems. The building of models is a way of thinking about a problem. The student conceptualizes the nature of the problem and proposes solutions to be tested and criticized. Models may, of course, be built from tangible things, or they may be highly theoretical—based upon behavior principles and mathematical computations. Mathematics as a tool for thinking has taken on new significance for all professions.

The trend toward group practice is another factor that influences innovation in training programs. Group practice enables specialists to collaborate in offering widely diversified services; it also permits the use of ancillary personnel—a practice best understood among engineers. Engineering really provides three levels of training: the technician (Associate in Science), the engineer (Bachelor of Science), and the professional man (Master of Science or higher degree). Possibly there is a fourth level, since the Ph.D. usually trains for research and development. In medicine, much use is made of nurses and technicians, but there has been resistance to the idea of educating physicians' assistants or associates. For this reason the experimental programs at the University of Colorado and Duke University (to be described in Chapter Eleven) are highly significant.

The tendencies toward socialization within our democratic society also affect the nature of the curriculum. The prolonged depression of the 1930s brought much greater socialized control over private business and industry. A public policy such as urban regeneration brings fresh attention to environmental design. Medicine is becoming more socialized—the turning point was the enactment of Medicare— and the graduate of the future must be prepared for the changing character of medicine. Colorful new courses are being introduced. The register for law at Harvard announces courses with such intriguing titles as Legal Protection of Environmental Quality, Legal Protection Against Hazardous Products, Urban Legal Studies, Land Use Planning, and the Prediction and Prevention of Antisocial Conduct.

In addition to change in course content, change in teaching is needed and is taking place. Much teaching has emphasized rote learning—note taking, memorizing, and performing laboratory experiments for which the answers are known. The innovative schools believe that there is a better learning theory and are discarding the stereotyped methods of the past. Lectures should have the role of orienting and interpreting, but not the role of reproducing what is available in print or otherwise. Versatility in teaching—selecting methods appropriate to the occasion—is required to achieve effective learning.

Many of the innovative schools rely heavily on the problem solving approach. The study of cases is one example of this approach. Schools of law and business administration for many years have used the case technique, with cases drawn from court reports or from business practice. This method has been successful as a way of training practitioners and of developing skill in decision making. Some professors in both areas, however, have turned toward devising problems in law or games in business. Certain problems in family law (as will be noted in Chapter Twelve)' simulate an actual case in which various psychological, sociological, economic, and other problems exist and greatly affect the legal aspect. Large-scale games in business administration involve groups of students who play various administrative roles, dealing with all of the functions of the enterprise and managing its affairs over a period of several years. The computer can compress the time for class use.

An important consideration in this type of education is to ensure the transferability of learning. The study of a problem is not merely to find the solution; the follow-through is a most important element. The student learns the most from a problem by developing generalizations that will apply to additional cases. The problems do not always have preformulated answers; instead, the class evaluates the relative merit of alternative solutions. Obviously, this method trains the student to reason, to find solutions for novel situations, and to become skilled in decision making. When unsolvable problems are attempted, there is an additional advantage: the student learns how to handle frustration in meeting problems for which all alternative solutions are inadequate; and he learns thus how to work—as almost all of our leaders in today's society must—in situations that are characterized by ambiguity.

Programed instruction has attracted the interest of many professors. Programing has certain merit in that it requires the instructor to think through his objectives fully and to use good principles of course design (continuity, sequence, integration). Programing also enables the student to learn at his own rate or in relation to the time that he devotes to study. By selecting, eliminating, and arranging the materials and methods, programing can result in an improved design. If not well done, programing, of course, can result in dull, wooden, and mechanical courses. But the fault can hardly be placed at the feet of programed learning as a new medium, just as the printing press can hardly be blamed when a faculty member writes or uses a poor textbook.

Closed circuit television has been used rather widely among professional schools with a high degree of success. The Medical School of the University of Michigan, for example, has superior television instruction. A surgical operation can be viewed by hundreds of students simultaneously (as contrasted with the old gallery where perhaps six students could get a partial view). The School of Law at Michigan provides an opportunity for students to view the hearings in the county circuit court by television. Computers are now available in many professional schools to assist with instruction, and they enable problem analysis to be carried on at a highly sophisticated level. In business administration, such universities as Carnegie-Mellon and the University of Chicago have made good progress in devising games of the type described. An especially significant study of the use of computers in instruction in engineering is being carried on at the University of Michigan. Although the goal is improvement of instruction, one result is that at least 85 per cent of the undergraduates in engineering schools today are acquiring some knowledge of digital computing techniques.

The adoption of programs for independent study is almost a revolution in teaching in many professional schools. Independent study requires a complete reversal of roles, removing responsibility from the teacher and placing it with the student. It is also a departure from the method of disseminating all known facts and skills; instead, the student studies selected problems and topics in depth. Giving the student more freedom for initiative and responsibility does not necessarily free the professor, however; the student needs much counsel, guidance and evaluation concerning his efforts. The objective is to deepen student learning, not to dilute it.

Departmental organization, so common within the universities, often restricts the evolution of the program. Schools of medicine in the United States are not as rigidly departmentalized as those in European universities where some departments are almost wholly autonomous, but barriers to new subject matter and to interdisciplinary collaboration do exist. Some reorganization that makes more functional sense and that permits greater coordination between the basic curriculum and the clinical study and experiences seems warranted. The new School of Medicine at the University of California, Davis, has created several divisions. They include divisions for sciences basic to medicine, surgical sciences, medical sciences, community and postgraduate medicine, and mental health. This device is aimed at securing more cooperation among the departments. At MIT, the program in business administration is kept flexible so that the ongoing research in the school can influence the evolution of the program.

The problem of career oriented departments has been noted. One new school of engineering has broken away from the standard department system and is organized with five functional divisions: physics which supplies the foundation; materials, energy, and information which are the columns; and systems engineering which provides the synthesis and capstone. In the College of Agriculture at Minnesota, the programs are becoming less commodity oriented in favor of basic processes and principles. The increase in the vitality of the doctoral programs in several fields is causing departmental walls to crumble. A few decades ago business administration and economics constituted a single program; later business departed in strongly applied directions. Now there is a growing tendency to turn to economics again for an understanding of the social forces that bear so heavily on business operations.

From the above analysis, we can see many possibilities for change in programs, content, teaching methods, and the organization of professional schools. To these should be added change in admissions policies and practice. The professional schools have been insufficiently conscious of the benefits of admitting students from disadvantaged segments of society. In a study of discrimination in admissions made in a legislative investigation in New York in 1946–48, we found that many institutions of higher learning had policies of discrimination and of favoritism. The instances were sufficient to cause the legislature to pass new legislation—the Fair Education Practices Act of 1948. In more recent years, professional schools have been making efforts to attract blacks and other minority students, but they have been only partially successful. Two things have stood in the way: high costs and requirements of scholastic achievement. The financial barrier must be removed through social action. The achievement tests are a barrier that needs reconsideration; there is not a high correlation between preprofessional academic achievement and success in practice.

Certain schools of law have been experimenting with new admissions policies, and with heartening results. Their Council on Legal Opportunity (CLEO) has been holding summer seminars to which students—nearly all of them graduates of southern Negro colleges— have been admitted who failed the legal aptitude test but who nevertheless seemed qualified to study law. In 1968, institutes were held at Harvard, Emory, Denver, and UCLA. Of the 160 students who enrolled, 120 completed the study and only eight of them failed. At least ninety-four enrolled in some thirty-one law schools. The tentative opinion of the educators involved is that the program has been entirely successful. Such success suggests that all professional schools should take a fresh look at their admission criteria, taking account of the social needs for professional services. It is these needs that should receive major consideration; too often it is the enhancement of the scholarly prestige of the faculty that receives first consideration.

A special reason for fresh policies at this time lies in the new motivation of disadvantaged students to return to their own communities to serve and lead. In medicine, it does not suffice merely to increase the number of black physicians. They will leave medical school with the same orientation as whites toward affluent patients and specialized practice. The medical faculty must reinforce the motivations of the blacks to return to the ghetto for service, for this is where the need for medical services is the greatest.

To assist in projecting plans and in effecting change, a staff for research and development is of great advantage. In large business enterprises and in governmental operations such staffs are accepted as essential, but only a few universities have created them. At the university they endeavor to anticipate future needs and trends, develop long-range plans, and are available to professors for consultations about course revisions and new techniques in teaching. Several medical schools—among them Case Western Reserve, Illinois, UCLA, Northwestern—have added staffs of this sort. Possibly the large impact upon medical education that Case Western Reserve is now having is due to the research and development activity that has taken place there during the past twenty-five years. Along with this activity at Case Western Reserve, a systematic reform of the curriculum also took place. Their experience confirms the view that curriculum planning should not be vested in a committee of department heads, for departments are divisive and their self-interests dominate their actions. As a first step in transforming its philosophy and programs, the Medical School at Case Western Reserve—the first of the pioneers—created a committee on medical education composed of venturesome faculty.

Change is not easy in professional schools for several reasons. Faculty members fall into grooves and find it difficult to accept change either within their own baliwicks or through sharing budgets with new ventures. Occupational orientation is very strong because a faculty member's reputation in part depends upon the post graduate placement of his students. Immediate incentives cause the future to be dimly perceived. Persons long accustomed to old models find it difficult to accept new ones; most of the faculty in engineering or business administration know less about computers than do their advanced students. Where practitioners are used, as in the clinical part of the medical program, their weighty voice is apt to be on the conservative side. Their interest is in conveying information about existing practice. Because of the way budgets function within a university, it is usually necessary to supply additional funds—not always easily available—to encourage innovations. Behind all of these impediments, there is not infrequently a lack of imaginative leadership within an institution.

Still other restraints are imposed from the outside. It is highly important for professional schools to be fully accredited; and the standards of accrediting agencies—by their very nature as watchdogs for the establishment—relate to the past and present and take little account of the future. Where licensing or certification are involved the laws, together with the regulations of the licensing boards, define the educational qualifications and lag far behind the current scene. Ways must therefore be found to take advantage of "equivalents" and to work with the licensing agencies in an effort to secure some liberalization of the provisions.

Nevertheless, changing social needs and revised thinking about good teaching and learning are necessitating innovations in professional schools. If one takes account of the revisions in particular courses, the sweep is wide. But the more significant changes that have been analyzed here are limited to a few schools, and they are widely scattered among the universities. The best opportunities for innovations seem to occur in two kinds of situations. One is clearly the newly created school; many such schools have recruited unusually alert deans and faculty who proceed with fresh perspective and design. The other situation occurs in the universities that have exceptional resources; they can afford to be more venturesome in adding imaginative, creative thinkers to the faculty. Perhaps, however, the cause and effect relationship is just the reverse: perhaps they get the money because they have ideas.

CHAPTER 11

MEDICAL
EDUCATION

ʃ❋ʃ❋ʃ❋ʃ❋ʃ❋ʃ❋ʃ❋ʃ❋ʃ❋ʃ❋ʃ❋ʃ❋ʃ❋ʃ❋ʃ❋ʃ❋ʃ❋ʃ

Following the Flexner Report of 1910, medical schools ceased to be merely an appendage to the medical profession and assumed a role of leadership. But with the passage of more than half a century, fresh innovations are again urgently needed. In the view of one leading medical educator and investigator, Lowell Coggeshall:

> It takes bold and intelligent leadership to recognize that we are living in a medical paradox and then to break more sharply from so many of the conventional educational, research, and service patterns. Although earlier successful, they no longer suffice.[1]

[1] Lowell T. Coggeshall, "Progress and Paradox on the Medical Scene," The 1966 Michael M. Davis Lecture (Chicago: Center for Health Administration Studies, Graduate School of Business, University of Chicago, 1966), pp. 2–3.

Our advancing technology, coupled with the knowledge explosion, is transforming American life. One of the incongruities of our time is that in the midst of affluence there exists a host of sociopolitical problems; many of them—population policy and eugenics, radioactivity, recreation and resource conservation, and pollutions of food, water, and air, for example—are also biomedical.[2]

One aspect of social change is the recognition of the human being as a focus of primary concern. We are not merely concerned with man as an object of scientific observation and treatment, but with his well-being and the quality of his environment. Leading medical educators are not without some recognition of this fresh perspective. Dean William Hubbard, for example, has described "a movement from the university commitment to the education of physicians to a university commitment toward education for the health of the people."[3]

During the years following World War II, the medical profession fostered a large shortage of physicians. The negative influence of the American Medical Association is well known.[4] The views of the deans of medical schools have been changing, but in 1947 at the legislative hearings on medical education in New York the deans of the nine medical schools in the state unanimously declared that the supply of physicians was sufficient. There was an interesting sequel to this confrontation. Following action by the legislature to establish two or more new medical schools, four of the same deans came to my office with requests that their schools be taken over by the state; and they presented data and charts to show how the schools could be expanded in size. The impact of the shortage of physicians on health services is shown by a Gallup poll released May 5, 1968, in which the figures of a nationwide sample reflect American opinion about the shortage. Gallup found that people believed the shortage of doctors to be higher than the shortage in any other occupation or profession: 39 per cent

[2] Albert Lepawsky, "Medical Science and Political Science," *Journal of Medical Education,* Vol. 42, No. 10 (October, 1967), pp. 905–17.

[3] William N. Hubbard, Jr., "Medical Ventures and the University," Report of the Thirteenth Association of American Medical Colleges (AAMC) Institute, Third Institute on Administration, *Journal of Medical Education,* Vol. 42, No. 7, Part 2 (July, 1967), p. 113.

[4] See Julius B. Richmond, *Currents in American Medicine* (Cambridge: Harvard University Press, 1969), pp. 50–60 for a summary of these influences; also R. Harris, *A Sacred Trust* (New York: New American Library, 1966) for the story of the political lobbying of the AMA.

of the interviewees cited physicians as in shortest supply, whereas only 11 per cent cited plumbers, the highest shortage in the skilled worker category. The two most recent directors of the U.S. Public Health Service have declared medical manpower to be the most urgent problem in health service.

Parallel with this shortage and partly induced by it is the rapidly rising cost of medical services. Obviously the availability of increasingly specialized services from physicians and elaborate facilities in hospitals account in part for the increased cost to the patient. Fees charged by doctors for simple checkups and other services, however, continue to increase. The median income of doctors has been rising much faster than that in other occupations. I believe that the student, while in medical training, becomes influenced toward materialistic rewards. He is assured that he can afford to pay high tuitions and to take out large loans because later he will have a high income; and the incomes of his clinical teachers confirm this impression.

In medical school the physician is taught to be an entrepreneur. This mode of practice is becoming less viable because patients' financial risks can be shared through insurance and social security systems. Coggeshall speaks of the "declining emphasis on the nineteenth century entrepreneurial philosophy of the physician's responsibility."[5] And an eminent sociologist, Talcott Parsons, criticizing the practice of physicians in pricing their own services, often leading to exorbitant fees, says that "the profession [is] wide open to the charge that they have abandoned their ancient and honorable devotion to the welfare of the patient."[6]

Medical practitioners have been so indoctrinated against "socialism" that they have been blind to the need for greater socialization of the benefits of good health. They confuse the political issue with the health issue. It is becoming imperative, however, that medical educators consider the implications for the future practitioner of systems approaches to the promotion of health and attacks on disease. The systems concept also represents a need to use teams of experts in attacking some of the ills of society. A characteristic of social change has

[5] Lowell T. Coggeshall, *Planning for Medical Progress through Education* (Chicago: Association of American Medical Colleges, 1965), p. 43.

[6] Talcott Parsons, "Social Change and Medical Organization in the U.S.: A Sociological Perspective," *The Annals of the American Academy of Political and Social Science,* Vol. 346 (March, 1963), p. 29.

been the emergence of problems that are comprehensive in nature. Sociopolitical problems, including those that are also medical in nature, require systems approaches. Schools of public health understand the problems, but in medical schools they receive minimal attention.

Several criticisms of medical education can be made, as can suggestions for change. Cyril O. Houle in a recent study of continuing professional education neatly epigrams an attitude. "If you teach a person *what* to learn, you are preparing him for the past. If you teach him *how* to learn, you are preparing him for the future."[7] The method of stuffing and memorizing so common in medical schools is preparation with materials, much of which will quickly become outdated. Furthermore, this method does not teach the student to learn.

There is an overabundance of knowledge. To quote the report of the 1965 Summer Study at Endicott House: "the medical student faces the unbearable task of seeking to master an overwhelming range of knowledge and skills that he may never utilize in his career—a fact of which he is well aware even as a student."[8] The problem is to select the learning materials and experiences that will launch the prospective physician with sufficient competency to begin his professional career and to continue his learning thereafter. As Beaton wrote in 1965:

> In the future the physician will no longer be a "graduate," a man who has finished his schooling and severed his connection with the medical school. Rather will he be an abiding member of the university and its medical college, continually refreshed by contact with it, continually contributing to its fund of knowledge.[9]

Laboratory work takes about 50 per cent of a student's time in the preclinical years. According to Ralph W. Gerard, this situation resulted

from the nineteenth century revolt from authoritarianism and didactic teaching; and it was a tremendously important advance. But

[7] Cyril O. Houle, "The Lengthened Line," *Perspectives in Biology and Medicine,* Vol. 11, No. 1 (Autumn, 1967), pp. 37–51.

[8] Oliver Cope and Jerrold Zacharias, *Medical Education Reconsidered: Report of the Endicott House Summer Study on Medical Education* (Philadelphia: J. B. Lippincott Co., 1966), p. 34.

[9] Lindsey E. Beaton, "Adaptation to Change: A Consideration of Possible New Relationships," *Journal of Medical Education,* Vol. 40, No. 1, Part 2 (January, 1965), p. 282.

over the years there has been a tendency to forget that the laboratory
was intended to give some firsthand experience with real nature,
and it has often degenerated into a set of rather dreary routine hand
exercises which teach the student nothing new, but are often repetitive and sterile. Laboratory teaching happens, also, to be quite expensive. In recent years a few people have become concerned enough
to make some experiments to determine whether this expensive,
time-consuming laboratory experience really pays off.[10]

As an example, J. B. Kahn, a professor of pharmacology at Northwestern University, for two years divided his class at random into two
groups: one group did regular laboratory work; the other group held
demonstrations and discussions instead. Kahn reported:

> The results were similar in both years. The conference group
> did slightly better than the laboratory group on the final examina-
> tion, but the difference was not significant and the course grades
> were indistinguishable; the laboratory group's mean National Board
> score was just under two points lower than the mean of the group
> which had had no laboratory. . . . It can be stated that investi-
> gators have been unable to find any effect of laboratory on the areas
> which have been examined.[11]

A fresh approach to laboratory instruction, the unit study
laboratory introduced at Case Western Reserve, shows much promise.
In this new laboratory, his home for four years, the student—simu-
lating his later practice—does his studying, learning, arguing, and lab
work. Ideally each carrell in this laboratory is equipped with a computer input–output terminal and has facilities enabling the student to
use videotapes of outstanding lectures, laboratory demonstrations, patient interviews and examinations, operations, seminar discussions, and
the like. With the exception of the anatomy laboratory, the large
laboratories that are used only a few hours each week can be eliminated, saving space and money.[12] In some schools the time given to
anatomy is also being substantially reduced.

The teaching of medicine lends itself especially well to the

[10] Ralph W. Gerard, "Medical Education and Health Science," an
unpublished paper, July 1967, p. 11.
[11] J. B. Kahn, "The Pharmacology Laboratory: Teaching Tool or
Sacrament," *Journal of Medical Education,* Vol. 40, No. 9, Part 2 (September,
1965), p. 872.
[12] Gerard, p. 18.

problem solving approach. It should not be tied slavishly to textual materials, lectures, and traditional laboratory experiences. Cases that permit role playing by the prospective physician provide excellent practice in decision making. One form of problem solving is to have each student undertake research problems. The horizontal cleavage that has existed between the basic sciences and clinical study is breaking down in favor of an interrelationship between the two, as at the Duke and Yale Schools of Medicine. A sound principle of education is involved. The idea that all of the foundation must be provided before the professional types of experiences are permitted is not valid. The interaction between theory and practice is an important component of learning.

The student's orientation to the patient needs to be cultivated from the beginning of his medical school career. When patient contacts are deferred for as much as two years while the student is immersed in the study of the basic sciences, he gradually becomes science oriented rather than oriented to the patient. His relationships with patients and especially his understanding of the psychosomatic aspects of health are affected in an important way. As Cope says:

> Something happens during their four years. The educational mold distorts their vision in such a way that they become increasingly centered on the exact sciences to the detriment of their interests in the behavioral and emotional aspects of the patient.[13]

Through scientific research knowledge is becoming ever more interdisciplinary, and comfortable watertight compartments no longer exist. The biological sciences influence knowledge in several of the professions; research findings in the behavioral sciences are essential to the understanding of man, his environment and his total well-being. In preventive medicine, the study of interdisciplinary subjects such as genetics or nutrition becomes highly important. For teaching purposes a distinction must be made between research that facilitates student learning and research that advances knowledge but often actually impedes the training of practitioners. According to one authority, Ralph W. Gerard, this distinction is significant:

[13] Oliver Cope, *Man, Mind, and Medicine* (Philadelphia: J. B. Lippincott Co., 1968), p. 22.

The introduction of research has been crucial in reorienting medical education and is an indispensable part of the clinical school. But the amount needed to direct attention to and give experience in the mode of inquiring is limited. After this has been achieved, much larger research commitments, however worthy for the advance of medical science, have little direct impact on medical education.[14]

New intellectual tools are available to university teachers. Medical schools have been making excellent use of audio and television instruction. One obvious use is in surgery where exemplary operations can be viewed by thousands of students. The tapes that are beginning to be available to practitioners are an important innovation in their continuing education. The potential in audio-visual aids, however, has been insufficiently exploited through interinstitutional collaboration, through utilization of tapes prepared by eminent researchers and lecturers, and through two-way audio-visual facilities. Use of these aids might also reduce the costs of faculty lectures.

The computer is having a profound influence on education for the various professions. Its utilization in research is universal. But the computer also holds great promise as a diagnostic aid and as a source of data about pharmaceutical products. The public will breathe a sigh of relief—and also save large sums of money—if and when doctors turn to the computer console rather than to the drug company salesman for information about illnesses and drugs.[15] These potential developments in practice indicate the present need for instruction in the use of the computer.

Because the overall objective in medical education has been changing, the study of cadavers and the diseases of mammals must be deemphasized, and the study of man as a living being must become the primary focus. The plan of having the student begin his study of medicine with the observation of a family in which there is a pregnant mother, as at Case Western Reserve, uses sound principles of education. The student observes the growth and development of the foetus and the living being, together with the health implications of the en-

[14] Ralph W. Gerard, "Statement for the Assembly of the Academic Senate," University of California, Irvine, May 23, 1966.
[15] C. May, "Selling Drugs by 'Educating' Physicians," *Journal of Medical Education,* Vol. 36 (1961), pp. 1–23.

vironmental pressures in and surrounding the family. In the laboratory, it is the living cell, not dead tissue, that stimulates learning.

Another dimension of this new orientation is provided when medical students, as at the University of Kentucky, are required to have experience in community center agencies, complementing their clerkships in hospitals. The indigent patient in the teaching hospital is there because he has an interesting or exotic disease; such contact for the student is highly important but does not attune him to the health problems of the slums. Realistic experience in the ghetto helps the student understand the impact of malnutrition on physical and mental well-being.

In preceding chapters I have given some attention to preprofessional education. Medicine has its own special problems. Medical schools have taken a lead among professional schools in requiring of the applicants for admission a substantial preprofessional education. The results are far from satisfactory. The total time required for the training of a physician is exceptionally long; the articulation between the premedical and the medical programs is inadequate; the repetitions are time wasting; and the intellectual skills, cultural interests, and behavioral activities of practitioners do not sufficiently reflect liberal learning.

The problem of wasted time must be attacked in every phase of the program. In the preclinical stage, three accepted beliefs must be questioned: that all of the content now given in the basic sciences is valuable and necessary; that knowledge and skills achieved in the premedical program need to be repeated or duplicated; and that the liberal arts foundation now given is the best one for doctors.

The preclinical areas take up about half of the student's time in medical school. Ralph W. Gerard comments on this portion of the curriculum:

> What is taught reflects exciting discoveries in these scientific fields; and a vast amount of detail has accumulated during the past decades because these areas have been essentially in the analytic stage, just digging out of nature what's there. They are turning now to the synthetic stage, one of the great triumphs of biology in the last decade or two which collapses detailed items into broad principles. There remains, however, much factual detail taught redundantly in courses under different departmental names, so that the medical student not only is exposed to a vast array of facts—

which may not be facts very long, which he will not remember very long, which at best are only a small fraction of the relevant facts—but many of these are taught to him two or more times.[16]

And in a study for the American Physiological Society, a committee reluctantly agreed that perhaps 10 per cent of the time that medical students were spending in physiology was needed in order to learn matters really essential to medical practices.[17]

After clarification as to what content and skills are foundational to medicine, the question remains whether much of this knowledge can be obtained before entering medical schools. In any event, is it necessary for the individual student to repeat things that he already knows? Improved high school preparation in mathematics and the sciences has already enabled undergraduate colleges to step up the quality of their work. Since learning throughout undergraduate and medical education should be a continuum, the teaching of basic sciences must be examined for unnecessary repetitions and duplications.

One of the problems causing poor articulation between the undergraduate college and the professional school is that the faculties of the professional schools have not sufficiently analyzed the achievements desired for the students who will be entering their programs. For example, certain intellectual skills are pervasive and would greatly benefit a student going into any professional area. Among these are some that have been discussed—quantitative skills, behavioral skills, conceptual skills, skills of analysis and synthesis, and skills of communication. When further defined, these skills might become instructional objectives that could largely be fulfilled at the preprofessional level. Now it is a hit-or-miss chance whether the student really acquires them.

Another problem in articulation stems from the practice of liberal arts faculties to require a major for graduation. The major is in itself a specialization. Some adaptations, usually in biology, are made for premedical students, but even this major may not permit inclusion of enough other subjects—notably knowledge and skills from the behavioral sciences. Literature on medical education often expresses the need for knowledge and tools from the social and behavioral sciences

[16] Gerard, "Medical Education and Health Science," pp. 11–12.
[17] Gerard, "Medical Education and Health Science," p. 12.

as part of the training of the physician, but it does not spell out with sufficient precision how this knowledge equips the practicing physician to better understand and help his patients. It is now an accepted fact that disease has social and psychological as well as organic or physical causes and consequences. Courses in the social and behavioral sciences help the medical and premedical student to develop a sensitivity to relevant social/psychological phenomena and a new frame of reference from which to view the sick, and indeed the healthy, person. However, the random choice of courses offered in the behavioral sciences (most of them sequential and hence unavailable) will not provide the student with the concepts and skills needed in practicing medicine. The needs, which are several and differ in type, include: better understanding of social/psychological relationships, the cultural and anthropological aspects of human growth and development, the relationship of emotion to disease and well-being, environmental impacts on health, the functioning of groups, and the social role of health agencies.

Many aspects of knowledge from the behavioral sciences must be taught in the medical school—for example, control of ovulation by the hypothalamus and emotional impacts on migraine headaches, heart disease, and strokes. Just as clearly, other knowledge could be achieved in the undergraduate programs—knowledge, for instance, about individual development, learning, communication, ethology, unconscious motivations, social systems, and culture. A number of medical schools have added psychologists, and a few have employed sociologists for their staffs. The men who are to teach in these areas should themselves undergo fresh training or retraining. However, to avoid duplications, much of this learning can occur on the premedical level, and here the definition of need is nebulous.

In considering the cultural–foundational aspects of the education of the physician, it is important to distinguish knowledge which is basic to the profession from knowledge which produces personal growth and cultural understanding and refinement. The public image of doctors is that they do not represent good liberal learning. Their liberal study has resulted in cultural veneer which becomes largely eroded during the long and confining study of medicine.

Several medical schools—Johns Hopkins, Boston University, and Northwestern, among others—in various ways have been attacking the problem of time condensation and seeking better articulation of the components of the cultural–foundational program. In view of the importance of this subject, both for the student and for the problem of costs this experimentation should be watched with deep interest.

Reorientation of the focus of medical education at the pre-doctoral level is needed. During the past quarter- to half-century the interest of medical faculties has drifted strongly toward research. Research has had generous support and the results have been of high value in understanding and conquering disease. The grants of money have been a factor in the enlargement of medical knowledge and in the support of medical schools. Constructive as this has been, the absorption of interest and energies in research has had detrimental effects. It has caused serious neglect of the teaching; it has influenced policies that restrict the admission of students and the class size; it has created extravagant demands for private laboratory space to the disadvantage of research faculty elsewhere in the university; and it has consolidated departmental structures that cause fragmentations within the school. Specializations not only impede the core programs in medicine, but later displace the general practice of medicine. This practice, in turn, has the effect of making the physician's services much more available to affluent patients than to those from low income groups.

Concentration must be, first of all, on the health of all of the people.[18] Most specializations could be moved to the postdoctoral level. If the physician specialized later in his career, perhaps on a sabbatical leave from his clinic or firm, he could better afford the cost. The focus in the predoctoral program could then be placed on turning out primary physicians, a term recommended by medical educators,[19] and on preparing graduates for later specialized study, if and when they decide to specialize. The program might also train certain medical associates.

The need for a new type of physician, the primary physician, was recognized by an exploratory conference on medical services and medical education, held at Ft. Lauderdale, Florida, in February, 1966:

As a "primary physician" he would use the resources of the [health-care] center, including paramedical personnel, to full advantage and

[18] William N. Hubbard, Jr., "Principal Recommendations of the Workshop on Medical School Curriculum," Report to the Association of American Medical Colleges, October 30, 1968, mimeographed.

[19] "The Crisis in Medical Services and Medical Education," Report on an Exploratory Conference, February 20-25, 1966, Ft. Lauderdale, Florida. Sponsored by the Commonwealth Fund and Carnegie Corporation of New York.

would be carefully trained to bridge the gap between maintenance medicine and the diagnosis and treatment of major disease and between the health center and the medical center.[20]

Such physicians, aside from being widely useful, would help meet the needs for elementary medical services in the urban ghettos, in thinly populated rural areas, and in aspects of community medicine.

The medical associate performs a different type and level of service in that he functions in a medical capacity under the guidance of a physician. An example is the *pediatrics nurse practitioner* now being trained at the University of Colorado School of Medicine with financial assistance from the Commonwealth Fund. The aim of this experimental program is to train public health nurses for increased responsibility in the care of children from low income families. According to the 1966 annual report of the Commonwealth Fund:

> The experiment is directed at the problem of providing adequate medical attention to groups most likely to be affected by the increasing national shortage of doctors—the rural and urban poor. The experiment also has implications as a demonstration of how the reach of doctors in general might be extended through the use of nurses with advanced clinical training.[21]

The program at Colorado

> prepares the nurse to furnish comprehensive well child care to children of all ages, to identify and appraise acute and chronic conditions and refer them to other facilities as indicated, and to evaluate and temporarily manage emergency situations until medical assistance is available.[22]

The field of pediatrics seems to be a natural field for this development. The training of midwives, a shocking idea in America, would also help. If such physicians' associates were available in this field, perhaps the mortality rate of non-white infants, which is double that of white infants, could be reduced.

[20] "The Crisis in Medical Services and Medical Education," p. 7.

[21] *The Commonwealth Fund Forty-Eighth Annual Report for the Year Ended June 30, 1966* (New York: Harkness House, 1966), p. 22.

[22] H. K. Silver, L. C. Ford, and S. G. Stearly, "A Program to Increase Health Care for Children: The Pediatric Nurse Practitioner Program," *Pediatrics*, Vol. 29, No. 5 (May, 1967), p. 758.

But if this plan is good for pediatrics, why is it not good for many other specializations as well? In surgery, for example, surgeons' associates with training in certain of the skills of surgery would probably do a much better job in assisting the surgeon than a general practitioner, who is often used. His training costs would be much less; and if the time required of the surgeon were less, the fee could be reduced.

Duke University is pioneering in this field. In a two-year program that involves both the study of basic knowledge and the development of skills in practice, the medical school since 1965 has been preparing a small flow of physicians' assistants. Provision has also been made for these persons to return, after they have gained experience, to train in skills that relate directly to the specialization of the employing physician or clinic. The huge number of applicants to the Duke program indicates that the potential supply of these students is large. (Incidentally, 80 per cent of the one thousand applicants in 1967 were former medical corpsmen in the armed services, where their motivations had been stimulated.[23]) Among the tasks that can be performed by physicians' assistants, according to the director of a similar program at the University of Washington School of Medicine, are: screening patients, performing parts of physical examinations, applying and removing casts, assisting at surgery, suturing minor cuts, taking x-rays and performing laboratory tests outside of office hours, assuming some administrative responsibilities, and being available to assist the physician whenever he is on call, day or night.[24]

The Colorado and Duke programs represent small beginnings of what is certain to become a nationwide movement. Enlargement of health teams through the addition of these new categories of personnel, physicians' assistants and medical associates[25] would open the medical

[23] Thelma Ingles, "A New Health Worker," *American Journal of Nursing*, Vol. 68, No. 5 (May, 1968), pp. 1059–61.

[24] The *New York Times*, Sunday, November 30, 1969.

[25] A distinction needs to be drawn between physicians' assistants and the professional for whom I suggest the new term "medical associate." The assistant belongs in the category of paramedical personnel in that he works continuously under the direction of a doctor. The medical associate, on the other hand, should be qualified to engage in diagnosis and therapy within the scope of his training, and should be licensed accordingly. The term medical associate parallels that of medical doctor, but also implies a team relationship. In Soviet Russia, the *feldsher* encompasses both roles, but I believe there would be advantage in making the distinction.

profession to students who cannot afford the longer course of studies now required of the M.D. specialist. And the addition of these practitioners should reduce the costs of medical services. These new health personnel are especially needed for neighborhood health centers.

The costs of medical services and of medical education have become alarming. They are prohibitive for many persons, and something must be done about the situation. The creation of sixteen new medical schools will help relieve the shortages of physician-specialists. But adding new schools is highly expensive, and adding specialists and research activity does not solve the basic social problem.

A much more economical plan would be to enlarge the present schools. There is, of course, great variation in the sizes of student bodies among the medical schools, and this fact demonstrates that the smaller schools could be enlarged—but I am also talking about increasing the enrollments in the largest ones. Enlargement of existing schools would be a highly important factor in reducing student-unit costs. More, the cost of expansion would be modest compared with the enormous sums required for new schools. Granted that the presence of sufficient clinical materials needs to be taken into account—an argument that has been considerably overworked—the real obstacle to increase in the sizes of medical schools lies in the attitudes of the faculties. These attitudes stem from obsolete notions about the need for large faculty–student ratios and small class sizes, and from self-protective stances that are concerned with research grants and with the supply of physicians.

To achieve significant increases in size, it is necessary to get rid of these obsolete notions. First, there is the question of justifying the faculty–student ratio which in medical education is so extraordinarily high. When the teaching of medicine was the equivalent of training apprentices through man-to-man relationships, the high faculty–student ratio may have had some justification. Today, the master under the apprentice system has become a vast array of stimulating contacts and experiences that flow from a variety of experts and a series of laboratory and hospital experiences.[26] This changed relationship between teacher and student suggests a number of ways to use the teacher more effectively and to cause the student to become more of a participant in his own education.

A related opinion, that the class size must remain small, prevails

[26] Parsons, pp. 27–28.

among medical educators. Class size is a matter of policy for the university, but the practice of limiting the enrollments in medical school is not open to the same scrutiny as are the classes elsewhere in the university. I should like to give an example of the limitations in two departments of a prominent medical school, with information taken from the school bulletin. The department of pediatrics lists twenty-five faculty and eighteen instructors. The maximum number of students permitted in the department's fifteen courses (all that are listed by this department)' are, respectively: 10, 2, 3, 5, 4, 6, 3, 2, 2, 5, 2, 3, 9, 6, 10. Several questions need to be asked: Is the flow of babies (clinical materials) as small as these figures suggest? If this school specializes in pediatrics, should not its flow of graduates in pediatrics be several times this large? If it does not so specialize, why does it offer such fragmented courses? Should this department, on its own, be attempting to include specialties where the cases are rare? Should not the study of rare diseases be removed to the postdoctoral level and studied in a limited number of centers?

Does this school illustrate the case where the pursuit of research is given more emphasis than is teaching? This impression is confirmed by the department of biochemistry, which lists twenty-four faculty (plus twenty-five fellows) and only ten courses. Why are ten courses in this basic science necessary for the education of physicians? What is the function of the undergraduate program in biochemistry in this university, and is the teaching in medical schools coordinated with it? Why does this large medical faculty admit only eighty students each year? The answer lies in the fact that most medical schools have become for all practical purposes research laboratories.

Of relevance to this point is the evidence from research in education that class size is not as important a factor in securing good educational results as once was thought. Sanazaro reviewed the literature and applied the findings to medical education. "The available data support the conclusion that class size itself is unrelated to objectively definable major components of the educational process in medicine," Sanazaro states. He adds that "It can be concluded that medical education of acceptable quality is relatively more economical in the larger schools."[27] Increasing class size is one way to control the costs of faculty and space and, hence, reduce the unit cost.

[27] Paul J. Sanazaro, "Class Size in Medical School," *Journal of Medical Education*, Vol. 41, No. 11, Part 1 (November, 1966), p. 1027.

Most predoctoral classes that enroll as few as two to five students should be doubled or trebled in size or eliminated—as is done elsewhere in the university. The need for producing more physicians at lower unit cost is a consideration of public policy and should take precedence over the whims of professors who limit their classes and fragment knowledge. This increase in class size could take place with minor increases in staff and facilities.

Still another approach to the problem of state and national costs for medical education is to apply the systems concept to the organization of medical schools. Forty-three states today have planning–coordinating commissions on higher education, which means that the state regards the public colleges and universities as a system of higher education. The systems concept involves large-scale planning and coordination, including differentiations of functions among institutions. But these commissions have seriously neglected the subject of differentiation among medical schools.

Applying the systems idea of medical education, should all medical schools be all-purpose schools? Of course, they really are not. The practical situation of finances limits the scope of activities for many of them. Also the characteristics of students differ among the various schools. H. H. Gee documented the differential recruitment and was able to classify the medical schools of the country into three clusters.[28] In one cluster the schools are well known for the proportion of graduates who go into teaching and research. The other two clusters of schools had student bodies with somewhat different characteristics. Yet, in spite of these facts, the medical school faculties behave as though all of the schools were identical.

In view of the quality and thoroughness of training needed, is there any reason why all medical schools prepare persons for the field of academic medicine and medical research? And should not this program have an identity of its own? Medical schools in general can limit the specializations that are taught to those needed in the usual practice. The teaching of other specializations can be concentrated in those institutions best prepared to undertake them. They are, to some extent, but I advocate a more drastic approach of identifying the teaching–

[28] H. H. Gee, "Differential Characteristics of Student Bodies—Implications for the Study of Medical Education," in *Selection and Educational Differentiation,* ed. T. R. McConnell (Berkeley: Field Service Center and Center for the Study of Higher Education, University of California, 1959), pp. 125-54.

research roles in specializations and also of removing more of the latter to the postdoctoral level. This arrangement would leave the preparation of physicians in the basic phase of medical study to the remaining majority of medical schools.

There is a further social issue involved in the manner in which new medical programs are planned. The people of New Mexico have taxed themselves to finance a new medical school. Their motivation has been to assure that the people of the state will have a supply of physicians. But if the new school follows the standard pattern, nourished by research grants from the federal government, the graduates will not become general practitioners for the county seat towns of the state. They will flee to metropolitan centers and to other states where the per capita income is high. Thus the people of New Mexico will have been frustrated in their basic objective, another case of mistaken role identity. Institutional pride has taken priority over social need.

In spite of the high cost of medical education, the average quality of medical practice and health care in this country is seriously inadequate. As one observer, Edward T. Chase, sees it:

> The American health care system, despite its scandalous costs, 6 percent of the gross national product, more than that of any other nation, is mediocre. The United States now ranks fifteenth in infant mortality (eleventh in 1961, fifth in 1950). Twelve nations have a higher life expectancy at age 60. In life expectancy for the population generally, the United States ranks thirteenth for males, seventh for females. Fifteen other nations have higher ratios of hospital beds to population. Only about 60 percent of American hospitals are officially accredited . . . seven countries have a higher proportion of doctors to population than the United States.[29]

Reflection upon these data reveals that they are concerned with the simpler issues of health, longevity, and supply of services, as distinguished from the question of competence in research and in medical specializations.[30] While going overboard for the more spectacular aspects of medicine, our medical schools have been neglecting the elementary and the mundane. Yet for substantial portions of our people

[29] Edward T. Chase, "The Doctor's Bonanza," *The New Republic,* April 15, 1967, p. 17.
[30] For a more complete analysis of the health problems of the country together with constructive suggestions, see Julius B. Richmond, *Currents in American Medicine* (Cambridge: Harvard University Press, 1969).

care at this level is the crying need. It is here that most of the innovations in curriculum, educative experiences, and teaching can be effective. It is this level of service which deserves from the medical schools fresh professional orientation and a dedication to service.

CHAPTER 12

ENGINEERING
EDUCATION

[decorative ornament]

In 1968 the American Society for Engineering Education published the report of a committee of the society that had been studying engineering education. Having devoted five years to studying themselves, the schools of engineering will undoubtedly be greatly influenced by this statement of goals. The report is an admirable one, but I should like to examine it from a special viewpoint—the impact of social change on engineering.

An Interim Goals Report, published a year earlier, had commendably advocated preparing the student for "accelerating technological change" and causing the student to become alert to "the changing needs and heightening and broadening aspirations of mankind." The Final Report, however, adds as the first objective, "To prepare the student, ideologically, for constructive participation in the competitive

148

profit motivated economy."[1] I should like to analyze this statement, for it seems contradictory to the data supplied by the committee. In addition, it is out of harmony with the traditional aims of universities and with the needs of our complex society. By the latter I mean such things as the motivations that should prevail in resource conservation and management, in designing new systems to solve complex social problems, and in the education of foreign students. I think also that the statement of objective suggests that the engineers accept technological change without accepting economic or social change. If so, the situation has implications concerning the breadth of training that engineers get in college.

Should a university, or any school within it, indoctrinate its students in a particular social ideology—even capitalism? To do so seems to pervert the objectives of intellectual inquiry. Without debating this issue (for much literature exists on the point), I shall go on to a second one —namely, the roles that engineers will play in society during the next quarter to half century. In addition to serving business and industry, either directly or through professional practice, engineers will undoubtedly function in government service, in philanthropically supported research and planning, in academic roles, and in programs of assistance to underdeveloped nations. Of the responding educators in the Goals Study, 70 per cent foresee an increased social role for engineering graduates, although that point seems to have been omitted from the phraseology of the first objective.

The contributions of engineers to the development of the resources of this nation fill a remarkable and commendable page in history. Now, as noted so well in the Master Plan for Engineering at the University of California,[2] the United States is in a period of resource protection and is moving into one of resource management. Resource development has taken place largely through business enterprise. Resource conservation and management are primarily social in nature. Much of this work has to be done by government or with the assistance and supervision of government. Indeed, the interests of profit-making industry are antithetical to aspects of the conservation

[1] "Final Report: Goals of Engineering Education," *Journal of Engineering Education*, Vol. 58, No. 5 (January, 1968), pp. 373–443.

[2] University of California Engineering Advisory Council, *An Engineering Master Plan Study for the University of California* (Berkeley: University of California, 1965), pp. 53–56.

of natural resources and of blight removal; and the costs of development in other cases are so huge as to be beyond the possibility of financial return in the near future. Thus resources management, extremely important to the welfare of future generations, cannot be left in the hands of private enterprise. To do so would be disastrous.

T. J. Gordon and Olaf Helmer prepared a long-range forecast, which I have mentioned earlier, for the RAND Corporation. They identified thirty-one breakthroughs that can be expected in science.[3] Many of them require systems approaches to achieve and apply. Systems such as the Tennessee Valley Authority, national defense, highways, and National Aeronautics and Space Administration could not have been undertaken by private enterprise alone, although the participation of private enterprise is highly valuable. The engineering-related problems and solutions of the future—congested population corridors, pollution controls, space communications systems, urban regeneration, desalination, and the development of fresh food supplies through photosynthesis—may in some part require collaboration between profit-motivated industry and the agencies of government. But realistically speaking, most of the basic research will have to be financed through government and nonprofit sources, and the development stages may take long periods with low expectation of financial return. To choose one example, the ultimate social benefits of planned corridor systems—not financial profit—should be the primary motivation for participation by future generations of engineers.

Engineers serve both government and private industry; of those in industry who possess the doctorate, about half are working principally on government projects. Of the income available for research in engineering, 84 per cent comes from federal and local governments. The report of the Committee on Educational Policy at the Massachusetts Institute of Technology notes "the increasing dependence of government on technical advisors."[4] Even so, an overwhelming portion of those with doctor's degrees go into academic work and research and development. The more fascinating of the research and development programs doubtless relate to systems-type problems, often too vast and

[3] T. J. Gordon and Olaf Helmer, *Report of a Long-Range Forecasting Study* (Santa Monica, Calif.: The RAND Corporation, 1964), p. 13.

[4] Massachusetts Institute of Technology, Committee on Educational Policy, *Changing the Undergraduate Curriculum at MIT* (Cambridge, Mass.: Massachusetts Institute of Technology, 1967), p. 4.

complex for industry to solve. These data do not contradict the merit in a free enterprise economy, but neither do they suggest an emphasis on competition and profit making as motivations for professional men.

Opportunities to provide professional assistance to underdeveloped countries, many of which have socialized economies, should not be overlooked. Also, among the full-time students at the graduate level in engineering are large numbers from foreign countries—25 per cent of the total. Their perceptions of social systems may differ from those of capitalism, and engineering educators need to understand this. The students need to be given the kind of training that will fit them to become constructive participants in their own economies when they return to their homelands.

Since engineering graduates are employed in occupations and situations that include both private enterprise and socially controlled institutions and governments, they must be oriented to serve humanity rather than a small competitive segment. Some leaders in engineering education sense this need full well. The Massachusetts Institute of Technology has been steadily broadening and enriching its program to give its students a broader grasp of social needs. In his annual report for 1966–67, Gordon S. Brown, Dean of the School of Engineering, spoke of a new challenge in engineering education now confronting MIT and said that "this challenge introduces new value systems, as these problem areas relate primarily to the civilian, rather than to the industrial, military, or space sectors of our society."[5]

In view of the kinds of challenges that lie ahead, the engineering profession must entice youth of greater imagination, intelligence, and potential creativeness into the field. Youth will be motivated toward an engineering profession whose primary concern is with the use of technology for the development of the good society. The youth of the country are reassessing many of the values that underlie our materialistically oriented society. (Perhaps it will be said that "hippies" do not go into engineering.) The movement among youth is a broad one, and it relates to many problems that require for their solution the participation of engineers.

One of the problems of all of the professions today is to step into the world of tomorrow, an interdependent world emphasizing

[5] Massachusetts Institute of Technology, *Report of the School of Engineering 1966–67, Annual Report* (Cambridge: Massachusetts Institute of Technology, 1967), p. 3.

human values above all other considerations. Schools of architecture, realizing that they now must take greater account of the human as distinguished from the physical factors, are broadening their approaches to city planning by adopting the concept of environmental design. Indeed, a study on the goals of architectural education, undertaken at Princeton University for the American Institute of Architects and recently published, states that "We are beginning to understand today, as we seldom have in the past, the way that changes in the physical environment are inextricably linked to changes in the social, economic, and political environment."[6]

In an affluent society materialistic rewards influence too much the motivations of professional men, who get caught up in the tide of large personal incomes and corporate profits. That this trend is of concern to the professional schools may be seen from the attention being given by alert medical schools to the shortage of physicians who are willing to serve at the family level and with disadvantaged groups, by schools of agriculture that are attempting to alleviate food shortages in underprivileged countries, and by schools of law through a restudy of professional ethics.

The men and women who are educated for the professions help more than any other group to make society viable. They solve the problems and the controversies and design the patterns for action. The more complex the society becomes, the more the professional men need to define their professional ethics and resolve to fulfill the code. An engineering education must include a broad cultural foundation, training in problem solving, and educative experience.

The Goals Report makes a plea for a more substantial cultural foundation for engineers, including knowledge from the humanities and social sciences. Will this goal be achieved by the current methods used by schools of engineering to supply cultural content? The programs are nearly all undergraduate in type; they are heavily loaded with technical subject matter and laboratory experiences. Students get a good foundation in mathematics. They also get an adequate foundation in science—but as a technical, not a cultural, subject. Programs are highly deficient in the humanities and social sciences. English, when taught, is "English for Engineers." Perhaps the schools, in practice,

6 Princeton University, *Final Report: A Study of Education for Environmental Design, A Report by Princeton University for the American Institute of Architects* (Princeton, New Jersey: Princeton University, 1967), p. 4.

identify cultural content with the ability to read, write, and calculate. Beyond that, they let the applied and technical content push other knowledge out of the way. This dilemma is real; the schools have not been able to put design into the planning of their own programs.

I have discussed the subject of breadth of education for all professions in Chapter Ten. The trend clearly is toward adding more of this content. As the professions mature, they become more sensitive to cultural values, but today there are additional factors. Of immediate concern to engineering is the recognition that the profession must deal with contemporary social problems and with the problems of the underdeveloped nations. New approaches for all students are needed, but for engineers, who combine their general and professional education within a four or five year span, there is the added difficulty of providing room for the subject matter and experiences. It does not suffice merely to require a year or two of preengineering education or to save room for electives. A fresh design for engineering education is needed— one that defines and injects liberalizing content and influence.

Schools in several professional areas have become concerned with their knowledge-stuffed, memorizing-based type of teaching. A few have acted to select more relevant materials and to make room for fresh knowledge from current research. Of more significance, however, is the possibility that the change may be the result of a major revision in objectives. If the study of engineering is not merely the study of technology but also of the dynamic impact of technology on man, this concept, too, argues for fresh approaches in engineering.

The vast accumulation of knowledge has caused educators to realize that it is impossible to stuff all of the available knowledge into a student during four years of study. But lengthening the period to five years does not answer the need; even if it were possible to cover all relevant knowledge, the result would not be wholly beneficial because knowledge becomes obsolete. As I have noted previously, skill in problem solving is one definite answer to this dilemma. If a student is trained to be a problem solver, in later life he can keep pace with the development of fresh concepts, knowledge, and techniques, and he can thus avoid getting into an occupational dead end or into a rut that reduces him to the technician level. The Goals Report advocates better training in problem solving, as well as the utilization of work-study programs and internships. Both recommendations have my emphatic endorsement.

Case studies represent a form of problem. They are thought provoking and provide good training in decision making. In schools of business administration, a distinction is made between a case that recites an actual situation and gives the decision that was made and a problem-case where the statement may be real or simulated and the student is required to arrive at his own decision. This distinction is highly important because, where cases are taught as a means of causing the student to learn what precedents exist for decisions, he is really being trained as a technician and not as a person who thinks for himself. In spite of the long history of the use of cases in schools of law, the method has come under considerable criticism. Professors of family law at several law schools have begun to devise cases with less emphasis on legal precedents and more emphasis on explicit analysis of the realistic problems of a family and its environmental situation. In some instances, professors from psychology, sociology, social work, and psychiatry have participated with those in law in the writing and teaching of such cases. The writing is done with a view to presenting the best possible teaching–learning problem.

The Goals Report might well have given more attention to ongoing experiments in the use of cases (such as those at Stanford, Massachusetts Institute of Technology, and the University of California) as a means of studying engineering. Cases can provide simulated experience as well as training in decision making.

I want to turn now to a further discussion of the use of experience as a factor in educating for engineering. Although the work–study kind of program was first used in an engineering school, it has too often been limited to an apprentice type of experience. From the employer's point of view, there are reasons for the limitation: the inexperience of the student, the ease of accommodating him on an elementary job, and the lack of continuity in the services that he renders. But it is these reasons which render it of the utmost importance that the desired learning experiences be clearly defined. There should be an evaluation by the student of his experiences, and an interweaving of the knowledge gained with that received through study at the college.

One objective of engineering education is to graduate the students with a high degree of competency for the engineering jobs at hand. The objectives of work-and-study can, however, include the liberalizing of the student in the sense of teaching him to become a keen observer of organization, of group processes, and of the impacts of environmental conditions on individuals, enterprises, and governments. These objectives relate to an important one included in the Interim Report: "learn to understand the major institutions of society —how they function (and sometimes fail to function)." Some of the liberal arts colleges that use the work-and-study plan place particular emphasis upon this point. An implication of what I have said about both cases and experience is that they will train technicians or educate engineers, depending upon the method of using them.

Engineering may be called a problem solving profession. In setting the goals for the next several years, the schools of engineering must give major attention to improving their methods of education in problem solving. As Charles Wales, speaking of both case–problem and programed instruction, has said:

> As it is impossible to equip each student with a lifetime supply of knowledge, why do engineering teachers try to do it? Would it not be better to teach students how to search for knowledge, where to search for knowledge, and how to use the knowledge they find?[7]

Many questions are being raised today about the internal organization of universities, and it is surprising that the Goals Report gave little attention to this subject. Organization is one of the important means through which goals are achieved. Moreover, the separation between means and ends is not—except in superficial ways— clean cut.

The kinds of problems that exist today for engineering education consist of the needs (1) to curtail departments (such as mining) that have passed their heyday; (2) to find the best ways to educate new types of engineers (for example, information specialists, systems engineers, or engineers in interdisciplinary fields such as bioengineering); (3) to achieve interdisciplinary collaboration, both for research and for teaching; (4) to maintain flexibility in the planning of students' programs to permit them to take advantage of interdepartmental and interdisciplinary offerings; and (5) to free the doctoral programs so that each piece of research can relate to a problem in engineering, regardless of departmental lines.

Beyond the possible adjustments required to supply such needs,

[7] Charles Wales, "Programmed Instruction: Key to Engineering Education for Tomorrow," *Journal of Engineering Education*, Vol. 57, No. 6 (February, 1967), p. 433.

there is the further possibility of undertaking a thorough reorganization of engineering subject matter. An example is the study of engineering made at the University of California, Los Angeles, directed by Allen B. Rosenstein.[8] This study made a thorough analysis of the objectives and content of engineering curriculums, and the study was followed by a synthesis of the essential elements surrounding fresh concepts about the education of engineers. The resulting design is revealed by *stems* of knowledge which I will describe later in this chapter. In engineering the difficulty of redesigning curriculum is intimately related to departmentalized specializations.

It is the tendency of all academic faculties to subdivide into harmonious groups related to specializations. Even so, they cannot keep pace with the fragmenting of specializations. A school, a division, or a department, therefore, should be identified for what it is: an administrative convenience and a group to which congenially related scholars can belong. Constrictions occur when a department extends its authority beyond these points to control students' programs and research. This is why some professional schools are resorting to a two-dimensional plan of organization. One aspect may represent the inputs of faculty services—budgets, equipment, and so forth; the other aspect may represent the outputs—student learning, research findings, and continuing education, the three types of faculty effort which are called programs.

The term *program* is in use at the Harvard Graduate School of Business Administration and at the College of Agriculture, University of Minnesota, for identifying concentrations of study. Both institutions aim to depart from occupation- or commodity-oriented curricula in favor of flexibility and unity. In a somewhat analogous manner, some institutions now program research around natural groups of problems —rather than along the usual departmental lines—on the assumption that this rather different cross section will influence the design of the curriculum. Instances may be seen at the Institute of Technology of Southern Methodist University and at the Alfred P. Sloan School of Management of the Massachusetts Institute of Technology. The organization of institutes and centers, so many of which are being formed, is similar but usually has little relationship to the educational program.

8 Allen B. Rosenstein and L. Cromwell, "Dynamic Analysis and Design of Engineering Curricula—The Information Base" (Los Angeles: Department of Engineering, University of California, Los Angeles, June, 1968), EDP4-68.

Indeed, the departments protect their own interests by insisting that this be the case.

The logic of curriculum formation seems to be to identify a core of subject matter that is relevant to all of engineering and to create a number of models of concentrated study for students. The faculty creates the core and models and also sets up criteria related both to the breadth and to the depth of study for the individual student's program. The student then may choose a model or devise variations from it as his program, conforming always to the criteria. The supervision of the student's program, however, is in the hands of a counselor who is not under the control of a departmental chairman but instead is responsible to a top counseling officer associated with the dean. The plan suggested here assures flexibility of individual programs. In like manner, research must be organized around programs that provide for teams of appropriate specialists.

An alternative to fragmenting the departments still further would be to reverse the trend and return to broad areas such as electrical, mechanical, civil, and chemical engineering. These groupings, analogous to the divisional plan for organizing the arts and sciences, are broad enough to include the large majority of model programs for students and perhaps also the bulk of research. The advantage of the divisional plan is that the walls within walls are reduced greatly in number. Thus the competition for students, the subdividing of research, and the rivalries over budgets are minimized. My discussion in Chapter Seven about departments in liberal arts colleges and the organization of graduate schools has relevance here.

Another mode of organization is the *stem* idea, as proposed by the study directed by Rosenstein at UCLA. The stems concept casts aside the usual departmental nomenclature and involves a reorganization of engineering programs around basic work in design, stems of materials, energy, information, and general education, topped by integrative programs relating to systems. A totally fresh approach to organization such as this is difficult because of the many constricting influences—especially the existing subunits, such as the professional societies—within the profession. The plan, however, has the advantage of departing from the somewhat outmoded occupationally oriented departmental structure.

As a means of doing advance planning, leading engineering schools—strong advocates of research and development—today might well establish research and development staffs of their own. These staffs, composed of men with competence to study problems of education, would evaluate students, curriculum, and teaching methods. They would provide the ideas, data, and recommendations addressed to changes that are needed in the schools.

Because of the growing size and complexity of higher education, it is desirable to differentiate among the functions of institutions. The principle applies equally to schools of engineering. The problem is most easily seen within a populous state where large numbers of colleges and universities are needed. If funds are distributed to institutions without a comprehensive plan of present action and future development, the funds are apt to be dissipated rather than mobilized for strength in support of particular functional purposes. This is why states are beginning to think of public colleges and universities as systems of higher education, the whole of each system developing along guidelines provided by a planning–coordinating commission and approved by the state legislature.

In any such planning, a distinction needs to be drawn between those programs that should be widely distributed geographically and those that require concentrations of resources for highly specialized programs and for advanced education and research. Because graduates of doctoral programs go into academic work and into research and development, these programs must have adequate funds to secure competent faculty and equipment. In advanced research, the quality of faculty production must act as a magnet for research projects and laboratories. Laboratories, when near the campus, tap the pool of knowledge in the sciences and engineering departments; and in turn, they are of potential aid in identifying doctoral research problems and in providing highly educative experiences at this advanced level.

In projecting trends in the granting of doctor's degrees, the Goals Report counted 101 schools in 1966 and estimated an increase to 150 by 1978. This would represent a growth of approximately 50 per cent within twelve years. Does this mean also that by 1990 the number would become 200 to 300? Although it is estimated that the production of doctoral degrees will number 8000 per year by 1978, it seems wiser to have fifty schools that emphasize genuinely advanced training, or even the 101 schools that now have doctoral programs, continue to perform this level of the educational job, rather than to encourage so many additional schools to jump on the bandwagon. The report recommends that the new graduate schools maintain high standards. But how can they, if resources are spread too thin? The problem doubtless centers in the psychological attitudes of faculty members. Faculties feel the urge to emulate those in the schools with the greatest reputations. They also want to qualify for research grants. If, however, this psychology is not redirected in some way, many hundreds of institutions will become inferior universities and will miss the opportunity to become excellent schools meeting goals that are different but not less important than those met by the prestigious institutions.

Embedded in the Engineering Education report is a recommendation which if more strongly emphasized might clarify functional roles. In discussing developments at the master's level, reference is made to the Master of Business Administration degree as a terminal type of degree. The MBA is not awarded to a student while he is on the path toward a doctor's degree; instead it serves the needs of students who are becoming practitioners. In a similar case, the Master of Public Administration degree is a highly useful degree in preparation for governmental service, whereas the dissertation and other features of a doctor's degree are not of any great benefit in the vast majority of positions. A master's degree of this sort in engineering is a highly commendable recommendation. The objectives of a program of this kind are such that they can be given wholehearted support by a professional faculty. The schools would be utilizing their resources in providing excellence of teaching in relation to objectives of distinct usefulness in society.

The report stresses the need for training more engineering technicians but is not clear about how this is to be done. Public community colleges and technical institutes are mentioned, and these institutions should be supported in this role. As noted also in the report, a differentiation can be made at the four-year and five-year levels because, as the report states, the recommendation of a five-year master's degree program does not mean that every engineering school should offer a program leading to a master's degree. Engineers are accustomed to thinking about systems. I am advocating that schools of engineering or engineering-type training be conceived of in systems terms, with various units within the system having clearly defined functional roles.

Since 1900 the engineering profession has grown much faster than many older professions, such as law, medicine, and the ministry. Schools of engineering have responded well to the need for practitioners, and it must be admitted that, in a technical sense, the United States has produced the best engineers in the world. Rather than resting upon their laurels, however, engineering schools must accept the fresh challenges before them. These cannot be met by adding more of the same thing. Society is changing; engineering is changing; and schools of engineering must make some fresh approaches to education.

CHAPTER 13

TEACHER
EDUCATION

♪☀♪☀♪☀♪☀♪☀♪☀♪☀♪☀♪☀♪☀♪☀♪☀♪☀♪☀♪

Teacher education should be the joint responsibility of faculties in general education and in professional education. Unfortunately there is little rapport between the two groups. Professors of the liberal arts and professors in education have grown apart for several reasons.

Professors in liberal arts, though conversant with history, have been slow to recognize the dynamic nature of the demand for more and more education in this country. The tradition of the liberal arts grew out of the monastery—where the classics of Greece and Rome were rediscovered, and was nourished in the universities of Europe—where higher education was a class privilege and its diploma a badge of cultural attainment and a ticket into the civil service. In this country, the liberal arts became basic to the rest of higher education, but in the minds of many they were meant for the intellectual few. Traditional liberal arts curricula have put their stress on the disciplines. Professors of education, on the other hand, have been influenced by the more flexible curricular developments taking place at the secondary level. They have been imbued by the philosophy of education for the many. Breadth of education is emphasized, not specialization.

When teachers with professional training in educating children and youth were needed for the public schools, the colleges and universities did not regard it as their obligation to supply them. So normal schools, and later teachers' colleges, were established. Thus there grew up a separate system of colleges for training teachers. This phenomenon was not limited to education. The earlier failure of the faculties in liberal arts to recognize the growth of various vocational and professional needs resulted in the establishment of a whole array of professional schools with specialized and applied curriculums—business administration, journalism, social work, and architecture, for example. And typical faculty members in the liberal arts look down their noses at the professors in all of these schools.

As is contended in Chapter One, the educational need in the United States is for a balance between cultural education and vocational education. More than that, the need is for a fusion of the two elements. Some trends toward such a fusion in the curriculum can be identified. Teachers' colleges have been moving strongly in the direction of providing general education content for their students. Their course offerings in professional education have not been reduced, but for the individual student the methods courses have been de-emphasized in favor of more general education. Most such colleges also now offer degrees in the liberal arts. The independent liberal arts colleges, too, have been providing the more elementary courses in professional education. Thus in some cases the two programs have been moving closer together.

When one speaks of *general education,* one taps another source of conflict in views. The conflict arises because of the nature of the usual liberal arts curriculum. The professor of history, philosophy, or mathematics thinks of his program as providing cultural breadth; and he contends that this is needed by prospective teachers. The professional educator answers that the usual liberal education merely pretends to provide breadth; actually it falls far short of this goal. The liberal arts college of today, he says, is a collection of specialized departments, and the student gets only fragments of knowledge plus a specialization. This type of education might prepare the research scholar for more intensive study, but it gives the potential schoolteacher inadequate preparation for teaching.

The concern of the academic man with research in his field is, of course, commendable. Extension of the horizons of knowledge is an essential function of higher education. But it is not generally the concern of the public school teacher. The teacher whose task is to prepare children for their future roles as participants in the democratic society and as persons of breadth of culture needs a genuinely broad education. The teacher needs to know a lot about life on earth and about the world that nourishes that life. It does not suffice merely to know a lot of mathematics or a lot about economics.

Professors of education are usually advocates of general education. The general education movement was an attempt to reorganize the content of education to enable the student to see life as a whole, to secure integration among fields of knowledge, and to study the more significant trends of history and the problems of humanity—to retrieve some of the values that were lost from liberal education a century ago when it lost its unity.[1] This viewpoint is shared by an increasing number of professors of academic specialties, but the progress is slow. In the meantime the advocates of reform are being charged with superficiality of approach and with "lowering of standards." The charge "lowering of standards" can, of course, be used to defeat any attempt to disturb the academic status quo.

Another conflict lies in the difference in views about the professional aspects of teaching. The academic professors scorn the idea that methods of teaching need to (or, perhaps, even *can*) be taught. They deplore the courses in teacher training, and there is some substance to their contention. Education courses have been multiplied and fragmented (just as the more academic courses have been). Worse than that, professors of education do not take the trouble to make their own teaching superior; they thus appear to be preaching something they do not practice. But it is a mistake to lump all courses in professional education into the methods category or to assume that a methods course, by its nature, must lack substantive content. A high

[1] Joseph Axelrod *et al., Search for Relevance: The Campus in Crisis* (San Francisco: Jossey-Bass, 1969).

quality methods course, in fact, typically has a double content. In the language field, for example, the content of the methods course derives from two rich fields of knowledge—modern linguistics and language learning psychology.

The curriculum in teacher education is now based more and more upon the findings of basic research—research in child growth and development, in individual and group behavior, in methods of teaching, and in evaluation. The academic man, immersed in his own specialty, is quite unaware of the advances in knowledge that have taken place in this area within the past half century, and more especially in the past few years. Professors of education, among whom the number with doctor's degrees is high, are today the products of scientific study and scholarship just as are other professors. The classes which they teach reflect their training.

Attempts have been made, with partial success, to secure answers to many difficult questions about the nature and growth of the child, the nature of learning, the conditions that facilitate retention, the processes of thought, the methods that facilitate or inhibit the intercommunication of ideas, the situations that promote or deter group morale and learning. How does the teacher go about educating the child of six, or of twelve, or of eighteen? With a phonetics manual in one hand and a ruler in the other? Or should he be sensible and apply the best present-day knowledge and techniques to the job?

There is some evidence of progress in reducing the conflicts described above and in carrying out the joint responsibility for teacher education.[2] Consistent with the expectations of teachers, the question of who should be educated is being answered by the public, as anyone can see by looking at the swollen high school enrollments and the trends in college attendance. The movement to experiment with meaningful breadth courses gains momentum year by year. And the experimentation is not intended merely for the education of teachers. Rather, it results from a growing awareness on the part of liberal arts colleges of a need to reorganize the curriculum. On the master's degree level, some academic departments have begun to wonder why they lose to education the candidates who should be in their subject area. This

[2] James C. Stone, *Breakthrough in Teacher Education* (San Francisco: Jossey-Bass, 1968) presents program models in which three elements have equally important roles: education faculty, faculty outside of education, and the educational system in the community.

scratching of heads has produced some courses (as in the sciences) that are better adapted to the needs of the high school or elementary school teacher. The schools of education on their part are enlarging their requirements of cognate courses. The findings of research are having greater impact on the training of teachers.

But better training for teachers is only a part of the problem of supplying our schools with good teachers. Another problem lies in the desperate need for more teachers. We are experiencing a shortage, and the shortage will continue for many years to come. The causes are several: deficiency in funds for education, inadequate salaries, disturbances by alienated children, and clashes between groups of parents. These factors promote feelings of insecurity and make teaching less attractive.

It need hardly be argued that our teachers should be well-trained. They teach our children. If we cannot always choose the person of natural aptitude for handling children and teaching them, we must increase the skills for doing so by careful training. If we use teachers of lesser intellectual aptitudes, we should strengthen the content of their education to insure adequate understanding. Because time is a factor, it is essential to do a better job of planning the whole program of education for teachers so that they will be prepared to function effectively. As I have noted above, this task requires the combined thought and energy of academic and professional men.

Why does teaching not attract the best students in college? Some of the reasons are obvious: The best students felt unchallenged and frustrated in high school and have blamed their teachers. Hence, familiarity with the world of teachers during the student's high school days removed the romance that Dr. Kildare and Perry Mason still continue to give other professions. Moreover, salaries for teachers begin low, cover only nine months, rise slowly, and end at a low ceiling. Teaching, either in the inner city or in the small community, is not much fun, and the small town does not supply the social wants of young men and women. Many college women choose a teaching major as job insurance and hence are not well motivated. Some of the courses are boring, as courses in any field can be; others, taken prior to teaching experience, do not have the significance for the student they might have if taken later. Education courses generally have a bad rating among college students.

Fortunately, this is not the whole story. It is not true that the best students always avoid teaching. That is one of those misleading generalizations. Aptitude tests given to freshmen entering the education programs of the state colleges of New York have shown that these students rank high in intelligence. Then, too, there is no assurance that the verbal and manipulative tests—that favor majors in English, mathematics, and chemistry—are necessarily the best tests of aptitudes for elementary and secondary teaching. The brilliant verbalist may be well fitted for creative writing or college teaching but poorly suited to teaching children whose vocabulary lags far behind his. The genius in calculus may be impatient with teaching the multiplication tables or beginning algebra to boys who are in the lower half of the IQ distribution, and these children must be taught.

Empathy—the ability to put oneself in the place of another person—is an essential qualification for good teaching. Do the tests that typically determine our judgments of student groups evaluate this quality? Do they, indeed, evaluate other qualities of personality and character or skill aptitudes germane to the tasks of a teacher? We know little as yet about testing for these factors. But until these results are in and counted, we cannot be too dogmatic about the qualifications of prospective teachers.[3]

Offsetting doubts about the intellectual qualities of teachers is one fact of which we can be certain: Teachers today have a better education for their work than teachers formerly had. Many persons still living began teaching immediately after a short course, taken after high school, at a normal institute. The normal school has disappeared in favor of the four-year teachers' college, which is now rapidly becoming a true college with expanded purposes and broadened curriculum. The trend in certification is toward a requirement of four years of college as preparation for teaching; some states require a five-year program, with most of the professional training delayed until the postbaccalaureate year. To apply for a state teaching certificate in most states, a student needs to have taken only one-sixth of his undergraduate credits in education courses; the highest requirement in any state is one-fourth. It

[3] Most of the data of this nature available thus far are reported in Volume II of Kenneth A. Feldman and Theodore M. Newcomb, *The Impact of College on Students* (San Francisco: Jossey-Bass, 1969), including also scores on the Omnibus Personality Inventory for student groups majoring in various fields.

is obvious, consequently, that the prospective teacher can be a broadly educated person.

There is little doubt that the trend in improving the preparation of teachers will persist. If a danger now exists, it is not that the prospective teacher will have too many courses in education but that he will suffer, as so many liberal arts students do, from the fragmentation and tendency to overspecialization of subject matter that still characterize so many undergraduate curricula (discussed in Chapter Seven).

It is possible—and here one must be speculative—that the teaching profession can become more attractive than it has been recently. In the past, the romantic appeal for young people was found at the frontier, in business enterprise, in journalism, and more recently in government. The frontier has disappeared; business has become big and tends to submerge the individual; journalism has had to compete more and more with other communicative vocations; and government is becoming an ever more complex bureaucracy. Many young people today are attracted by incentives other than money.

Education, on the other hand, has become America's frontier; it is through education that the children and youth of today find opportunity for personal identity and advancement. The significance of this statement is most apparent in the actions of black parents who strive to assure their children an education. The increasing rate of attendance at college can be accounted for only through an increasing belief in education, a belief that lies deep within the minds of the American people. The beneficiaries of education share this conviction. For many, preparation to become future teachers is an expression of that interest. The increasing rate of attendance in college means that larger numbers of students are coming from families of lower socioeconomic status. Will such boys and girls turn to teaching as a career, which for them has high prestige? For those who desire to return to their own communities for service, teaching is a natural vocation.

Pressure from the general population for more and more education produces one telling effect. The strength of education is cumulative. The children of a parent who has completed elementary school attend high school; the children of a high school graduate aspire to college. Thus each new generation pushes to a higher level of culture. Education is an aspect of our standard of living. Even though taxes are disagreeable to pay, there is no doubt about the ability of government to finance education. The problem is merely one of priorities, and education must rank high. I suspect that most parents today, if put to this test, would even sacrifice such possessions as the second car or the extra television set, if need be, in order to keep their children in school.

But the shortage of teachers, and especially the shortage of good teachers, points up a serious problem—that of educating the individual. Mounting numbers of children are being accommodated in limited facilities and taught in increasingly larger groups. How can we give the individual child the opportunity he deserves? How can the traditional American emphasis on individual growth and achievement be maintained?

At first glance, the answers to these questions seem to depend wholly on increasing the supply of qualified teachers and providing adequate financial support for the schools. These actions are, of course, essential. But the problem cannot be fully understood, or resolved, without giving further consideration to two recent developments in American education.

The first of these is the changed organizational pattern of the public school. The ungraded school has given way to the consolidated, graded school. This fact is well known, but the implications are little understood by the public. The ungraded school had the significant characteristic of providing individualized instruction. I recall that, starting at age five, I was in the third reader by the end of the first year. I recall also a couple of big fellows who at age sixteen were still plodding away at the elementary level. The curriculum was narrow, the teaching was often inexpert, and the social grouping left much to be desired. But each pupil moved at his own pace. Growth in the number of school children and the development of good roads upset that program. The high school, too, became popular, and it set out to serve a broader clientele with a more diversified curriculum than had the earlier preparatory school.

The present-day organizational differences, then, are two. First, the consolidated school is graded, which means that it is horizontally stratified by age groups; second, the curriculum is much larger and more varied. The result, too often, is the individual is submerged and ignored. Nearly everyone advances year by year in a common pattern (to keep with the social age group). The program is geared to the average pupil. The brighter children are held back, unstimulated and without sufficient incentive to live up to their capacities. The emphasis is on curriculum rather than on individual learning.

Educators know that the educational results from the changed pattern have not all been good. They also know that we cannot retrace our footsteps. Not only is retracing physically and psychologically impossible, but it would sacrifice many of the gains that have been made. In this situation many educators have turned to the philosophy of John Dewey as the way out of the dilemma. His concepts of individual growth, of the development of the whole person, and of the use of educative experience in learning how to live better have had a distinct appeal to teachers. The influence of Dewey helps account for some instances in which teachers have tried progressive methods.

Unfortunately, those newer methods were not uniformly successful. Much harm was done to the progressive school movement by ill-prepared teachers who attempted to be progressive without sufficient understanding of the underlying theory. Much was done in Dewey's name that was a vitiation of the principles for which he stood. A child-centered school does not mean one that is chaotic! The child should participate in the planning in order to become better motivated and to gain an understanding of what he is trying to do. The school should be one in which the focus of education is on the individual, and thus is similar to the earlier American pattern.

This illustration brings me to the second recent development in American education. I have said elsewhere that we are learning how to educate better through knowledge gained from research. The solution to the problems I have just mentioned must be found through continued experimentation and research. Some progress has already been made. Research findings have been stimulating, and indeed exciting; they show clearly that many of our concepts of education need revision and that better methods of instruction can be found. For example, it is now clear that there are marked differences in the physical maturation of children who are the same calendar age and that there is a close parallel between physical maturation and mental growth. Furthermore, the University of Michigan studies in child growth indicate that the differences in intellectual achievement levels among children become greater as age increases. At the time of graduation from high school, the achievements of pupils—as they appear in standard tests—have varied in the Michigan experience as much as eight grade levels. Yet all of the pupils receive high school diplomas. The significance of this situation does not relate so much to the meaning of the diploma as to the differences among youth of a given age. The college professor who assumes that all freshmen are equally ready—or equally unready—for his courses is overlooking an important factor.

The younger teachers of today have been much impressed by recent research on learning and teaching. They have studied under professors of education who are informed about the findings of research. The conscientious teacher wants to use the new knowledge in developing fresh approaches to counseling and teaching. This means, among other things, that he can no longer teach reading in the good old-fashioned way. More important, it means that he must attempt to find ways to differentiate the learning of the children to accord with their individual aptitudes, maturity, and needs.

American education has been exhibiting some of the growing pains that are natural to a transition period. In spite of these difficulties we cannot go back to the little red schoolhouse. Nor will we go back to the reading–writing–'rithmetic formula. Our expectations in life are too great; our society has become too complex to permit so simple a solution. In an earlier period our educational goal was literacy for the common man to enable him, as Horace Mann contended, to vote intelligently and be a good citizen. A handful of the best students—or children from the "best" families—went on to prep school and to college. Today this situation has changed profoundly. The future citizen must not only be literate; he must have an awareness of his environment and the means to improve it. He must have a measure of understanding of the government, the developments in nuclear physics, and the problems of Southeast Asia. He needs creative and scientific skills, and appreciations of music, art, and philosophy. In short, a high school education has become a must and a college education will soon be a must as well. Thus we have discarded the narrow educational ladder, intended for the few, in favor of a pyramid, up all sides of which youth are climbing for more and more education.

To achieve these goals for the individual, we must prepare more good teachers. This objective has become one of the most important functions of our colleges and universities. It is, perhaps, the function which has taken on more importance than any other.

STUDENT AND FACULTY
PERCEPTIONS AND STATUS

~~~~~~

PART **FIVE**

CHAPTER 14

DESIGN FOR INNOVATION IN TEACHING

𝄞✳𝄞✳𝄞✳𝄞✳𝄞✳𝄞✳𝄞✳𝄞✳𝄞✳𝄞✳𝄞✳𝄞✳𝄞✳𝄞✳𝄞✳𝄞✳𝄞

Having discussed many ideas for change in programs of higher education, I should now like to suggest a method for effecting change. The methodology will have special relevance for the design of curricula and for the design of individual courses of study or learning experiences. Methodology is of the highest importance in such planning because most college courses are regurgitations of the creation of someone else's mind: what the instructor himself learned as a student, his attempts at emulating other professors, or his reiteration of a textbook. Obviously, such courses are not innovative. College curricula too often are the result of beliefs about tradition and prestige, plus accretions that are fragmentary and for the most part based on professors' special interests and talents rather than on the talents and needs of students. Such accretions pass the curriculum

173

committee on a courtesy basis because of a given professor's prestige, as a result of logrolling, or simply by virtue of conformity with a pattern that characterizes a nearby prestige university.

It is apparent that when a teacher has not sufficiently thought through his objectives or assimilated the ideas and content of his subject, his instruction is mediocre and his course a bore for the students. A comprehensive study within the liberal arts area at a large university has revealed that in the opinion of the students the courses were not as good as the faculty. Paul Klapper, a keen and experienced observer of college teaching, spent some years at the University of Chicago in a specially created position devoted to a study of this subject. He concluded that the largest single obstacle to genuinely effective teaching was lack of clarity of purpose.[1]

The young instructor initially receives no help in the design of his courses, or else he must teach the standardized product as approved by the department. After five years or more of stumbling effort, he arrives at the point where he can throw himself more fully into his teaching; he is at last able to make the course his own. It is too bad that this does not happen sooner. And it is even more unfortunate for the students that many instructors never rise above heavy dependence on a text that someone else has written or on materials and ideas which were current when the instructors were students. A more fruitful approach is to use a systematized technique in planning. The beginning teacher needs to be aware that the process of analysis and synthesis can be applied in course design just as it has been applied in his graduate research.

I should like now to describe a model for planning. The first step in such a model is to make a survey to determine needs, an especially important step when establishing the bases and the broader objectives of a curriculum. In Chapter Six I described briefly the survey

[1] Paul Klapper, "The Professional Preparation of the College Teacher," *Journal of General Education* (July, 1949), pp. 228–44. The Chicago faculty was unusually concerned with this problem during the heyday of the Hutchins College, as the literature of that period shows. In addition to the article by Klapper, see also Joseph Axelrod, "The Technique of 'Group Discussion' in the College Class," *Journal of General Education* (April, 1948), pp. 227–37; J. Axelrod, B. S. Bloom, B. Ginsburg, W. O'Meara, and J. Williams, *Teaching by Discussion in the College Class* (Chicago: University of Chicago Press, 1949); and A. M. Hayes, "Teaching," in *The Idea and Practice of General Education,* ed. F. Champion Ward (Chicago: University of Chicago Press, 1950).

method used in New York state in planning the state technical institutes. In Chapter Seven I have referred to the consultations held by the University of Wisconsin with citizens of the community of Green Bay when the program for the Green Bay campus was designed. The techniques of such surveys are widely used by social scientists, by doctoral students, or by anyone engaged in empirical research; they do not need further description here.

An alternative to the survey, however, is methodological analysis, recently used in two rather different situations by Daniel Bell, a sociologist, and Allen Rosenstein, an engineer. Bell, on behalf of Columbia University, made an analysis of objectives and content of curricula in general education. His findings were published in his book *The Reforming of General Education.*[2] His conclusions are fresh and propose substantial change. Rosenstein, under a grant from the Ford Foundation at the University of California, Los Angeles, made a thorough analysis of innovations in the field of engineering practice and of the content available for teaching. His findings were published in a series of reports, one of which applies the method to the design of curricula in all professional fields.[3]

Ralph Tyler, former director of the Center for Advanced Study in the Behavioral Sciences, has been one of the most original thinkers on curriculum planning. His *Basic Principles of Curriculum and Instruction,*[4] devoted to the design of a curriculum, includes the matrix for analysis that I have used in developing the method for course design which is outlined in detail below. The procedure is usable for either an entire curriculum or an individual course of study. It can also be used in planning other educative experience, such as off-campus work, travel abroad, and so forth. Too often these programs are plunged into without the necessary analysis because they are the innovative thing. Much greater and more positive values are derived by students if the desired results are well defined and the experiences outlined, with both the objectives and the principles of continuity, sequence, and integration in mind.

[2] Daniel Bell, *The Reforming of General Education* (New York: Columbia University Press, 1966).

[3] Allen B. Rosenstein, "A Study of a Profession and Professional Education" (Los Angeles: Department of Engineering, University of California Los Angeles, 1968), EDP 7-68.

[4] Ralph W. Tyler, *Basic Principles of Curriculum and Instruction* (Chicago: University of Chicago Press, 1950).

Planning must involve three stages: analysis of objectives, analysis of materials and methods to be used in achieving the objectives, and preparation of the syllabus or plan of action. If a survey of needs has been made, the analysis of objectives should be based upon the findings. In the first stage of planning, making detailed analysis of his objectives—including the achievement outcomes he expects of his students—it is important for the teacher to interrelate the aims involved in the learning by the student with the content of the subject matter. Most college teachers do not make such an analysis. They simply make a brief outline, usually of the subject matter to be taught, adding textbook assignments or references. It is not even uncommon for a textbook to be used as the outline, with no use made of the principles of learning.

A cross-sectional chart or matrix is a useful device. On one axis the instructor can list the six to a dozen of the most important broad objectives that he is seeking for the students. Some of them should be to add to the student's knowledge of facts and principles; others might relate to growth of skills in problem solving, in search for materials, in praparation of bibliography, or in concrete practical applications of knowledge gained. Still other objectives might relate to changes in attitudes and growth in appreciations. This frame of reference can be diminished or enlarged in telescopic fashion. Start with three broad objectives—such as knowledge, skills, and value perceptions—and then subdivide into more concrete objectives.[5]

A special problem is to take account both of objectives that are unique to the particular course and of those that are pervasive in many college courses. The former are usually uppermost in the teacher's mind. The latter, such as growth in intellectual skills and in appreciations and attitudes, are not achieved in any one course but rather as a result of persistent attention in all courses. But achievements of this kind must not be taken for granted; it is precisely the failure to define clearly such objectives that results in mediocre teaching.

On the second axis of the chart should be listed the subdivisions of content which are the general basis of the course and necessary in

[5] A taxonomy of education objectives (in two volumes, one volume dealing with the cognitive and the other with the affective domain) lists in detail the many different kinds of objectives a college teacher, or one on other levels, may have. Benjamin S. Bloom, *et al.*, *Taxonomy of Educational Objectives* (New York: Longmans Green & Co., 1956).

working toward the stated objectives. These content subdivisions are broad in scope, similar to those that instructors use in developing the outlines of their courses. The content chosen must be directly related to the broad objectives. But let us be clear about one thing: objectives come first, for you must know what you want to accomplish before you can choose the specific content wisely. One alternative to the listing of content topics is a series of major questions or problems that make up the broad content of the course; these are followed by alternative possibilities of specific content that illustrate and give insight into the problems.

Since the chart is cross-sectional, it is now possible to use the rectangle at each intersection of the two axes to insert specific outcomes that will be expected of the students. These are stated from the viewpoint of the learning expected of the student, rather than from the viewpoint of what the instructor will do. Each assists in the achievement of a broad objective by drawing on some phase of the content; thus is the essential interrelationship secured. This exercise, it will be seen, forces the instructor to think through to the end of his course exactly what he expects the student to have learned. These outcomes can number as many as one hundred or two hundred in total. To these the student can add objectives of his own. The manner in which the instructor has made his analysis assists the student to make adaptations to meet his perceived needs.

Eliminations at this stage are just as important as inclusions. Elimination is a step too often neglected, and the result is a course stuffed with information or—as eliminations are made on an ad hoc basis later—a hodgepodge of extraneous topics. Eliminations clarify the focus of the course, highlight the more significant things, and assure that the student has time and opportunity to do well what is expected of him. This budgeting of the content also leaves room for the student to pursue inquiries of his own choosing.

The analysis, as made on the chart, also enables an instructor to coordinate his course better with other courses available to the student—both those the student studies concurrently and those already studied or scheduled for the future. The instructor is in a position to control the content and to eliminate phases that would be duplications.

The second stage of the planning process is part of the analytical procedures and carries the thinking one step further. Having defined the general objectives and each specific outcome expected of the student, the instructor is now able to choose materials and methods to best accomplish them. Thus, from the outset, he keeps an open mind about ways and means, and he avoids making tacit assumptions or emulating the methods of others. He is able to introduce variety instead of drawing upon a single method. This analysis proceeds in relation to each objective, both general and specific. The major criteria in making these decisions are as follows: What are the best materials and experiences and what is the best method (or methods) for accomplishing this particular result? Here again, the teacher considers many possibilities, then makes selections for use in the final design of the course.

The third stage of the planning process is synthesis, bringing together in orderly form for instructional purposes the results of the preceding analyses. This becomes the instructor's plan of action. Assuming that the student is given a copy of the final plan, it becomes an aid to his learning. (The student will have such a copy if he has himself participated in formulating the plan.) He then has concretely in hand the objectives of the course, the materials available for his study, the resources at his disposal, and the instructor's expectations of him as the course proceeds as well as upon its termination. Furthermore, the student has greater assurance that his instructor will make a fair and thorough evaluation of his work because expectations have been clarified and used as the bases for examinations and total evaluation of performance.

After such a plan is formulated, the instructor can decide which portions of it are to be included in the course syllabus. A statement of the purpose or purposes of the course is essential. In this statement, the general objectives as defined in the analysis can be drawn upon, with appropriate emphases. Whether the more specific achievements expected of the students are included in this section of the syllabus is a debatable point; they probably are more logically included in a discussion of the units of instruction rather than as a part of the statement of course purposes. Some instructors also like to place in the statement of purposes a few leading or provocative questions to set the tone for the course and arouse interest.

Next, a description of the course procedures would seem to be logical: an indication of the principal media of instruction, the responsibilities to be assumed by the students, and the availability of the instructor for conferences and professional help. If a time schedule has been planned, it also appears in this section.

A brief indication as to how the student's progress is evaluated is reassuring to him. It also causes the instructor to consider carefully in advance how this is to be done. The instructor, having retained his chart of expected student achievements, has an array of potential bases for examination questions. The chart can be especially helpful in devising objective types of questions in large numbers. To the extent that it is so used, the student's knowledge is thoroughly and fairly sampled. Again, having thought out a plan of action in advance, the instructor has greater assurance that his evaluation is consistent with his objectives.

The principal items in the syllabus compose the several units of instruction. These are now selected from the final draft of the chart of analysis and arranged in the best order for instruction. In presenting each unit, the minimum requirements are: a brief statement of its objectives; an outline of topics, questions, or problems that serves as the basis of study and of class procedure; and bibliographical references.

The same principles that are used in the study of curriculum apply in preparing the syllabus. The course must have good continuity. That is it must, if possible, relate to what has been learned already; each segment of the course is an element in a continuous chain, with sufficient referral to previous points and questions and with sufficient intervals of review to assure that the thread of the course stands out clearly and that the content is mastered as the student proceeds. The structure of the course must also take account of the principle of sequence, not only to interrelate properly with other courses but to assure that study is proceeding wtih increasing levels of difficulty, depth of penetration, or scope of comprehension. Integration is necessary not only to provide integrity within the course itself but to assure that the knowledge achieved in this course is interrelated with knowledge gained by the student in parallel or cognate courses.

The design of a course is something in which the instructor can take considerable pride. It is his creation, just as the design of a building is the product of the training of an architect or a painting the result of the skilled hand of the artist. It is an expression of his professional skills. If, at the conclusion of the planning, the instructor is not convinced of the merit of the course, he should not give it. If he is convinced of the merit, he can approach his students with full self-confidence, enthusiasm, and conviction; and these qualities make a tremendous difference in teaching effectiveness.

The plan is one that he can show with confidence to his professional colleagues and to his administrative superiors. There is a prevailing sentiment among college professors that the courses they teach are no business of any other member of the faculty; and there is even a tendency to be secretive about the content and methods used in courses. This attitude is in striking contrast to that of the architect who wants to place his name on his buildings so that the design is attributed by all to his genius. The introversion of the professor militates seriously against developing the potential strength of the faculty as a group. Each member of a faculty has a personal stake in developing the highest professional tone and work of the entire group through both teaching and research. It is the colleges with strong faculties and, hence, with good reputations that attract the best students and the interest of professional colleagues. These institutions also are able to secure more adequate resources with which to carry on their work. By exchanging course syllabi faculty members secure the criticism of colleagues, make certain of good coordination of courses within the total structure, and inform the faculty so that they can counsel students accurately. There is advantage in showing the design of courses to the department head, the dean, or the president, and discussing the course with them, for then the instructor receives the benefit of their professional criticism.

I have described in some detail the procedures for designing a good course of study because it seems to me to be basic to educational purpose. The procedures apply equally to the design of a curriculum. Both the survey of needs and the definition of objectives are essential in planning innovations in curriculum or in courses—indeed also for adopting innovative methods for the use of educative experience. If the results confirm the merit in a proposal, the faculty can move toward implementation with conviction and disregard those who question or deride it. Innovation in program is based upon objectivity in planning and evaluation.

I have been concerned here with a description of planning activity by the faculty. Planning activity is certainly part of their role as teachers. There is distinct advantage, however, in faculty–student collaboration. When students fully understand and accept the objectives of a course or a curriculum, they are much better motivated to learn. And participation in the planning is likely to result in a higher degree of acceptance of a course by the students. Because of the way in which time schedules structure a program, it is often necessary for faculty to do the preliminary planning; if so, student feedback can be used as a basis for modification and redesign for the next occasion. An alternative is to make the planning of the course the first unit of the course.

When the need for a new program has been projected by students or by members of the community or of a profession, the importance of having their active participation in devising it is obvious. The uses made by public community colleges of advisory committees from the community have already been mentioned. In many instances their contributions are constructive, and their interest helps to assure the success of the program. The black studies proposal is one program where student and community participation is essential. The dominant aims of such a program must be kept in mind: to educate for self-identity; to lift a whole people—the black people—to a new level of self-respect, confidence, and sense of belonging; to discontinue the melting pot view of American society in favor of the development of a plurality of cultures. These aims must be achieved with the involvement of the students and, through them, the people.

I have not intended here to stress a particular method at the expense of others. Rather, I want to emphasize that creative design involves systematic thinking and planning. Method need not be frowned upon as an example of professional pedagogy; it is the process of problem solving—analysis and synthesis—used by scientists and professional men. It is a way to effect change.

CHAPTER 15

STUDENT
STATUS

In the short space of five years, beginning with the Free Speech Movement at Berkeley, students have revolutionized their role in the college. They have shifted from the carefree and pampered progeny of an affluent society, content on campus to play games in Mickey Mouse government, to a generation of youth burdened and disillusioned by the ills of the world, seeking a better way to live and insisting with substantial influence that the university also change. College students, in spite of instances of irritating and disturbing actions, are raising serious questions about the university as an educational institution and about its role in society. They are determined to live their own lives and not to be thwarted by conventions inherited from Puritan times. They are revolting against the paternalism of college administrations.

The egalitarian movement in higher education is another influencing factor. Institutions are being pressured to respond to the needs of students of varying ages, abilities, and interests and to provide services for the disadvantaged segments of the population. Students are demanding action on problems relating to their civil liberties and to the design of the educational program. On these matters there are profound differences of opinion. Colleges are undergoing a transition from a position of responsibility for the protective care of students *in loco parentis* to a position of treating and counseling students as young adults. Presidents and deans are caught between opposing forces that represent strong views on each side of the subject.

To appreciate the change that is taking place, it is necessary to consider briefly the history of colleges and universities. In earlier times, before the public secondary school became universal, the general age of the student was much younger—commonly fifteen to eighteen. Also, most colleges had preparatory departments and thus large numbers of students who were adolescents. Until comparatively recently colleges were predominantly private and often church-related; the idea of having a lay person rather than a cleric as president is also recent. In the past colleges were strongly oriented toward the inclusion of religious and moral teaching in the curriculum, and part of the college's role was to influence the moral behavior of the students. Students were disciplined, fined, or expelled for violations of rules and regulations. A century and a half ago these regulations were very confining. On the ground that they "should not learn to be playful," Cokesbury College disciplined students who remained in their bath for more than one minute.[1]

Today the typical entrance age of college students is eighteen, and the average student age is much older. Indeed, among urban universities the average age is well above twenty-one. Preparatory schools have been eliminated from college campuses. At the other end of the age continuum large numbers of students are enrolled in professional schools and in graduate education. Programs in adult education have grown by leaps and bounds, especially in urban situations where the commuting is easy. The result is an increase of older part-time students —most of whom are married, have families, and live at home. These

[1] W. H. Kilpatrick, *Source Book in the Philosophy of Education* (New York: The Macmillan Company, Publishers, 1924), pp. 4, 5.

students hold jobs, many to support themselves, others to gain independence from their parents.

Since World War II, the percentage of students attending public institutions of higher education has grown rapidly and now considerably exceeds the percentage attending private colleges. Public universities do not view the teaching of religion and morals in the same light as do church-related institutions; indeed, they are prohibited from indoctrinating in particular religions. The prevalence of automobiles (and parents do provide them)' makes it impossible to "keep diligent watch" over coeds, as Horace Mann once advised the University of Michigan to do.[2] Mann also cautioned the faculty not to let coeds board promiscuously in the village and his methods evidently worked. He confided that in four years of experience with coeducation his institution (Antioch College)' had not had a single incident of what people at that time called "an accident."

Two other trends have been affecting the college situation. One is the growing permissiveness of parents and the parental discarding of older disciplinary forms. The other is that children have become more sophisticated. In part this sophistication is the result of today's methods of communication and transportation, with the exposure of knowledge and ideas that come through radio and television. Parents today typically treat their children of college age as adults; they serve them cocktails, discuss sex freely with them, and admit them to family discussion when future plans are being weighed. When fathers attend fraternity parties, they become just as drunk as sons, sometimes more so. Some mothers are now giving the pill to their daughters in college. But it should also be remembered that young men are now eligible for the armed services draft at age eighteen and can vote at the same age.

The practice *in loco parentis* is no longer tenable. However, many parents continue to expect colleges to maintain this relationship. At least one parent has said: "If my son dates a Negro girl, I want the university to tell me." Parents will permit their eighteen-year-olds to accept jobs in distant cities without daily supervision, but when the youth go to college, the older image of the institution prevails. Parents are not alone in their concern. The general public, or at least that

---

[2] Correspondence between a faculty committee and Horace Mann in the archives of the University of Michigan.

segment of it who become agitated about student behavior, also thinks that a college should discipline its students.

One role of the president and his administrative associates is, unfortunately, to protect and extend the image of the university. The image needs to be good, not necessarily in the academic sense, but in fulfilling public expectations. Universities are dependent on the public (or public bodies) for funds, and for the maintenance of environmental conditions that attract students and permit effective operation. College presidents and their deans sometimes are confused because they have not sufficiently analyzed the changes that have been taking place. In their zeal to defend their institutions against hostile attacks from parents and the public, they frequently paint images of the campus which are inaccurate and misrepresentative, arousing false expectations. In the days when smoking by women was highly controversial, I recall one college president who remarked that his university had strong rules against women smoking; yet he added with a wink, "But we know that they *do.*" Policy and practice are not always the same thing.

The concept of *in loco parentis* must be laid to rest, because it is dead. A program of counseling must be substituted, with a staff of professionally trained personnel. Administrators do not work sufficiently with faculty and students to develop a positive policy and a rationale for it. An effort must be directed toward educating the student and developing *group* concern for an environment conducive to good education. Tensions in the area of student behavior are inevitable, but they need not mount to proportions of magnitude.

College administrators often assume an arbitrary authority, that they no longer possess, over students. Their authority is curtailed by a recent trend in court decisions to identify students' rights with civil liberties, and, hence, to require that colleges use procedures that protect these rights.[3] Heretofore, presidents and deans have also assumed that

[3] M. M. Chambers, *The Colleges and the Courts Since 1950* (Danville, Ill.: The Interstate Printers and Publishers, 1964); also *The Colleges and the Courts, 1962–66* (Danville, Ill.: The Interstate Printers and Publishers, 1967). The same point is illustrated in an instructive way in Robert B. Yegge, "Emerging Legal Rights for Students," in *Stress and Campus Response: Current Issues in Higher Education 1968,* ed. G. Kerry Smith (San Francisco: Jossey-Bass, 1968).

the college had the right to determine—when the rules and regulations were not fully obeyed—who could enter as a student and who could remain. Many administrators continue to act on these assumptions, but the assumptions are no longer valid. Some states have enacted fair education practice laws which require equality of opportunity in admissions on grounds of race, color, and national origin—and also in the case of creed, except when the institution is clearly under the control of a religious body. Under such a law, the aim of which is to protect the applicant from discrimination, any student who feels aggrieved can apply to a public official, an ombudsman, for assistance in having his case objectively considered. New York enacted the first such law in 1948, and other states have followed. Parallel with this legal development, courts have become increasingly willing to hear the complaints of students who accuse their institutions of arbitrary actions, especially in cases of dismissal.

Precedent for student cases exists in the protection afforded faculty. Colleges and universities have generally accepted the principle that faculty members are entitled to hearings when their tenure is questioned. Most of the national organizations of colleges and universities have adopted uniform policies concerning academic freedom and tenure. Consistent with these, individual institutions have codified their procedures, sometimes with only minor variations. Similar agreement has recently been reached by many of the same organizations on the rights and freedoms of students. Leaders in the movement for this reform have been the American Association of University Professors, the Association of American Colleges, the U.S. National Student Association, and the National Association of Student Personnel Administrators. Speaking of the procedural standards in disciplinary proceedings, the Statement says:

> In all situations procedural fair play requires that the student be informed of the nature of the charges against him, that he be given a fair opportunity to refute them, that the institution not be arbitrary in its actions and that there be provision for appeal of a decision.[4]

[4] *Administrator's Handbook: Understanding the Joint Statement on Rights and Freedoms of Students* (Chicago: College and University Business, n.d.).

These requirements are essentially the same as those laid down by the courts in recent years when the principle of due process of law has been applied to student cases.

Administrators tend to be impatient with this new development, partly because it is time-consuming and partly because it prevents the president from showing the public that "proper" discipline has been promptly administered. Some administrators, of course, do not believe in the new method at all. Thus institutions often support arbitrary action instead of fair play and due process. But a change is taking place.

In addition to seeking change in their status with respect to their rights to equality of treatment and due process, college students seek to participate in determining policy. They feel that they have something important to say to administrators and faculty and, indeed, to the governing board on the issues that they are identifying. The subject of control in higher education, including student voice, is discussed in Part VII, but I would like at this point to make a few observations of relevance to student status.

The problems that confront administrators usually arise from one of two sources. The first is the insistence of the more militant student groups that the college take leadership in social action. This view is strongly opposed by faculty who are research minded—rather than action oriented—and who believe that the main purpose of the university is adulterated if its energies are not given fully to the exploration of knowledge. The view is also opposed by most trustees and administrators on the ground that off-campus action involves unwarranted interference in the affairs of others. Thus an issue is joined between two factions, each of which feels deeply that its stand is just. I have discussed this issue in Chapter Four and taken the position that the college must be an instrument for social action. The dilemma for the administration, however, arises from the resulting conflict of interest. These deep-seated views must be reconciled if institutional viability is to be achieved, but reconciliation takes much communicative effort and time.

Whether or not the college as an institution engages in social action, it is important to maintain freedom of action for individuals and for groups who, acting for themselves, make it clear that they are not speaking for the institution. To avoid frustrations, which encourage confrontations within the university, it is essential to avoid restraints on off-campus political and social activities. Governing boards and autocratically minded presidents are seriously in error when they endeavor to limit these freedoms. Furthermore, from the civil liberties viewpoint, they have no right to do so: Students are also citizens. Indeed, if the theory that I have discussed under the subject of experience has merit, an active role by a student in community and other public affairs gives him habits and skills for participation in later life. Such participation is an expectation within the democratic context. Without these habits and skills, the alumnus ends by doing no more than sinking into his easy chair, reading the sports page, and watching television.

The second problem confronting administrators arises because of student pressures for change within the institution itself. Interestingly enough it is the students, and those of the best intellectual quality, who today express the greatest sensitivity to the consequences of social and educational trends.[5] Sometimes they have excellent ideas for institutional reform. The needling activities of national and local groups, along with the irritations they produce, result in constructive contributions. Unfortunately, though, administrators have resisted ideas to the point where student aggressions now frequently turn toward the achievement of student power rather than toward the solution of educational problems.

I shall not endeavor to offer a panacea for the problems of student confrontations. A few observations may be made, however, with appropriate tentativeness. Although the militants, and especially the revolutionists, are not large in number, they feel deeply about the issues they raise; some of the deficiencies in society—at this stage of civilization—are so glaring as to cause large numbers of students and faculty to sympathize with the militants. Demonstrations of feelings on this order of magnitude cannot be suppressed by police action, and to use police for this purpose plays into the hands of the demonstrators. The impact of the youth movement has been pronounced, as witnessed by the change in the opinion of the American people about the war in Viet-

---

[5] Paul Heist (ed.), *The Creative College Student* (San Francisco: Jossey-Bass, 1968); also Nevitt Sanford, *Where Colleges Fail* (San Francisco: Jossey-Bass, 1967), has a chapter called "Education for Creativity" in which he discusses the "creative" student.

nam and by the decision of many colleges to institute programs in black studies.

I am not sufficiently naive to think that all disruptions and violence suddenly will cease. It is becoming clear, however, that violence provokes responses in kind and brings political backlashes. Student leaders have proven themselves good planners and strategists. Hopefully they will recognize that violence does not promote their ends—with the result that evolutionists will part from revolutionists and the latter will subdivide into splinter groups.

Administrative finesse is needed to steer debates about all issues onto the rational ground that should be characteristic of a university. This means, in part, leading these institutions to a broader concern for issues than has been traditional in colleges. Late as it is, it is still essential to reorganize the institutions to give representation in decision making to the major interest groups, including students, and to set up procedures for an attack on the vital problems.[6]

College students are engaging in a widespread—indeed worldwide—movement to enlarge student participation. Agitations on particular campuses are coordinated, and to some degree directed, by national organizations of students which include the U.S. National Student Association and Students for a Democratic Society, both of which advocate a substantial measure of control by students. Administrators are resisting this movement; faculties, generally, are opposed to student participation in academic governance. Both, however, have been making concessions to the students—a negative stance. What is needed, as I shall contend in Chapter Twenty-One, is a new theory of college government.

[6] For a discussion of student activism, see Edward E. Sampson and Harold A. Korn, and associates, *Student Activism and Protest: Alternatives for Social Change* (San Francisco: Jossey-Bass, 1970).

CHAPTER 16

FACULTY MOTIVATIONS AND INCENTIVES

In this time of change, the motivations of many faculty are out of harmony with the interests of students. One result is neglect of faculty–student learning relationships. Professional schools are preparing their graduates for specializations and motivating them to serve mainly affluent clients, slighting the less privileged portion of our population and the less attractive needs of our society. Both neglects are attributable to the value emphases of our materialistically oriented society and to incentives—such as research grants and large consulting fees—that foster these motivations. Professional men and women have been losing their sense of call to duty in favor of competitive living and elitist prestige. The manner in which graduating physicians solemnly take the Hippocratic Oath for human service, then rush forth to make a killing financially, through specialized practice in areas where the per capita income is high, shows the hypocrisy of the oath and the true impact of the medical school. It is the thing to do, and the professors join in setting the example.

The problem of incentives is also important to the practical operation of colleges and universities; salaries for teachers have lagged behind those in business and several other professions. The attitudes of colleges toward fringe benefits have also been affected by the growing interest in plans for social security, for protection against hazards, and for reducing the impact of taxes—plans that are increasingly common in business and industry. The colleges and professional schools have been faced with a shortage of faculty. The shortage has created competition among the institutions for the services of teachers and research staff. This competition has stimulated the institutions to greater activity in their effort to induce the holders of advanced degrees to remain in the service of the college and not be lured into business and government. The situation has caused colleges to increase monetary inducements and to neglect appeals of a more intangible nature which have a high degree of attractiveness for persons with intellectual interests. Now that the supply of college teachers is becoming adequate, the nonmonetary incentives will become more important in securing the desired personnel.

It is the incentives that cause a person to accept employment with any organization. To some degree, incentives can become standardized; but it is usually a combination of several incentives—some of which are objective and some of which are quite intangible—that accounts for the decision an individual makes to accept or reject a job offer. Indeed, he may be fleeing from another position where his security is threatened, rather than merely being tempted by the new one.

Incentives may therefore be either positive or negative. Positive incentives bring to the individual what he perceives to be additional advantages to him. Negative ones take the form of reducing or eliminating disadvantages of his existing situation or his future. Incentives can also be characterized as either concrete or intangible; monetary or nonmonetary. The most obvious concrete incentive is the salary; but there are a number of others. Intangible incentives pertain to the individual's sociopsychological situation and his value judgments pertaining to it.

In writing about the theory of incentives Barnard distinguished between two classes, those "that are specific and can be specifically offered to an individual; and second, those that are general, not personal, that cannot be specifically offered." He called these two classes specific inducements and general incentives, and he further categorized these as follows:

> The specific inducements that may be offered are of several classes, for example: (a) material inducements; (b) personal nonmaterial opportunities; (c) desirable physical conditions; (d) ideal benefactions. General incentives afforded are, for example: (e) associational attractiveness: (f) adaptation of conditions to habitual methods and attitudes; (g) the opportunity of enlarged participation; (h) the condition of communion.[1]

Material inducements include money, physical things, or physical conditions. Personal nonmaterial opportunities include those that enhance prestige, professional reputation, or personal power. The importance of desirable physical conditions is seen in the significance faculty attach to offices, access to libraries, and private laboratories. Ideal benefactions include satisfaction of personal goals, pride of workmanship, emphasis upon scholarly environment and achievement, and the ideal of service to youth. By associational attractiveness, Barnard meant social compatibility—feelings of compatibility or incompatibility among persons with different cultural backgrounds and values. Barnard, who placed considerable emphasis in administration upon fluency of communication, contended that when incompatible people work together communication is difficult and decreases, leading to low morale and inefficient performance. Personal habits are difficult to change and should be taken into account—again as a means of satisfying the psychological urges.

Barnard's third category, the opportunity for enlarged participation, has psychological appeal to college personnel. The assistant professor who moves from a distinguished university to a small college does so because he has been offered an advance in rank and a departmental chairmanship. A man of senior rank at a small college moves to a junior position at a large university because of opportunities for personal research, work with graduate students, or specialization in subject matter. By the condition of communion, Barnard referred to feelings of personal comfort in social relations demanded by gregarious

[1] Chester I. Barnard, *The Functions of the Executive* (Cambridge, Mass.: Harvard University Press, 1942), p. 142.

instincts or the need of security. A college or university as a community of scholars who may attain tenure certainly has this intangible appeal to educators.

It is useful to distinguish further, with relevance to the academic scene, between monetary incentives and nonmonetary ones. Monetary incentives in a college ordinarily will include salaries, fringe benefits, assurances of future monetary income, and other inducements that have monetary significance. Salaries are essential inducements because they provide subsistence. The needs of individuals for subsistence will vary considerably depending upon their personal resources, their dependents, and their habits of living. That salaries do not have large meaning to college teachers or teachers in general is evident from their demonstrated willingness to continue to teach in spite of relatively low incomes. On the other hand, where there is competition among institutions for the services of teachers and administrative officers, the relative financial inducements offered become influential. A prime example can be seen in medical faculty. The policy of the American Medical Association in restricting the number of physicians entering the profession created an acute shortage of personnel; now that sixteen new schools are being launched, there is severe competition for the services of medical faculty.

To raise some questions about the relative importance of salaries to academic men is not to suggest that they should be underpaid. In our individualistic and competitive society, we have taken advantage of teachers—because of their willingness to continue to teach for small compensation—by failing to give them adequate salary recognition. Considering the significance to society of higher education, including both education and research, it is clear that society greatly undervalues the services of college teachers. If other conditions of employment deteriorate—as the result of public indifference about educational facilities, research in nonscience areas, academic freedom, and so forth— salaries may have to be raised substantially to attract a large enough and sufficiently competent staff to remain in the profession.

Monetary fringe benefits invariably accompany salary. Although they may vary widely from institution to institution, they commonly include provision for retirement and various types of insurance. Most colleges provide allowances for sabbatical leaves, related to the individual's salary and to a given number of years of service, during which the individual is not necessarily expected to perform a direct service for the institution. The University of Michigan, for instance, promises its faculty upon their retirement for age an additional year of salary as a consultant to the university. Of a similar character is the terminal salary. Another inducement is the salary increment schedule, the subject of some controversy. Some participants feel that insufficient consideration is given to merit, on the other hand, the schedule does provide some feeling of security because the individual, from the outset of employment, knows the full scale and the increases in salary that he can anticipate receiving. Increment schedules appear to be of greatest usefulness in a situation where there are large numbers of employees whose work is closely similar in character; those who do similar work or make equal contributions get similar rewards.

There are other kinds of fringe benefits. Some institutions provide housing for faculty or subsidize the ownership of housing through the sponsorship of mortgage loans. Colleges sometimes encourage better teaching or research by special award; this is one way to stimulate achievement and to indicate the emphases that the college places upon particular kinds of achievements. An antidote to the common emphasis on research is to provide special recognition for superior teaching. Still another example is health benefits for the professor and his family. Some colleges with established health services make these available to their faculty, for there is obvious advantage in keeping staff in good health.

The opportunity to earn extra income is also a monetary incentive, and may include royalties from publications or inventions, salary from part-time positions, and fees earned from consultations. Presumably every young scholar is offered the possibility of writing books which will produce royalty income. Successful textbooks for subjects that are widely taught in school or college can produce large income. Most college professors, however, do not write with this income in view; they are apt to write irrespective of the prospects for financial return, because the recognition accorded is more highly valued than is the royalty. And scholarly papers and books are even more highly valued by the employing institution than are the textbooks. Writing and publication are encouraged by colleges and universities, and hence it is the custom to give the teacher the privilege of retaining the income from them. This practice is also in keeping with the free enterprise philosophy—the American way.

The part-time salary becomes an administrative problem when

the employing arrangement has not been made sufficiently clear. If the person is employed for part of his time by the institution and part of his time elsewhere, there remains only the question of performance in relation to the agreement. But where a man is employed full-time by the institution it should be assumed by both parties that the institution should enjoy his full attention and services. The third situation arises when the college teacher or research worker also engages in a consulting practice. This is common among the faculties of schools such as medicine, dentistry, engineering, business administration, and law. Instances, however, occur in all departments; psychologists, economists, and chemists engage in private practice and are in demand as consultants with industry, government, and the military services. The opportunity to engage in these consultations is prized by the individual both because of the outside income and because of the experience gained and the prestige acquired. Many institutions permit or condone this practice, both to obtain and retain high quality men and because of the belief that this outside experience increases the competence of the men for service to the university. However, a balance must be found between the value of this opportunity as an incentive and the disadvantage of it as a disruption to the work of the institution. In too many cases, the professor is off-campus earning a fee while the students are marking time doing "independent study" or waiting endlessly to have dissertations read. When consulting activities are uncontrolled, the institution defrauds its students.

Students have been challenging the ethics of professors who lend their services to produce war materials (napalm, for example) or to strengthen the industrial–military complex. Doubtless, many men have had motives of patriotism. But the underlying issue is war as a blight on society and the manner in which the products of consultation (napalm, nerve gases, and poisons) are used. Should universities be involved in activities through which humanity is destroying itself? The grants of funds and the consulting fees take on an unsavory aspect. The issue presents a dilemma for the university because, when such research is dropped by the university and private laboratories enlarge their activities, some of the most competent professors will be tempted to change employment. Rigid plans for regulating the consulting practice or for dividing the net fee income have been tried by a few institutions—notably the University of Chicago—but they have not worked well. Cooperatively formulated standards seem to produce the optimum results that are mutually beneficial to the individual and the institution. However, a major reorientation of the motivations of professors is needed.

In professional work, inducements other than monetary ones can be highly influential. Persons who work at routine employment in factories, stores, or offices can usually purchase the things that satisfy them in life if their monetary income is sufficient. Hence, the wage they receive is a weighty consideration. The condition applies for many of the nonacademic employees of a college as well; but the faculty— and those administrators who may be classified as educational leaders —derive many satisfactions from their employment that cannot be purchased outside of it. This is true because of the intellectual nature of the task and the professional satisfactions that accrue from it.

The college professor ordinarily has emerged from his graduate study immersed in his subject. He has devoted a considerable amount of time, has expended money for tuition and other necessities, has sacrificed the opportunity to earn money (and often has been supported by his wife)—all evidences of his earnestness. If, by chance, he has done a commendable dissertation or has had it published, he will have experienced a creative satisfaction. A career as a college teacher seems to him to be a natural projection of a satisfying experience of the past. Many college teachers have been willing to accept minor beginning posts in universities, where their teaching is on an elementary level and where they may have to do departmental chores, because of their incentive to get started well in the profession.

Added to this is an element of idealism. Teaching is a bit analogous to preaching or to social service in that some individuals feel the call. They are attracted to the idea of serving youth. They believe in education as a foundation for civilized society and the means through which man may project his further development. They are motivated toward the exploration of knowledge in the hope of making some substantial contribution to knowledge. Unfortunately, this feeling of mission seems to be diminishing.

College faculty invariably seek membership in professional societies. A young economist feels elated to attain membership in the American Economic Association or to succeed in publishing an article in the *American Economic Review*. He beams with satisfaction if members of the profession write him in commendation of his scholarly efforts. If he has published a book, he searches the journals for reviews and glows or quivers depending upon the tone of each one. The academic man is strongly attached to the ideal of scholarship and seeks to emulate the scholars whom he has come to respect. The colleges stimulate this type of scholarly activity because they believe it produces better education; they also cater to these satisfactions in the individual by emphasizing production in scholarship when making monetary and promotional awards.

A number of other factors influence a man's decision to choose college teaching as a profession. In most countries, a professor is accorded high recognition by the public. In America he is treated as a public employee of little standing and is the subject of suspicion when he fulfills his role as a critic of society. On the other hand, the federal government turns to college professors repeatedly for expert help on the problems confronting it. Another consideration high on the list of any prospective teacher is the freedom he is given to express himself. He has become committed to the ideal of academic freedom. College positions, after a period of trial, normally result in tenure—which means security of position with freedom in scholarly research and in teaching. The true scholar is a man of considerable integrity in relation to his special knowledge, and he prizes academic freedom highly. He may refuse to join a staff or may depart from one where he senses that the institution does not sufficiently protect academic freedom. Because of public hostility toward academic freedom, it is fortunate that the organizations of professors can maintain a solid front in support of the principle.

Rank is also an important consideration. The use in college faculties of hierarchy ranks is common. There may well be a difference in opinion as to whether the faculty should be subdivided among professors, assistant professors, instructors, and so forth; but there seems little doubt that institutions use this scheme of rank to provide additional satisfactions. Teachers who are on their way up eagerly await their successive promotions. The ranking of faculty has serious negative aspects, however. Length of service rather than professional merit is often the criterion used in making the promotion. The system induces much competition clouded by campus politics, and the result is often vicious infighting. Where there exist rivalries among schools of thought (as in Japanese universities, for example)', or differences in ideologies, the pressure toward conformity with the power structure in order to gain promotion is unrelenting. When ranks become skewed toward the high level, the situation brings about rigidities that inhibit change in the staff and, hence, in the program. Institutions would be better off if they could free themselves from the ranking system. It is unfortunate that the community junior colleges, which have been free of this system, are now moving to establish faculty ranks.

Every college teacher feels a need for participation with his peers in decisions respecting educational policy and program. He is strongly motivated by the traditions of his profession in relation to the prerogatives of the faculty. Participation is satisfying to the members of any group and has genuine meaning. Because the role as teacher or researcher requires intensive contemplation and study, congenial working conditions are important to the college professor. Since these special appeals of college teaching as a profession are nonmonetary, it is important to note that research on the practices of industry has demonstrated what might be called the diminishing value of monetary incentives. It is clear from these findings that the value of monetary incentives decreases as income increases, as the creativity level increases, and as group consciousness and morale increase. Correspondingly, under these circumstances, the relative effectiveness of nonmonetary incentives rises. It is a misfortune for America that the values of our materialistic society cause so many men to fall into the trap of worshiping competitive incomes. Life is too short, men are too busy to enjoy the fruits of excess income, and you can't take it with you.

For a time during the postwar period, the salaries of teachers fell seriously behind those of other personnel while the cost of living rose steadily. The colleges needed to take action on salaries and did so. Too much emphasis, in fact, was placed upon this form of incentive; not enough attention was given to other satisfactions. One result was the rise of the teachers union with its labor-oriented emphasis on salaries and working conditions. Professional mission and satisfactions have been subordinated to material considerations—a loss for society.

And the public has itself to blame. Parents want their children to have a college education, and thus congest the institutions with students. But at the same time they do not want to pay the costs. They prefer to use their money for a second television set and a second drink. Yet education is the most important activity in society: health, economic progress, and cultural advance are the end products. In America, we must take a new look at our priorities in values—and when this is done, it will be easier for the college professor to take a fresh look at his motivations and satisfactions. It is in the mutual interest of the public and the professors for colleges and universities to provide their faculty with adequate monetary compensation and then to be able to highlight the professional satisfactions.

CHAPTER 17

FACULTY LOYALTIES, CONFLICTS, CONSENSUS

The nostalgic view of a college depicts it as a group of professional men and women, under the leadership of an educator, who arrive at unity in goals and esprit de corps in action through rational discussion and consensus in decision. Some institutions achieve this healthy state. But more realistically, a college is a place of marked differences in goals, of intergroup jealousies, of subgroups striving for power, of administrator–faculty haggling over decisions, and recently of confrontations with students who object to established policies. It is fundamental to relationships between administration and faculty that faculty be recognized for what they are—professional men and women. It is true that they are employed by the institution and that in a technical sense they are employees, but the attitudes that prevail among employers concerning their employees cannot be transported to administrator–faculty relationships.

A dominant factor in a college or university is the loyalty of faculty to their professional interests. They have interests and loyalties beyond the institution that produce compelling motivations. The individual professor's loyalty to his particular college may equal and, indeed, exceed that of the employees of any business organization. He may be entirely happy with the satisfactions being derived from his employment by the college, and he may easily sense in the college an opportunity for a lifetime career that has depth of meaning to him. He may be throwing his energies wholeheartedly into the ongoing activities of the institution. The presence of outside interests and loyalties does not necessarily mean an absence of interests and loyalties internally; the outside influences, however, have a large effect upon his attitudes toward his professional career and his particular institution.

The faculty man ordinarily belongs to several professional societies within his discipline—for example, a man teaching French at a California college may belong to the Modern Language Association of America (MLA), the American Council on the Teaching of Foreign Languages (ACTFL), the American Association of Teachers of French (AATF), the Foreign Language Association of Northern California (FLANC), Philological Association of the Pacific Coast (PAPC), and other associations for faculty working in comparative literature, in the humanities, and in linguistics. It is in the professional society where the teacher meets and associates with colleagues who have the same primary academic and scholarly interests as he. In the society he finds opportunity for creative participation, notably through his writing and through appearances on programs and work on committees. It is from these associates in the profession that he gets much of the recognition that has the highest meaning to him. Indeed, it is usually the professors who receive the greatest recognition from professional colleagues outside who are the most valuable to their colleges or universities; and the craving for this recognition helps produce the superior results within the institution. Furthermore, the teacher's judgment—as to the appropriate subject matter to be taught, theories to be analyzed, research to be undertaken, and even the methods to be used —will largely be determined by the influences of his colleagues in his professional area, most of whom will be outside the institution in which he is a teacher.

An incidental effect of these professional ties centering on the discipline, however, is that they tend to solidify the personnel within a teaching department. It is not only the individual professor who seeks the recognition of his colleagues outside; all the members of the department of instruction to which he belongs seek this recognition also. To a considerable extent, there is a pecking order of departments among institutions. The members of a faculty of a lesser-known college seek the respect and commendation of the members of the same department at neighboring universities, and all departments seek the approbation of those departments at other institutions that are perceived as being superior to their own. Thus the graduate faculty in a department at a prestige institution may wield extensive influence upon the curriculum, methods of teaching, library collections, and scholarly efforts of the undergraduate departments in other colleges.

Such influence has several consequences. The ability of the administrative officers within a college to plan for and implement change is lessened. The mobility of college professors is promoted, and this leads to a degree of instability within each institution. Since outside recognition is usually given on the basis of productive scholarship rather than on evidences of good teaching, individual institutions find themselves emphasizing research at the expense of teaching.

The professor probably also belongs to nondiscipline associations, notably those that promote his professional interests and perquisites or cross disciplinary interests. These are many, but examples are the American Association of University Professors, the American Association for Higher Education, the American Federation of Teachers, the American Association for the Advancement of Science, and similar organizations or chapters at the local and regional level. Such organizations may be classified roughly as trade associations or employee pressure groups, and they exist to facilitate the exchange of knowledge, to protect academic freedom, or to struggle for better wages and working conditions. Some of them purposely create conflict in order to promote change.

The typical faculty member is apt to have strong convictions about his role in society. These convictions stem from academic traditions and from ethics, relating to college teaching and scholarship, that emanate principally from the professional organizations. Because he is sensitive to some grave deficiencies in society, he often participates in civic organizations and activist movements.

In describing professional interrelationships in this way—both those focused on the disciplines and those based on interests of other sorts—I am endeavoring to portray the context within which administrative relationships must be established and actions taken. The administrator must recognize the many strengths that ensue from the influences—stimulations toward intellectual alertness and activity, pressures toward good standards of achievement, the creation of wholesome traditions, the support of particular institutions—that derive from the total profession. After recognizing the true nature of a problem, the administrator can take steps to induce cooperation and action. Inevitably the steps include faculty involvement in preparing the way for the desired action.

It would be incorrect to say that faculty have divided loyalties, in competition with one another, because the outward influences are not antagonistic to the inward ones. Indeed, the college itself actively promotes these outside associations and enjoys the consequent recognition given to individuals. However, the faculty member does have dual loyalties; he will ordinarily be committed to objectives that are, on the one hand, institutional and, on the other hand, professional. The impacts of these two types of loyalties may on occasion produce tensions, and in such cases the professor needs to determine which loyalty has priority.

In all organizations, including colleges and universities, there is bound to be a certain amount of conflict. In considering conflict it is important to distinguish between critical, rational debate and emotional disagreement and antagonism. It is the essence of a university that it constantly examines unanswered questions. Progress is made in the discovery of new knowledge brought about by inquiry that explores at the periphery of present knowledge. Frequently there is a difference of opinion about the correct theory pertaining to some matter. Sharp differences of opinion may arise and be debated vigorously. The objective in these cases is the truth, and the method of search should be rational debate based upon critical inquiry. The explorations of these differences of opinion can be the very process through which the institution achieves and maintains vitality. An institution involved in such explorations is said to sustain a high degree of intellectual ferment. An administrator must be able to perceive the true nature of disagreements of this sort and assist in resolving them by encouraging critical inquiry and rational discussion.

Conflict, however, can also occur in a manner that creates

emotional strains within the organization. Differences of opinion often degenerate into feelings of hostility. The feelings of an individual can easily spread to others, and presently the organization suffers from the presence of two or more conflicting groups. Individuals or groups attack one another and reduce tendencies to unite in support of the whole institution.

John D. Millett, who discusses conflict and consensus at some length in his book *The Academic Community,* lists four principal causes of conflict: the violation of role expectations; the reality of interdependence among persons and groups; the existence of barriers to full and spontaneous communication; and a lessening of the sharing of values and perceptions of reality.[1] Each of these causes of conflict can be reduced by administrative action, by identifying the cause and instituting corrective procedures. Roles can be more clearly defined than they commonly are; through institutional research, information can be obtained in the form of opinions about role perceptions and preferences. It is possible to itemize and classify the functions of a departmental chairman and to gather the opinions of the departmental faculty, their perceptions and preferences, concerning the degree of participation desired.[2] With this information, the administrator is able to carry out his responsibilities with a larger degree of acceptance by his colleagues.

Interdependence among individuals and groups can be frustrating at times, because some persons are ready to move before others are. One of the tasks of leadership is to foster good understanding of the nature of the interdependence. Another task is to keep alert to the causes of delays and inconvenience; efforts must be made to bring the lagging elements into harmony with those that are progressing more rapidly. Still another task of leadership is to keep the whole group aware of and in sympathy with the larger goals of the institution. To achieve these group goals, the constructive efforts of all are required.

The fourth cause of conflict, the lessening of the sharing of values and perceptions of reality, is the most difficult to deal with because it usually involves groups that become antithetical. Student

---

[1] John D. Millett, *The Academic Community* (New York: McGraw-Hill Book Company, 1962), p. 231.
[2] David L. McKenna, "A Study of Power and Interpersonal Relationships in the Administration of Higher Education," (unpublished dissertation, University of Michigan, 1958).

groups challenge the values to which professors and trustees have subscribed. Differences arise within the faculty between those who believe in social action and those who advocate scholarly objectivity. There is the clash involving pressure groups for the folk culture and for the super culture.

In a period of transition of values, as in the present period of changing sex mores, conflict of opinions and feelings is inevitable. The problem is not to find ways to suppress it, but rather to direct the controversy toward constructive resolution. Patience is needed, for time is required in making a major change in thought and habits; impatience leads to violence, and violence polarizes people. Violence by demonstrators and violence by police are equally negative modes of action. The role of a university is to pool the strains of ideas, subject them to rational analysis, and help to set directions for the future. Conflict in ideas is stimulating and educative. When issues relating to values are raised, the institution must promptly initiate action to create study and experience situations and to begin research on the subject. A college must avoid putting its curriculum into pigeonholes; instead, it must maintain flexibility of pattern and the ability to mobilize resources from any relevant discipline.

A tendency of any group that is subordinate to an administrative officer is to be self-protective. Faculty bodies are no exception to the rule. Indeed, the members of any faculty are so sensitive to certain prerogatives, especially those relating to academic freedom, that they rise automatically to the defense and support of any individual who appears to be under attack by the administration. For this reason, the administrative officer can get himself into a very hot seat if he does not take unusual care in handling the situation. The major associations of colleges and universities and the American Association of University Professors have agreed upon principles relating to academic freedom and tenure and to the procedures to be used in such cases. The faculty has an expectation of the highest degree that it will be sufficiently represented in the study of the charges, the hearings of the case, and the decisions made or recommendations forwarded to the board of trustees.

Academic freedom is at the heart of the profession of college teaching and research. It is no wonder, then, that faculty members feel so keenly about the protection of academic freedom. A problem for the administration can arise if faculty members are not fully informed about the relative merits of a case. If they have not considered sufficiently the distinction between a pretenure case and one involving tenure, their frame of reference with respect to the case will differ considerably from that of the governing board. These conditions are well known to every administrator and he must endeavor to anticipate these problems. It is largely up to him to persuade both the governing board and the faculty of the need for established procedures that meet the approval of both parties. Inasmuch as there is a statement of principles and procedures, endorsed by forty educational associations and hundreds of colleges and universities, that statement can form the basis for the action by the particular institution.[3]

The procedures involve participation of representatives of the faculty, and the faculty in effect shares with the dean and the president the responsibility for the recommendations that are made. Faculty members initially are protective of the position of any one of their number. If there is sufficient merit in the charges, patient effort by the committee can enable the faculty to see the disadvantage to them, as a group, of retaining a man who is not worthy of membership in the group. On the other hand, faculty members usually know individuals better than the administrative officer does, and they may be able to reassure the officer about the integrity of the individual and his professional competence. Even in cases where the administration and the board act contrary to the wishes of the faculty, good procedures, if they have been followed, can help to minimize the area of conflict.

The evaluation of the work of faculty members is a sensitive area, and this evaluation is highly important. In any given faculty, however, there is always vocal opposition to any procedures for evaluation. There exists the general belief that evaluation should be strictly for the self-improvement of individuals and not in any way be related to rewards or dismissals. Because of the prevalence of these attitudes, it is essential for the administrative officer who feels that evaluation must be made to do two things. The first is to convince the faculty that every chairman, dean, and president has to evaluate the services of the faculty—it is an essential part of his job, a fact that became clear to

[3] American Association of University Professors, "Academic Freedom and Tenure—Statement of Principles, 1940" (Washington, D.C., 1941), pp. 40–46. For an interpretation of the statement, see Algo D. Henderson, *Policies and Practices in Higher Education* (New York: Harper & Row, Publishers, 1960), pp. 208–9.

me as I served in those roles. The administrator can raise the issue as to whether the evaluation should be highly informal, based heavily upon hearsay and regurgitated student opinion, and upon direct contact with only a small segment of the faculty member's activities—for example, his participation in departmental meetings, or whether it should be made in some orderly fashion and based upon objective data. Second, he can involve the faculty in determining what is to be evaluated, whose opinions are to be collected, what evidence is to be considered, and what general procedures are to be used. For example, faculty evaluations by students, when used, often are ineffective because the faculty think they are being judged solely on the basis of student opinion. But research relating to student opinion in evaluations has shown that it has a high degree of validity and reliability; so student opinions definitely should be obtained. However, an evaluation that is based solely upon these opinions invariably meets with hostility from the faculty, and these emotional feelings largely negate the purposes of the effort. Several additional criteria of effectiveness are available and any good administrative–faculty committee can select the ones it thinks appropriate.[4] In administering the program, it is important that the faculty as a whole understand the uses of the criteria.

Regarding administrative–faculty collaboration, E. R. Guthrie, a dean at the University of Washington, for a number of years used a procedure that secured good results and received substantial support from his faculty.[5] To illustrate the procedure, let us take the case of a faculty member who is scheduled for consideration for promotion. This faculty member is asked to nominate from among his colleagues persons he would like to have participate in the evaluation, and the dean gives assurance that a majority of the members of the committee will be selected from the individual's own nominees. The individuals, as individuals, then proceed to make evaluations in reports to the dean. When the results are obtained, the dean seeks a conference with the faculty member and reviews the collated findings with him.

This procedure has several advantages: the individual being

---

[4] Ruth E. Eckert, "Institutional Conditions Favorable to Faculty Improvement," *Improving College Instruction* (Washington, D.C.: American Council on Education, 1950), pp. 165–77; also Algo D. Henderson, "Evaluation of Teaching Effectiveness," *Improving College Instruction*, pp. 144–56.

[5] Edwin R. Guthrie, "Evaluation of Teaching; Progress Report," (Seattle: University of Washington, 1954).

evaluated cooperates and takes principal responsibility for selecting the persons who will do the evaluating; the conclusions are the findings of the man's peers and not merely the asserted opinion of the dean— thus the dean can deal with the faculty member quite objectively without getting himself involved emotionally; and the procedure brings the administration and faculty together into working harmony, with the results available to the individual and also to the administrator. This procedure portrays constructive possibilities for the dean and faculty to collaborate together in a highly sensitive matter.

Embedded in my reasoning about the kinds of group situations I have just mentioned are two principal points. The first is the importance of fact finding. The skillful administrator makes certain that he has adequate information—or as full information as possible. This is necessary so that better decisions can be made and he can deal objectively with the group without becoming emotionally entangled in assertions he really cannot support. The second point is that any institution must have well-defined personnel procedures. Personnel procedures pay dividends in any organization, for nonacademic personnel as well as for college professors. Referring once again to the peer perceptions of faculty members, however, it can be seen that the faculty is highly sensitive to the manner in which they are treated and to the professional level of the treatment.

A related subject is the use of consensus as a mode of making decisions in a college or university. It is not possible for an educational institution to make optimum progress by means of fiat from a board of trustees or from high administrative officers. The perceptions of both faculty and students are of high value, and acceptance by the faculty of a proposed action is essential. Should decisions be made on the basis of regular parliamentary procedures including majority vote, or should efforts be made to obtain more genuine consensus? When decisions are made that have to be implemented through general faculty actions, the majority decision, if it is only that, can mean only the semblance of a program, without reality of content or continuity. Or it can result in a strong and unusual program which lasts only as long as it is protected by the strong persuasive personalities who promulgated it originally. A good illustration of this second case occurred at the University of Chicago when, under the force of Robert Hutchins' persuasiveness, a recalcitrant faculty by a narrow vote adopted a radical change in the organization of the curriculum. This change was implemented and remained in effect under Hutchins' presidency and chancellorship; but soon after Hutchins left the university, the faculty again revised the program, retreating in several substantial ways from the original plan. Hutchins later confessed that if he had been more patient in endeavoring to persuade the faculty to support his idea with genuineness of commitment, more of the elements of his program might have survived.[6]

The moral seems to be that something more than a mere majority is needed to produce substantial permanent change. Change cannot be effected merely by formal procedures or legal action. Such actions may be necessary and may pave the way, but the college dean or president, or other sponsors of change, must take time and make an effort to persuade the faculty as a whole of the desirability of the course of action. Within a small faculty the timing of this ripening of opinion usually is apparent. At some point, the question of consensus can be raised; and unless there is vigorous opposition, decisions may be implemented. In a larger and more unwieldy faculty group, however, it may be necessary to vote, and action has to be based upon the vote. When the vote is close, it is a signal to the administrator to initiate additional procedures of discussion and clarification.

Sometimes another impediment to good spirit and action arises. Parliamentary procedures are intended to insure fair play and orderly discussion, but they can be used by power conscious cliques to monopolize, to stall, and to increase their own leverage in voting. This is another reason why informality leading to consensus is a wise policy whenever it seems feasible. Representative faculty committees, under the group participative model (discussed in Chapter Twenty-One), can be instrumental in securing optimum results. The ability to obtain a substantial consensus in a faculty depends to a considerable extent upon a pervasive understanding of goals and a substantial commitment to them. Consensus depends upon the adequacy of communication— or rather intercommunication—between administration and faculty on essential matters. It depends in considerable part upon the acceptance by all parties concerned of the procedures being used. The administrator must weave all of these elements together to secure a high esprit de corps.

[6] Robert M. Hutchins, *Freedom, Education and the Fund* (New York: Meridian Books, 1956), pp. 185–86.

In this discussion, I have placed considerable emphasis upon the determination of goals and the commitment of both faculty and administration to these goals. In a larger sense, the commitment must be to the profession of college teaching. It must be toward inducing intellectual alertness, intellectual freedom, and intellectual inquiry; and it must be conducive to the cultivation and maintenance of a feeling of genuine pride in the profession.

ADMINISTRATION AND LEADERSHIP

PART **SIX**

CHAPTER 18

ADMINISTRATION-FACULTY COMMUNICATION

꧁꧂꧁꧂꧁꧂꧁꧂꧁꧂꧁꧂꧁꧂꧁꧂꧁꧂꧁꧂꧁꧂

The flow of communication in a college is greater than that in any other organization, yet in faculty-administration relations it is often ineffective. Furthermore, communication between administration and faculty is deteriorating. What is causing the deterioration? What is the nature of the problems? What special situations require the constructive use of communication? As a basis for analyzing this subject, I repeat that a college or university is a distinctive organization, composed of professional men and women, and requires mutually supportive efforts.

Deterioration of communication results from inadequate use of the group process in problem solving. As the administrative structure becomes more complex, the faculty are overlooked in consultations about policies and problems. They are given information and directives about decisions that have already been made by staff. The causes of this subtle change are not difficult to discern. One basic cause is the drive for efficiency in operations and in administration. To secure greater efficiency, more line officers are required, and procedures are developed for action and for control. The complexity that comes with size and with diversity of problems necessitates sufficient staffing to permit the delegation of responsibilities. These responsibilities naturally center around functions. The net effect is a vertical structuring of the administrative pyramid.

The pyramid constantly grows taller. The principal educational leader, the president, is removed further from the deans and the faculty. A cabinet of vice presidents, most of whom have nonacademic responsibilities, meets frequently to coordinate their work and incidentally to make decisions about plans and programs. A staff is recruited to define and analyze problems and to provide the administrators with recommendations. The deans must often resolve the problems of budget and personnel in conference with staff assistants rather than with the policy-forming officers.

In building this organization, however, certain principles must be kept in mind. After delegating responsibilities to others, the president should function at the policy level. Policy formation is a matter of professional concern and is of great interest to deans, department chairmen, and faculty. They must participate. A distinction must be maintained between administrative coordination on the one hand and institutional planning and policy formation on the other. The administrators need to meet in order to coordinate their roles, but this coordination involves administrative problems only. Policy formation and program planning are different. For these purposes the top-level council, or cabinet, presided over by the president, must be weighted strongly with academic personnel. This cabinet must work not for efficiency but for effectiveness in formulating and achieving educational objectives.

Another cause of deterioration of communication within the institution is the tremendous increase in communication with parties outside the institution—with legislators, donors, state agencies, churches or other sponsors, parents, alumni, and members of the community. Their interests bear realistically upon the college and need skillful handling, but they are not of greater importance than the interests of the faculty. If the institution is to have the vitality that makes exterior communication easy and effective, ways must be found to place appropriate emphasis upon both areas, interior and exterior.

The effect of this deterioration is to increase the flow of downward communication—a characteristic of business and military organizations—and to diminish the flow of upward and lateral communication. Effective two-way communication must be a primary characteristic of colleges and universities. The change that is taking place has two serious consequences: reduction of the role of the faculty in decision making and distortion of the values used for decision making. Faculty are treated as employees rather than as professional men, and criteria that derive from finances and public relations become the basis for decisions about academic policy and program. Furthermore, in the absence of good two-way communication, the informal network, the grapevine, becomes agitated and potent, intensifying the antipathy of the faculty to the administration.

To secure the desired influence within the institution requires skill in communication as the basic element in the group process. Elementary skills, such as writing and speaking, can be taken for granted, but skills involved in achieving effectiveness and high group morale cannot. The utmost skill is needed to deal with problems that stand in the way of good relations between administration and faculty.

Any organization requires unity to secure the best results, and unity depends upon consensus on the goals of the organization. At first glance, the essential goals of colleges and universities seem to be well known and not in need of discussion. The college or university, however, has tremendous diversification in interests, and the attention of the specialists who compose a faculty is devoted primarily to their particular professional goals. To overcome this tendency toward discreteness, it is necessary to have considerable agreement about overall goals. Loyalty to the specialization and loyalty to the institution must be reconciled. The overall goals need to be accepted if the individual goals are to be consistent and to contribute to institutional vitality. To achieve this result requires active leadership by the president and other high administrative officers. Each year there is an infusion of new members on the faculty and they need to be brought into discussions of goals sufficiently to make them integral members of the group. In any situation where an educator wishes to create a program that has distinctiveness, it is advisable to have extensive discussion and gain acceptance of proposals.

Faculties generally have the feeling that although they receive voluminous amounts of mimeographed information and directives, they are insufficiently consulted about problems. An increase in the complexity of the organization does not change the fact that faculty members have professional responsibilities. Harold Dodds, the former president of Princeton, suggested that presidents always follow "the practice of consultation."[1] In the large university, extensive individual consultations may not be feasible. It is possible, however, to organize the faculty so that representatives of their own choosing—perhaps as an executive committee or a senate—share in the process of defining, analyzing, and solving problems.

Today administrators are making frequent use of staff members who are expert in doing studies and preparing alternative recommendations. This is excellent administrative technique. Such expert staff should also be available to committees of the faculty studying problems of importance. In this way, the efficiency of the committees is greatly enhanced, and much faculty time is conserved.

Administrators, badgered by matters awaiting their attention, often do not listen carefully and patiently when consulting with deans, department chairmen, and faculty. The person with whom the administrator is talking quickly discerns that the administrator's mind is wandering. The result is a feeling of frustration about the effectiveness of communication. Two-way communication involves listening as well as speaking or writing. It is important to invite opinions and to hear what is said. It is essential to hear complaints, because this is a means of keeping informed about current problems being discussed through the informal channels of communication. The acquisition of good information is a continuing problem. Henry Wriston, when he was president of Lawrence College or Brown University, took his morning walk—before he looked at his mail—among the laboratories, the library, and the offices.[2] This is a commendable practice. Equally commendable was the informality of Emil M. Mrak, chancellor of the Davis campus of the University of California; plainly visible in an office behind glass, he waved to people as they walked by. This, too, is communication. It is not as feasible in a large institution, but there as elsewhere it is

[1] Harold W. Dodds, *The Academic President—Educator or Caretaker?* (New York: McGraw-Hill Book Company, 1962), p. 72.

[2] Henry M. Wriston, *Academic Procession* (New York: Columbia University Press, 1959).

essential that an executive take the initiative in communication and not become a slave to the mail, the telephone, and a flow of appointments with persons who demand a share of this time. Every president must keep in sufficient personal touch with the faculty and staff to set a tone that favors good communication. Many of the more routine office obligations can be discharged by a good assistant.

Even so, the president comes under enormous pressure for personal involvement. The institution must turn to staff, and indeed to organized procedures, to gather information. Objective data and objectively collected samples of opinion are needed for decision making. The administrative device for this is the office of institutional research, equipped with staff trained in research and in the use of computers. Many institutions today have been establishing such offices, finding that they are invaluable as a means of facilitating and improving decision making on the campus and of providing information in the conduct of off-campus relations. An informal source of information is the grapevine. It exists in all organizations. Colleges and universities are especially given to it because of the intermingling of students and faculty. It is therefore highly important for the administrators also to have knowledge of the content of the informal communication. Ways need to be found to plug in to this network. Administrators must be aware of the phenomenon of entropy, the tendency of messages to deteriorate when passed orally from person to person. The third receiver in the chain, or the fifth or the tenth, is likely to hear a message that varies considerably from the one originally given. The original message must therefore be clear and concise, free from possible ambiguities or misinterpretations. When the administrator sends a message, he should get a report on what is received; it may differ from what he intended. A good practice, following oral communication on any important matter, is to send a written confirmation of the discussion or the principal points involved.

Insufficient reporting is another problem. Three types of reports are especially useful in administration. The first analyzes a problem and presents recommendations for decision making. Faculty committees that study problems are notoriously inefficient in making such studies. It saves time and results in clarity if the chairmen of such committees are given some instruction in problem solving. The final draft of the report, whether going from administration to faculty or the reverse, needs to contain enough discussion of the issue to be convincing about the care with which the problem was studied.

The second type of report is the annual budget of the institution. Budgets are concrete expressions of plans for the year. The persons who are responsible for working with sections of the budget should participate in the formation of it. If they have agreed upon the plan of action, it will be carried out more effectively. Departments and subgroups need to see their portion of the budget, when finally authorized, so that they are aware of the scope and of the limits of potential action. This is a means of defining authority and of fixing responsibility. In addition, summaries of the overall budget should be made available for widespread use within the institution as a means of securing the highest possible degree of cohesion in action. The budget is not a classified document to be kept in the locked files of the president and the business manager.

The third type of report is the periodic report expected of every functional department, school, and other subdivision, usually for the academic year or the operating year. There is great value, however, in preparing summary reports at shorter and longer intervals, especially at five- or ten-year intervals. Such reports enable the institution to consider trends and to evaluate changes, if any have been taking place. The periodic report relates achievements to original plans, brings unresolved problems to light, and projects future needs. It can also be a basis for making administrative determinations concerning the performance of subdivisions, the quality of leadership, and the relation of particular achievements to overall goals. This report is therefore a part of the process of evaluation, and evaluation should always be one of the steps in the administrative process. The better the evaluation, the better the decisions that can be made.

Administrators need to be aware of the barriers to good communication. A universal one is psychological in nature. Individuals who are involved in a hierarchical structure are sensitive about their status. Vice presidents of firms stand in fear of their presidents. Persons in second and third echelon positions, seemingly very secure ones, often have great feelings of insecurity. These feelings impede upward communication. Persons who are lower in status hesitate to offer suggestions to persons who are above them. They seldom criticize persons above them, at least directly. It is therefore advisable to reduce these feelings of tension. Friendliness of manner can help. An open office door, as

Herbert Hawkes of Columbia once said,[3] implies an invitation to any faculty member to step in and confer. Not many do so, but the invitation gives them the feeling that there is no barrier. The persons higher up in the administration need occasionally to extend invitations to others to offer suggestions. Another procedure is to meet with persons in groups, because in a group situation the individual feels more secure and is less afraid of the consequences of voicing criticism. He receives psychological support.

Other barriers arise from the causes of conflict. One of these is due to interpersonal conflicts, rivalries, and differences in value judgments. When persons come to have conflicting views about matters, they tend to reduce their communication. This merely exaggerates the conflict and deepens the differences about values. Insufficiently defined roles are the source of another barrier. Differences in ideas about roles may lead to conflict and, therefore, lessening of communication. Understanding about roles is necessary if the responsibilities involved are to be carried out fully.

The quality and vitality of an institution depend to a large extent upon the morale within the faculty. I have commented earlier about the importance of achieving unity of purpose and consensus for action. These are essential if good morale is to be maintained. The more positive the attitude of the group as a whole toward the expressed goals of the institution, the greater the enthusiasm with which the individuals contribute to those goals. Participation in defining and maintaining goals leads to better understanding and acceptance of them and, consequently, to better morale. Participation in making other decisions leads to greater effectiveness in solving problems.

Rensis Likert, director of the Institute for Social Research at the University of Michigan, has said that the most effective organization is one in which the members are mutually supportive.[4] Conditions which bring concern for the welfare and achievements of others are conducive to a supportive atmosphere. The degree of this support within the group is in part determined by the quality of leadership exercised at the top level. One way to induce support and to give it to others is to commend individuals and subgroups for their efforts and achieve-

[3] Herbert E. Hawkes and Anna L. Rose, *Through a Dean's Open Door* (New York: McGraw-Hill Book Company, 1945).

[4] Rensis Likert, *New Patterns of Management* (New York: McGraw-Hill Book Company, 1961).

ments. Criticism, unless constructive, tends to have an opposite effect. The administrator does well to commend individuals with judicious frequency, even when the commendation is coupled with constructive criticism.

Low morale is often the product of rumor. Assuming that the administrator maintains good contact with the grapevine, he needs to make certain that ill-founded rumors are counteracted as quickly as possible. Ordinarily it is possible to do this by supplying the correct information. I recall an occasion at Stanford University when I picked up a rumor that was causing much talk in men's rooms and at dinner parties. The faculty knew that because of depressed economic conditions certain railway bonds in which the university allegedly had a large investment had declined in market value. They feared for the future of the university and for their own security. As one college president to another, I discussed the rumor with Ray Lyman Wilbur and expressed the belief that faculty morale could be substantially improved by giving the faculty the facts about the investments. Swinging toward me in his swivel chair, Wilbur exclaimed, "Why, that's none of their damned business." In my opinion this view was mistaken. It overlooked the purpose of communicating fully with the faculty. Such communication is essential in maintaining good morale.

With innovation in higher education a favorite topic among academic administrators, many presidents and deans are eager to effect changes in organization and program. Many, if not most, of the significant changes in American higher education have been initiated through the leadership of such officers, who wish to reach the faculty more effectively. This situation raises the question: How does an administrator go about securing acceptance of change when the tendency of all groups is to resist change?

An idea for change must be shared if there is to be genuine acceptance. An exchange of ideas and of opinions must take place to develop consensus and support. In presenting an idea for discussion the administrator must be prepared to make some adjustments. He must listen to counter-ideas and carefully examine their merits with the group. If there is merit in a counter-idea, he needs to be willing to modify his own position.

Individuals or groups with firmly entrenched attitudes need to make considerable readjustment in their way of thinking before accepting change. But readjustment seldom occurs as the result of a single conversation or discussion; reeducation takes time. For this purpose, the workshop is a convenient device. The workshop enables a group to examine a problem long enough to permit all arguments and all implications to be considered. If the original proposal was a good one, discussion usually changes the ideas of the individuals involved. I recall an instance when the president of a small liberal arts college, without any preparatory discussions, asked his faculty to launch certain new courses in general education. This proposal met with consternation because the faculty had not been asked to share in his thinking. One faculty member exclaimed to me, "What does the president think he is doing anyway? I have been teaching a course like that for several years." This anecdote leads to the observation that new ideas will seem to some individuals to be threats to their security. It is therefore essential to explain a proposal fully, giving information about its purposes, its limitations, and its anticipated effects.

Many administrators are surprised and become much concerned when hostility breaks out between two subgroups within the faculty. In such situations the administrator must know how to take a lead in healing the breach. Ordinarily the hostility develops when there is a difference of opinion over goals or norms. Theodore Newcomb, the social psychologist, explains that this difference is the beginning of a downward spiral of communication.[5] When one group perceives another as hostile to it, communication diminishes. As communication diminishes, the beliefs of the respective groups diverge more and more. Communication must be started on some common ground. Because neither group is likely to take this step, the administrator needs to be sensitive to the situation and to take positive steps toward reversing the spiral of communication.

Administrators need to understand group processes and the techniques for correcting abnormal situations that develop within groups. Ordinarily the key lies in communication. Effective communication in administration involves more than issuing information sheets and directives. Ideas and problems must be shared with the faculty, and the faculty must be given leadership. The use of influence, rather than the exercise of authority and power, is the most effective mode of administering the academic program of a college or university. The desired influence can be attained only through effective communication.

    [5] Theodore M. Newcomb, *Social Psychology* (New York: Dryden Press), 1950, pp. 243–63.

CHAPTER 19

PERCEPTIONS
OF LEADERSHIP

The image of the college president
in America is that of a kindly man of superior intelligence who sparkles
with ideas and leads his faculty and students in the pursuit of goals
that are wholesome and lofty. "Be ashamed to die until you have won
some victory for humanity," cried Horace Mann when he was president of Antioch College.[1] Our image grows out of the respect we feel
for such men as Charles Eliot, Daniel Gilman, William Rainey Harper,
Arthur Tappan, Francis Wayland, Benjamin Wheeler, and Andrew
White, who transformed the narrowly conceived curriculums and the
provincial colleges of the United States into comprehensive and vital
institutions. They and other educational leaders introduced the sciences

[1] A quotation inscribed on a memorial shaft to Horace Mann at Antioch
College.

222

into the curriculum, nourished learning with research, launched programs that revolutionized agriculture and the technological process of industry, and elevated the study of the professions. Men of their mold created public universities that brought higher education within the reach of all qualified youth. Under their dynamic leadership colleges and universities became, within the short period of a century, models that have been emulated by institutions around the world.

The image remains, but the situation has changed. The institutions have grown in size and complexity. The governing boards, usually composed of business-related men, fail to differentiate between a college and a business. Presidents must function largely through staff. They are farther removed from their faculty and students, while faculty and students demand greater participation in policy determination. Publicity about colleges today highlights the college as an institution of widespread public interest and brings to the institution a strong interaction with its environment, often with results that inhibit freedom of action. The services rendered to industry, institutions, and government in turn bring a degree of dependence upon these agencies, particularly for financial support. Dissident students and faculty raise issues that involve both institutional and public concern. But the modern college likes to widen its appeal for funds and for students, and this interest draws the leaders into increasing activity on the public relations front.

These and other conditions have submerged the college president in the ongoing business of running his institution. An alarming portion of his nervous energies flows into activities related to promotion, public agitations, plant, and business and finance; and thus he often neglects his primary role as educational leader. There are good reasons why the academic administrator—whether he be president, vice president, provost, or dean—must exercise constructive educational leadership. In particular, he must take the lead in defining goals and in achieving consensus relating to them; he must attain operational unity for the institution, while stimulating diversity within the program; he must set in motion the processes of evaluation of the results obtained through teaching and research; and he must coordinate and synthesize planning for the future and make decisions that implement policy. How can he do these things when the daily problems of operations and the demands of the public absorb his time? How can he be both administrator and educational leader? How can the academic administrator in a college or university best function in his role?

Historically, three trends have influenced thought about the nature of administrative leadership.[2] One was the development of leadership in the military service or under authoritarian governments. This leader was the commander, king, or boss. An army, for example, trained for battle to accomplish a single objective, and time was of the essence. The army functioned best when the decision-making authority was centrally focused and orders from the top were obeyed. The boss perception still greatly influences our thinking. Engineers endeavoring to apply scientific principles to management created the second trend. F. W. Taylor,[3] among others, introduced techniques for studying factory operations to make them more orderly and efficient and to reduce the time and increase the skills for each step in a series of operations. As a result business management instituted piece rates for pay, systematic processes for the assembly lines, and quantity–quality controls over products and inventories. Scientific management has made a deep impress on American enterprises.

The third movement probably has been generated by the complaints of labor, effectively voiced through their increasingly powerful unions, about speed-up pressures, sharply competitive practices, and layoffs of men. Foremen with stipulated quotas for production bore down on workers to secure desired commendations and bonuses or to avoid boss-inflicted penalties. Labor began to assert its right to participate in determining goals, working conditions, and rewards; and industrial relations thus became a subject of study by experts trained in the behavioral sciences. These studies and other research in these disciplines have been accumulating evidence about the attitudes, motives, and reactions of men and the value of developing the human resources of an enterprise. Although short-time results can be secured by pressure methods, the long-run advantages of a mutually supportive approach in management are apparent.[4]

[2] For more complete treatment of this topic see: Roald F. Campbell and Russell T. Gregg, *Administrative Behavior in Education* (New York: Harper & Row, Publishers, 1957), pp. 82–118; Albert Lepawsky, *Administration* (New York: Alfred A. Knopf, Inc., 1955), pp. 77–106; and Warren G. Bennis, "Leadership Theory and Administrative Behavior: The Problem of Authority," *Administrative Science Quarterly*, Vol. 4 (1959–60), pp. 259–301.

[3] F. W. Taylor, "Paper 1003: Shop Management," *Transactions*, American Society of Mechanical Engineers, Vol. 24 (1903), pp. 1337–1480.

[4] Rensis Likert, *New Patterns of Management* (New York: McGraw-Hill Book Company, 1961).

All three approaches to administration have made their contributions to theory, and the skillful manager of today draws on the wisdom derived from all of these sources. Positive leadership has its values (Marshall Dimock calls it administrative statesmanship[5]); systematization is basic to organizing and programing; and the human relations approach induces good morale and productivity.[6] It must be borne in mind, however, that in a college the paramount factor is the human factor. A college is people—people with ideas, people who are there to learn.

Several distinct types of leaders have been identified. In practice such classifications are not mutually exclusive, but they nevertheless define primary types, each of which sets a certain tone within the organization. I present these characterizations in the hope that they will assist the administrator in evaluating his own personality, his relations with the members of the group, and his methods of administration. They can help him to determine a philosophy or approach to his role as leader. The terminology used here has been influenced by the literature relating to group dynamics, but it has applicability in administration when the administrator is viewed as a group leader.

The four types of leaders are: directive (authoritarian), permissive, group participative, and laissez-faire. The directive leader predetermines the results he wants achieved, assumes command, issues orders, calls for performance, and determines rewards or penalties. The permissive leader is democratically oriented; he has objectives in mind, but he gives to the members of the group a high degree of autonomy and is flexible in his attitudes concerning variations from the objectives, standards of performance, and incentives. The group participative leader carries the responsibility of group leadership but engages the members of the group with him in determining the goals and methods, in implementing them, and in evaluating the results. The term laissez-faire is used to depict the situation that is essentially leaderless; the man designated as leader functions basically as convenor of the group and then simply becomes an ordinary group member. From what I have already said in this book, it should be clear that I advocate leaders of the group participative type for colleges and universities.

[5] Marshall E. Dimock, *Administrative Vitality: The Conflict with Bureaucracy* (New York: Harper & Row, Publishers, 1959).

[6] For an interesting chart that compares by elements the classical theory of management with the human relations approach, see Bennis, p. 288.

Further differentiation between types of leaders can be made. An example is the administrator who operates man-to-man. This leader establishes direct contact on an individual basis with each of his staff or with his subordinates. He handles each problem directly with the subordinate concerned and, to a degree, segregates the one individual from his fellow workers. This pattern is commonly used by directive leaders.

A second example is the administrator who works with his principal staff or his subordinates within a circle. His leadership (of discussion, for example) involves two-way communication with each person in the group or round-table functioning where everyone is in communication with all others. This leader works with the group as an organism. He becomes, in effect, a member of the group as well as the person with principal responsibility. On all matters that are relevant to the interests and welfare of the group, he invites their participation. They share in determining objectives, in setting standards, in determining methods, and in appraising results. The leader of this group is essentially the group participative type.

This brief characterization of leadership types provides some background for a discussion of models, theoretical or practical. The model of a nostalgic image is the president who was known as "prexy," essentially a paternalistic type who furnished the ideas, directed operations firsthand, and concerned himself with the welfare and advancement of his group. This model is not appropriate for the complex conditions that prevail today. I do not mean to disparage, however, the role of the leader in giving expression to ideas, whether they come from his brain or result from his role as a catalyst. Nor do I want to deny the importance of having good communication within the organization; it can provide the administrator with the requisite information for decisions. But the college president today, to be effective, can be neither paternalistic nor authoritarian in his style of leadership.

A second model might be analogous to the presider at a town meeting. It has been the custom among small colleges for the faculty to have frequent meetings, with the president or dean presiding. At such meetings, the faculty has conducted much of the business of the organization and has even passed judgment on the behavior and achievements of individual students. When colleges were small, the plan had much to commend it. With growth in the size of faculties and the initiation of supplementary procedures to facilitate decision making, the town meeting method is less justifiable. It no longer is possible for everybody to decide everything. Refinements in organization have made the decision-making process more systematic and professional. Participation has been streamlined, and some amount of streamlining is essential in larger institutions. Even the faculty, important as it is for them to meet as a body, have been discovering group processes (the executive committee or the academic senate, for example)' that provide genuine representation, are less cumbersome in decision making, and preserve the collegial pattern of organization.

Faculty who believe that the older type of faculty meeting gives to them the final power must realize that this system can be manipulated by an administrator. The administrator knows that attendance is not good and that individuals present vary from meeting to meeting. Hence he can introduce proposals when the group is skewed in his favor, appoint committees that are stacked, and reintroduce ideas that may at first have failed of acceptance. If he advances a large number of proposals, he can swamp the cumbersome machinery and count upon some of them to survive. Persistence by the administrator enables him to win, because in some institutions few of the faculty become genuinely concerned and really study the problems.

Faculty meetings can also be controlled or stymied by organized minorities. They line up at the microphone, challenge procedures, and in other ways frustrate the majority, many of whom leave the meeting before the important votes are taken. But these illustrations are, perhaps, cynical views both of faculty interest and of administrative leadership.

Another model derives from business administration. The assumption is that the most efficiently operated college, like the efficiently operated business enterprise, is the best institution. But efficiency to the businessman is efficiency in the use of money; for a given expenditure of funds, a predictable result must be achieved. Members of governing boards of universities initially have the business model in mind. In relation to the nonacademic aspects of the operations, the model has a measure of validity: a central heating plant should heat efficiently; the productivity of typists or of janitors is measurable in relation to production standards. In short, the line–staff relationships for nonacademic responsibilities have a degree of similarity to those in business.

There are strong pressures on colleges to be more businesslike in all of their methods. Increased enrollments, requirements for new programs and new equipment, and demands for more research have caused institutions to greatly increase their budgets. Inasmuch as they are not in position to earn their own income sufficiently to be self-sustaining, institutions must secure appropriations and solicit funds. But legislators, desirous of avoiding increased taxes, look for other solutions to this dilemma. Members of boards of trustees, plagued with the need to get appropriations and raise money, demand that institutions reduce their costs. At every hand there is pressure toward greater financial efficiency, and efficiency requires a strong executive who will enforce procedures to effect economies.

The business-model type of leadership, however, fails badly when applied to the primary features of an educational institution. The reasons derive principally from two characteristics: the faculty is composed of professional staff who perceive themselves as peers of the administration; and the products of the educational and research programs are highly intangible.

Furthermore, theories of administrative leadership in business are changing, and these changes are bringing the leadership role closer in nature to the traditional role in education. The earlier business leader was the self-assured executive who, keeping his eye on sales and studying the accounting reports, issued orders that flowed down the lines of authority controlling every aspect of the business operation. The newer type of administrator mobilizes the available human resources toward the achievement of cooperatively established goals, with results that are evaluated through procedures in which there is general participation by the affected parties. Many large-scale businesses and industries now use the group process principle in management.

No doubt there are many causes for this change in the pattern of leadership in business administration, but two of them stand out: it has been discovered that greater productivity is secured when the total group of managers and employees constitute a closely knit, well-motivated, and goal-directed organization; and because of the increasing complexity of organization and of technological advances, members of the staff derive authority from their individually superior technical knowledge. These two reasons are applicable in a college situation. Faculty members are inherently creative persons who achieve the highest level of performance in teaching or research when they participate actively in determining the goals they are seeking and the methodology to be used. Faculty members also are highly educated persons, each competent in a specialization, each an authority in his particular field. Better educational results are achieved when there is a degree of deference on the part of the administrator to this type of technical authority. Thus the business model has some contribution to make to education but, as usually perceived by financially minded men, it is not appropriate for use in an educational institution.

For some purposes a model exists also in the political field. Education is a public function and questions about provision for higher education are questions of public policy. A college or university that is chartered by the state and relies heavily upon the state for its funds is a public corporation. The task of maintaining public receptivity to and approval of the work of the institution is essentially a political one; the task of securing the appropriations of funds is political; and the relationship of the particular institution to the system of public higher education requires the continuing use of political finesse. The president of a state university or the director of a community junior college, in order to achieve some objectives, must be a man who understands the art of politics. It must quickly be added, however, that the politician does not qualify for the role of educator. The successful political leader makes progress by a mode of compromise that secures sufficient public support to permit action to be taken. The university, on the other hand, has the function of searching for truth. It serves its function best when it pursues inquiry into unresolved questions and controversial issues and examines alternatives to the status quo. Educational leadership therefore must come from persons who understand the nature and purpose of intellectual inquiry. The academic leader must not bow before public hostility or pressures, or indeed to indifference. He must courageously support scholarly inquiry even in the face of public opposition. These concepts are basic. Like the model of business administration, the political model is not always appropriate for use in an educational institution.

Still another possible model is that of the administrator as mediator. Some students of organization, after studying what actually takes place, have found that the processes that involve decision making pervade the organization. Decisions are not always made at the top. Indeed, very few actually are so made. It is sometimes said that the best administrator is one who makes the fewest possible decisions, having delegated the responsibility largely to others. The best decisions are made locally, because that is where the best information lies and where the responsibility for implementation must also lie.

One characteristic of a college or university is its complex and decentralized nature, and the college is, therefore, an extreme example of decentralized decision making. It is also an organization of many and diverse subgoals, not all of which can be harmonized readily. To secure sufficient unity within this anarchy for the organization to function as a whole, the chief administrators must spend most of their time mediating among the conflicting interests.[7]

Granted that there is much truth in this description of how a complex institution operates, the model seems inadequate. Institutions of higher learning have a highly significant role to play in society. However generally the goals may be phrased, they serve as a focus for the subgoals. They establish long-run aims that provide a sense of direction. The results of the activity of the institution as a whole must also be evaluated, however informally or methodically this is done. Perhaps the time given to these functions by the leader is small, but this is no measure of their importance in the life of the institution.

The overall goals need to be derived sufficiently from the thinking within the group to gain acceptance and commitment by the group. But the academic leader, because of his many activities exterior to the institution, can provide many fresh ideas and outside perspectives for consideration. Even while mediating conflicts, he must bring fresh perspectives to bear in influencing the thinking of the parties at interest.

The final model that I will discuss is the problem solving one. Problem solving represents the application of the scientific method of analysis and synthesis to the process of making decisions. It implies having a methodology for identifying problems, for describing the factors that bear upon a particular problem, for collecting needed data, for using the data in analyzing the factors, for arriving at potential solutions, and for choosing the solution that seems best. Following implementation, the decision must be subject to review, involving systematic evaluation as the occasion demands. A good administrator selects staff who possess skills in this methodology or trains the committees in such procedures. A good leader interposes his influence if the conflicting interests threaten to produce a stalemate. The ideal leader

[7] Clark Kerr, *The Uses of the University* (Cambridge, Mass.: Harvard University Press, 1963).

plays many roles—as stimulator, critic, teacher, and catalyst. He anticipates problems and initiates procedures for clarification. Within his functional role, he selects from the recommendations the alternatives for decision.

In this book I have placed much emphasis on group participation as a mode of operation within a college or university. When problem solving within the context of the institution as a whole is considered, it can be seen that widespread participation, usually at the level at which the problem exists, is highly benefical. The favorite form for this participation is through faculty committees. The committees, as has already been noted, are notoriously inefficient. Logrolling reduces many good ideas to insignificance; careless procedures often produce warped or wrong conclusions. If faculty committees are to survive in the modern university, the members must learn to use problem solving procedures. Doubtless they know how, but often they do not perceive that the method is relevant to committee work.

Each of the models of leadership I have described has plausible application within the college and university. From each, some perceptions about the nature of leadership can be drawn. Within the institution, the situations vary and so should the style of leadership. The styles that are natural to individuals vary. Of all the models, the problem solving one, involving appropriate group participation, seems clearly to make the best fit. This seems the best way for the skilled president, dean, or chairman to gain optimum consensus in defining goals. When the goals of the individuals or subgroups harmonize with and advance the overall goals, optimum productivity is attained. The administrator advances the quality of work and the prestige of the institution through the motivations and incentives of strong, creative individuals. Group participative structures harmonize with traditions and feelings about the roles of officers and faculty. Problem solving, analogous to the scientific method, utilizes systematic methods for group thinking. Within the framework of problem solving, the institution can attack any issue that is presented by faculty, students, or other parties.

CHAPTER 20

ADMINISTRATORS FOR THE FUTURE

The custom among colleges and universities is to select as administrators, and more especially academic administrators, persons who have established reputations as scholars. This custom is undergoing some change, and the change has special relevance to the need for innovation in higher education.

Scholarly distinction is a good criterion—provided another dimension to the qualifications is added. Colleges and universities need persons of substantial intellectual interests and understandings in policy-determining posts. This has not always been true, for in earlier decades it was the almost universal practice to employ religious leaders as deans and presidents. In the more strictly academic positions today, it is unthinkable to give leadership responsibility over academically specialized men to a person who has no knowledge of the field of specialization. For example, a school of law needs to be headed by a person trained in the law, or at least in political science. A person in a similar position in engineering, medicine, or professional education— or as a department head in specialized subject matter—must also have as part of his qualifications a grounding in the professional area or the disciplines basic to the area. A shift from this basic philosophy would almost certainly endanger the goals and the quality of our institutions of higher education.

It does not follow, however, that one cannot design a program to prepare men to be college and university administrators. Two general types of such programs already exist. In one the participants are selected on a postdoctoral basis and gain varied and intensive experience in administration as interns. The advanced degree may be in any academic discipline or professional area. Thus the individual enters with specialized knowledge in a particular field—law or engineering or economics or the classics. A variation of this program is one that involves internship, but also includes the experiences of reading, critical observations, seminar discussions, and research papers.

The second type of program is at the predoctoral level; individuals enter the program with substantial background and a master's degree (or higher) in cultural or professional subjects, and they pursue doctoral studies in higher education. The basic education insures that the individual has breadth of education and some insights into a specialized area, while the studies in higher education add both depth and breadth. Included are elements of the history and philosophy of higher education, organizational theory, administrative behavior and processes, principles of student learning and curriculum development, and concepts of human development and relations drawn from the behavioral sciences. Doctoral dissertations based upon the research procedures of historiography, conceptual models, or the scientific method complete the requirements for the doctor's degree.

Both types of program are available at the University of Michigan's Center for the Study of Higher Education, which I directed for sixteen years. Since these programs are commonly questioned by academic scholars, a portion of this chapter is devoted to a discussion of the ideas involved.[1] First, however, the role of the college and uni-

[1] See also Algo D. Henderson, *Guidelines for Planning University Programs To Train College and University Administrators* (Paris: UNESCO,

versity administrator needs some description and analysis. For what is
he being trained? An analysis of this role is essential to demonstrate the
value of preparation for administration.

Higher education has three primary roles: to stimulate and
direct student learning, to discover knowledge (research), and to render public services. An academic administrator needs to have reasonable understanding of each of these functions of the institution.

Students may learn through having knowledge pumped into
them at lectures given by scholars. More insightful learning, however,
takes place when students are active rather than passive, when they
are well motivated, when the mode of learning is built upon previous
skills and habits of learning—and there are many variations among
individuals, and when evaluations of the students' progress are made
through joint faculty–student endeavors. There exists a body of knowledge about learning and about ways to devise curricula and experience
situations that facilitate the educational process. An individual with a
Ph.D. in psychology might have this understanding; one with a doctorate in English literature probably would not have it.

A scholar, as the name implies, has engaged in personal research and therefore has an understanding of research requirements
and procedures. It is helpful to the administrator to have a thorough
comprehension of research techniques. But in his busy office, he will
not be able to pursue personal research, and thus a high level of training in this respect is unnecessary. The administrator does need to be
aware of the contributions to social progress that have come through
research. He needs to be sensitive to the essential problems of our time
in order to know where to place emphases in research. The value of
allocating resources to applied research in the university may be dis-
puted, but the existence of such research cannot be. The administrator
consequently must have a sympathetic attitude toward the role of the
university in both applied and pure research, even though this attitude
may not be a residual product of his own scholarly work. In any case,
he must know how to promote the interests of the institution in the
research area.

Related to research as well as to teaching is the vital problem

1970); and Algo D. Henderson, "Higher Education as a Field of Study in the
University," in *On Higher Education*, ed. D. F. Dadson (Toronto: University of
Toronto, 1966).

of maintaining academic freedom. The scholar, without question, understands the nature of academic freedom and the need to protect the institution in this respect. The best protection, however, may not be simply a protective wall built around the institution. Pressure groups who are aroused because of some controversy have ways to breach such walls. If the administrator is to guard the integrity of the institution, he must have knowledge of the experience of colleges and universities with the concept of academic freedom, and he must be aware of ways of dealing effectively with those who seek to limit or destroy it. As a principal spokesman for the university, the administrator needs to have exceptional understanding of human relations and of how to mobilize support.

Nearly all colleges and universities, sometimes to the dismay of the academically minded faculty, render substantial services to the public. Indeed, such services as continuing education are becoming increasingly valuable to the public. Elsewhere I have discussed the role of the college or university in the community and in society generally, noting the effective work of the land-grant universities, of medical schools, and of public community colleges. I have also discussed the issues concerning relevance that confront urban-related institutions. The transition in viewpoint from scholarly disdain about public services to understanding support for them (the extremes in attitudes, perhaps) is highly important. Of equal importance is the need for understanding the manpower requirements of the nation, not only for advanced specialists, but also for middle manpower—the product of technician training. The latter requirement demands recognition of the constructive role of community colleges and technical institutes, even though many university professors question their contribution to higher education. Those professors are wrong.

Each of the three broad functions of higher education requires administrative orientation toward the social purposes at stake. Academic scholars seldom are alert to research relating to learning, and they are often indoctrinated with negative attitudes toward applied research and public services. It is in the social interest to have positive educational leadership. Academic leadership involves ethical and social values. Breadth of cultural background is a highly desirable element in the education of the future administrator, but he needs also to be a student of the philosophical bases of policy determination. Historical perspective and some of the ethical bases for making value judgments can be derived from an understanding of the history of higher education. Indeed, the history of human learning is as much a substantial discipline as any other aspect of history—perhaps even the segment of greatest importance in this era of swiftly moving intellectual achievement.

Scholars generally impress one as being progressive in their particular specialization but hesitant about joining in change that might affect their environment or the university in general. The administrator must be progressive in general outlook, however, and not merely protective of the status quo. His role as an educational leader demands that he be a catalyst of ideas. To the extent that fresh ideas and experiences stimulate his imagination—and they often do—he acquires the dynamic quality of leadership that is refreshing. To some extent his role is that of innovator. For this reason, he needs to be open-minded about existing objectives, programs, teaching methods, and internal organization and processes. He is frequently called on to make value judgments about relative emphases within the program and about new methods of accomplishing goals. Stimulations derived from his observations of exemplary institutions and from empirical research help to provide the background of attitudes and skills with which to implement his ideas. The preparation of the administrator in this respect can make the difference, for the institution, between the perpetuation of stereotypes and the exploration of fresh concepts and methods.

Another area of concern for the welfare of the college or university is the style of leadership of the top administrative officers. Our heritage has given us primarily the vertical hierarchy, a structure that requires a directive type of personality at the top. He issues commands, delegates authority, subdivides the work, approves incentives, and evaluates performance. Communication is primarily downward. Persons who have not had sound training in the theories of organization and the processes of administration will emulate some model, good or bad, or take the course of least resistance. The usual result is a bottleneck administration, authoritarian in nature.

Along with the style of leadership go the essential skills. Human relations skills are concerned with group dynamics—that is, how to cause a group to work effectively together toward commonly accepted goals and with mutuality of support. Involved also are techniques for maintaining loyalties, overcoming conflicts, and securing consensus on agreements.

In any model of organization the administrator has roles as organizer, delegator, coordinator, and evaluator. Assuming some graduated experiences in administration, he acquires a degree of finesse in each of these roles. On the other hand, if he has been a student of the theory of organization and administrative behavior, he is a critical learner during his apprenticeship positions and, on the average, he achieves a higher level of skill in each of these roles.

Incidentally, many scholars accustomed to supervising intensively every small detail of the research projects on which they work carry this habit into administration. In our complex institutions, these academic administrators frequently fail because they create a tremendous bottleneck in decision making. They also become fatigued with routine decisions and never have time to reflect upon or participate in discussion about matters of major policy or future planning. They are too tired to supply any creative vitality. The good administrator not only knows how to delegate portions of his authority but does delegate authority in large measure for various reasons: to give his subordinates an adequate role, to place most of the decision making at the level at which the operation takes place or where the best information is, and to relieve himself of decisions about routines so that he can be more imaginative and creative in his role as leader.

The academician is also much influenced by the prejudices of his colleagues about evaluations of teaching and of research. An administrator obviously must make evaluations. But sometimes, being timid about doing this openly, he resorts to subterfuges. In effect, then, much of his evaluation is based upon regurgitated opinions, mostly student complaints. The whole process of evaluating the work of faculty members is badly conceived and deplorably administered. Here again relationships between the evaluator and the faculty member must be one of mutual confidence, and this in turn depends upon the introduction of valid methods of evaluation which both parties agree are in their mutual interest. This situation requires a knowledge that is very different from that gained by the academic man while teaching or doing research in his specialized department. He must realize that the area of evaluation also has been researched and that substantive knowledge is available.

An aspect of major importance with which administrators must deal is that of planning and development. The better institutions today are projecting plans five to ten years forward. But planning is only possible if goals are thrashed out and adopted. Goals must be projected a few years in advance in order to enable gradual shifts to be made toward new objectives. Projection of goals assures that change will actually take place.

In setting goals and determining programs, the administrator must be able to visualize the college or university as a whole and to weigh the relative merits of various aspects of the program. He needs to balance the old against the possible new. He must become institution-minded instead of department-minded. Indeed, he must become fully conscious of the role of the institution in society, and he must carefully weigh the potential contributions of the institution to the growth and development of that society. The worm's-eye view of the specialist is out of place at this level of operation.

Certain forces in our dynamic society are leading toward greater interdependence among institutions, with the result that our concept of higher education is changing. Where formerly the individual college or university catered to the demands of individuals, now the state searches for talent, establishes a system of institutions to supply the needed services, and insures equality of admission for students. Under a coordinated plan, the roles of particular units of the system are identified, interchanges of resources are fostered, and provisions are made for common access to reserve libraries, data banks, and cyclotrons. The new college administrator must be aware of the changes in interrelationships that are occurring; he must acquire some understanding of the philosophy underlying the systems concept and of the models for making it function in the social interest.

I have been discussing the role of the administrator in order to answer this question: Does the person who is an authority on a particular subject—on petroleum geology or Chaucer or French literature—really have the best preparation to become a college or university administrator? He certainly needs to be an academic man; but academic specialization alone is not sufficient qualification. Because of the nature of the several facets of his role as an educational leader, he needs other training and experience. I shall turn now to a brief discussion of training programs.

If the budding administrator already possesses a doctor's degree in a specialization, there should be some provision under which he can gain the understandings and the competencies that come from the study of administration and of higher education. If, however, his interest in becoming an administrator is aroused prior to his obtaining the doctorate, it is possible for him to study for the doctorate in administration. The justification for this doctoral program is found in the substantial professional knowledge of organizational theory, administrative behavior and process, and history and philosophy as related to higher education. I want to be more specific about the content of these subjects, but since I have already discussed the reasons why most of these items have significance in training administrators, a list of descriptions will suffice here.

Value systems applicable to the mission of the college or university

Historical perspective relating to the roles of institutions of higher education and to the social contributions of these institutions

The problems of higher education; public policy relating to their solutions

Learning theory; the characteristics of students

Curriculum and the design of learning experiences; variable modes of teaching and of learning

Student counseling; student governance

Manpower needs; trends in the utilization of educational personnel

Innovations; factors influencing or inhibiting change

Organizational theory and administrative behavior and processes

Human relations problems and techniques—individual and group

Function, authority, influence, and power; communication in administration

The impacts of informal organization including overlays of authority, influence, and power that arise outside of job pyramid structures

Financial planning and administration

New management techniques

The economics of higher education; the role of educational institutions in the economic and technological development of society; higher education as a social investment in the future

The political process and the involvement of the university

The nature of academic freedom and modes of maintaining freedom in teaching and in research

Constrictions on the institution arising from the interests of the several publics; the roles of the publics in promoting the welfare of the institution

This list comprises the special areas of knowledge with which the doctoral student should be familiar. The items on the list can become the focus of courses of study and seminars; and within each area may be found problems that can be used for individualized study and for theses.

Some programs in higher education include both teaching and research. Research may include empirical studies or fresh syntheses of data, concepts, models, and generalizations which can create a ferment of critical inquiry by faculty and students to enlarge the learning. As a result, much needed contributions can be made to understanding higher education, its goals, its students, its functioning as an institution, and its responsibilities to society. A program for preparing college administrators is a program for the whole university and, hence, knowledge should be sought from many fields in addition to professional education. The behavioral and social sciences, including public administration and business administration, have special contributions to make.

The best training for a potential administrator involves more than doctoral study, of course. The value of experience as a factor in education has been stated in Chapter Two, and the reasoning which applied there applies here. Experience may be gained in one of two ways. The first is through a beginning job which follows the termination of study. Whether this is valuable depends upon the nature of the learning experiences. Often the job consists of routines; the more skilled the person becomes as he repeats a task, the more valuable he is in this task—but he is denied opportunity to progress in learning. Or he may take direction from an individual who is himself a poor administrator, and thus may learn bad attitudes and habits. It is possible, however, to provide good learning experiences on a regular job,[2] which can be made a type of internship.

True internship is the second method of gaining experience. It should provide objectives that have been defined, a variety and pro-

[2] Edwin Allen Penn, "The On-the-Job Experience: A Method of Preparation for Students of College Administration" (unpublished doctoral dissertation, Columbia University, 1966).

gression of experiences, opportunities to observe the organization as a whole and the process in some detail, and stimulations to learn. When internship experiences are interwoven with seminars or other discussions of theory and practice, the intern gains the most intensive type of training for administration.[3]

Following the lead of such institutions as Columbia, Stanford, Michigan, California, Minnesota, and Florida State, substantial progress has been made in developing advanced degree programs in higher education. An even earlier program at the University of Chicago was highly effective. A considerable flow of mature students have received the doctor's degree in these programs, have been well placed in leadership positions, and seemingly have been successful as administrators.[4] The demand from students for this type of program is great, and the demand from colleges and universities for the graduates of the program is large. These demands have led many universities to launch doctoral programs without sufficient attention to the quality and number of faculty, to the content of the program, and to the quality of the students being admitted to the departments. The many facets of the study of higher education cannot be taught well by one or two professors working alone; teachers in this field must themselves be active students of the area and must have time for this purpose; most professors whose specialty is in professional education at the secondary level have only a makeshift preparation to teach in this area. But there is a severe shortage of well-prepared faculty; the materials available for instruction are scarce and in considerable part must be drawn from other disciplines; the flow of research reports in the field is improving but is still weak.[5] If we are concerned with supplying a high type of intellectual leadership in higher education, students must be selected with these conditions in mind. The ultimate value of these programs depends not upon the number of doctoral degrees that are granted but,

[3] Patricia Jean Manion, S.L., "An Investigation of Selected Programs of Administrative Internship in Higher Education" (unpublished doctoral dissertation, University of Denver, 1967).

[4] The amazing growth in this type of program is described in James Rogers, *Higher Education as a Field of Study at the Doctoral Level* (Washington, D.C.: American Association of Higher Education, 1969).

[5] W. B. Martin and Dale M. Heckman, eds., *Inventory of Current Research on Higher Education* (Berkeley: Carnegie Commission on the Future of Higher Education and Center for Research and Development in Higher Education, 1968).

rather, upon the nature and quality of the training given to students.

The changes in institutions of higher education discussed in this book are manifold: the growth in size and complexity of our colleges and universities, the increasingly heterogeneous population of students, the interdisciplinary movements, the innovations relating to teaching and to program, the problems of creating and maintaining an educative environment, the increase in publicity and its impact on the public, the need to persuade the public about the values of higher education in order to produce an adequate flow of income, and the need of society for positive contributions toward solving the problems of society and helping to promote its further development. To cope with these changes requires knowledge and skills different from those possessed by most scholars who have been trained only in specialized disciplines. These changes demand that universities experiment further with programs designed to give future college and university administrators special preparation for their roles.

CHANGE IN GOVERNANCE

PART **SEVEN**

CHAPTER 21

CONTROL

¡[decorative rule]

The student drives to gain partici-
pation in college government, the demands by black groups for control
over their own programs, the moves by faculty to create faculty senates
as a means of dominating in academic areas, the agitations from the
public to crack down on the colleges—all these conflicting demands
for power raise once again the issue of control in higher education.
Control today has many facets—legal, educational, and behavioral,
and the latter includes such influences as informal communication, the
tactics of pressure groups, the sociometric pattern, and varying styles
of leadership. For the public colleges and universities, the problems
relate both to the governance of each institution and to that of the
systems of institutions.

Although colleges originated when students associated together

245

and employed a tutor, by the sixteenth century the practice of charter-
ing colleges as corporations was well established. The move to require
incorporation was a result of the church–state rivalry for control of the
institutions; the corporation was a device used by the state to gain a
measure of supervision and control. In many European countries, the
universities became instruments of the state; those in Germany were
launched by the state.

Harvard, founded in 1636, soon discovered that its board of
overseers, composed of magistrates and clergy, was inadequate; and in
1650 the college requested a charter from Massachusetts Bay Colony.
The charter, following the English practice of faculty governance,
designated the president, five fellows, and the treasurer as the members
of the corporation. It was intended that the fellows would be faculty.
However, through the influence of the overseers, the faculty members
gradually were displaced by clergy and lay personnel. This process,
much opposed by the faculty, continued until the board was composed
wholly of nonacademic members. Yale from its beginning had a board
of clergy. With few exceptions, the early colleges and universities in the
United States followed the Yale example. The displacement of the
clergy by business and professional men occurred during the nineteenth
and twentieth centuries.

A Supreme Court decision involving Dartmouth College in
1819 fortified the corporation as an entity with continuity. For private
colleges, the charter was construed as a contract with the state and not
subject to *ex post facto* revision by the state. The Dartmouth decision
assured valued protection to private colleges—but this rule of law does
not apply to public colleges because a state may not make contracts
with itself.

In 1784, an issue arose in the state of New York as to whether
King's College should be made a state institution. The legislature established the University of the State of New York under a Board of Regents
for that purpose. By 1787, a broader concept was worked out under
which the University of the State of New York was defined as an
agency of the state to serve as an umbrella for the whole of higher
education, private and public, in the state. King's College, renamed
Columbia, was given operating autonomy, and provision was made for
the establishment of other colleges and universities. Over the years,
the Regents acquired authority to develop plans for higher education,
charter institutions, initiate and coordinate state colleges, accredit col-

leges, supervise licensing in the professions, grant degrees, and investigate fraudulent and discriminatory practices in higher education. The concept of higher education as a statewide system, including subsystems, however, did not become widely implemented until after World War II, when public planning–coordinating boards proliferated. Today, more than 80 per cent of the states have statewide boards, concerned primarily or wholly with the public institutions.

The following discussion deals with four issues: control as it influences educational policy and programs, including the vital role of the faculty; the participation of students; possible models of governance based upon behavioral theory; and the concept of system as applied to higher education. In Chapter Twenty-Two I discuss more fully the status of the college as a corporation and the reform of the governing board.

Kenneth Boulding's portrayal of the dichotomy between the folk culture and the superculture (which I have mentioned in Chapter Four) explains why so much tension is created among the forces that influence the college.[1] Probably what most disturbs the radical left on our campuses—who seem to believe that American society is becoming decadent—is that they see little hope for its transformation while the institutions of higher education are so much under the control of prevailing vested interests and provincial thinking. But a more fundamental question for higher education, I think, is: How can the university best undertake its intellectual role in exploring all of knowledge and in searching for solutions to controversial problems or problems that do not have pat answers?

An important function of a board of trustees is to interpret the university to the public. Yet, the trustees do not share in the campus culture. The attitudes of most of them are molded through the prevailing public opinion—the folk culture—and those members who stand for public office must to a degree cater to that opinion. To protect the academic freedom of the faculty, presidents tend to keep the board so busy with financial and other affairs as to leave them no time to become acquainted with the main work of the institution. As a result, communication is minimal in an area where the board feels it has the legal responsibility. Also, because of the potential for conflict between

[1] Kenneth Boulding, "The Role of the University in the Development of a World Community," in *Higher Education in Tomorrow's World*, ed. Algo D. Henderson (Ann Arbor: University of Michigan, 1968), pp. 135–41).

the institution and the public constituency, the president is required to spend an inordinate amount of time on public relations. Thus, presidents are even less able than formerly to serve adequately as the liaison between faculty and trustees. With little understanding and appreciation of the campus culture, how can trustees be expected to protect it from environmental forces that are hostile to change and innovation?

A major problem in governance is that the persons chosen for high administrative offices seldom have any training for their roles or any knowledge of sociological concepts relating to organizational and institutional processes. Inadequately prepared presidents assume too much detailed decision-making responsibility, become serious bottlenecks, and use authoritarian methods. Our large institutions are evolving cabinets of presidents and vice presidents who, meeting weekly for coordination, make decisions from which the faculty are excluded. The institutions, as a consequence, are coming to be operated by oligarchies, most of the members of which are nonacademic. As I have stated earlier, hostility and conflict exist where there is a divergence of goals. If boards of trustees are to continue to exert full legal authority and to assist the universities in securing funds for their operation, board members must understand better the primary purposes and ongoing work of the institution.[2] I question whether such understanding can be gained under the prevailing mode of institutional governance.

To carry out its role, the institution (in legal theory the governing board) employs professional personnel—the faculty. Sometimes the charter stipulates that the faculty shall conduct the educational program; but, of course, this matter is subject to the tacit consent of or approval by the board. Customarily, boards in varying degrees delegate to faculty responsibilities relating to the admission, progression, and graduation of students, to the formation of educational programs, and to research. We should not overlook the influence of this tradition, which works reasonably well. Instances of intervention by the board, however, are disconcerting and occasionally endanger the institution because of the conflicts that are aroused. I believe that one reason such situations occur is that presidents do not sufficiently educate their boards about the academic program.

I wrote the amendments to the charter of Antioch College

[2] Morton A. Rauh, *The Trusteeship of Colleges and Universities* (New York: McGraw-Hill Book Company, 1969).

which brought faculty and student representatives into the decision-making process. For fifteen years I presided over the meetings of the Administrative Council and the joint meetings of that council with the Community Council and also with the Board of Trustees. Participation by both faculty and students—who were represented on each of the two councils—was highly constructive and beneficial from the president's viewpoint, and otherwise, and I do not remember any instance in which either faculty or students failed to conduct themselves with the best interests of the college in mind. This long experience, during the Depression and war years (years of trauma, turmoil, and change), has prejudiced me in favor of participative plans.

Antioch developed two frames of reference for its organizational structure. First, it differentiates between the academic program—the admission, teaching, and graduation of students, as well as research, all of which were deemed to require professional knowledge and judgment—and the function of living and working together as a community. The academic program is considered to be primarily a faculty responsibility, but it includes a certain amount of student participation, with a minority of students sitting on all faculty committees. The community is thought of as a composition of both students and faculty, with students in the majority and consequently deserving of larger representation on the committees of the community government, although some faculty are included.

A second differentiation is between policy–program formation and administrative implementation. The Administrative Council devotes itself to policy making and program planning, including the allocation of resources and the selection and retention of primary personnel. The administrative officers work within this policy and have their own meetings for implementation and coordination. The council includes the president and representation from the administration, but the administrators are not in a position to dominate decisions. Through these devices the faculty and students play realistic and influential roles at the highest level of decision making. The Administrative Council also elects one-third of the trustees, with some interesting consequences in the choice of members: some trustees are academicians, some of them are blacks, and some come from the fields of agriculture and labor—to mention certain interests that were not previously represented on the governing board.

The distinction between policy making and program operation, a concept advocated by Woodrow Wilson, is important within the educational institution. When implemented through a structure such as the one Antioch uses, it enables faculty and students to participate in the formation of goals and programs and leaves the administrators free to administer.

Students today are asking questions that must be studied and answered. There are fresh breezes blowing across the facade of higher education, but they are having difficulty penetrating the ivy and the ivory. Frustrations and demonstrations result. These students intend to be heard, and their voices must be included in our discussion of academic governance. If included in a systematic way, the students would have less cause for disruption; and they would accelerate the process of change that is so badly needed.

A residual benefit to the plan of student participation with the administration and faculty is the additional dimension given to their education. To take leadership, to share responsibility, to attain the skills and habits of civic activity, and to feel the consequences of the successes and the mistakes that flow from group decisions—all these experiences provide learning which brings growth and maturity. Our society badly needs people with this type of training and experience, and it must take place during the college years, which are the maturing years. Students who do not have this experience slip easily into the typical alumnus mold, content simply to earn a living and watch television.

I want to make it clear that I favor student participation, but that I reject student control. Let me emphasize again the value of administrative leadership and the value of placing considerable weight on the judgment of the professionally trained faculty. Since participation by the faculty is essential and participation by students desirable, a brief examination of two contrasting participative models for their relevance to the college and university situation is useful.

The first might be called a model of negotiation and mediation. It derives from a recognition of conflict potential in a given enterprise. One fairly recent development in business enterprise has been the evolution of collective bargaining. The procedures of negotiation—and when necessary, mediation—of agreements about goals and working conditions have brought substantially increased recognition and benefits to labor. At times, however, negotiation arrives at an impasse, followed by disruptive and costly strikes. Nevertheless, union movements do exert on institutions and enterprises, pressures that achieve desirable reforms. From the union point of view, this model is good. Applied to the academic situation, the model calls for recognizing students, faculty, and trustees as separately organized interest groups. These groups can negotiate issues relating to goals and methods, and the administration or an outside party can mediate in cases of conflict.

An impediment to the effective operation of this model, however, is the tendency of faculty and student groups to polarize. With faculty, polarization occurs through the competition of academic interests and nonacademic perquisites, and with both faculty and students there are ideological polarizations. These are not merely variations on the conservative—liberal continuum; they also flow from the influence of noninstitutional organizations—American Federation of Teachers, American Association of Higher Education, American Association of University Professors, Students for a Democratic Society, Black Student Union, Third World Liberation Front, and National Student Association, for example. Each of these groups is interested in exerting power within the college. The question arises: Who represents whom? Mediation between factions usually means mediation between the institution—those who possess high-level decision-making authority —and a particular pressure group (or groups). A group agitates concerning a certain matter, negotiation takes place, and hopefully a viable solution to the problem is found. This is the manner in which this model of government can be constructive. Since we know that this sort of bargaining takes place in colleges, as well as in industry and government, we must recognize that this influence in governance exists, even though it is not shown on organizational charts.

Doubtless we will see more of this activity before we see less, given the currently expressed need of students and faculty to participate and the pressures from some groups to extend their power. Confrontations and disruptive tactics have, in fact, caused institutions to make concessions and thus have demonstrated their effectiveness. This model does not fit well the internal organization of a college, however, because bargaining among three authoritative bodies is complex and leads to stalemates. Furthermore, education by its nature demands more than compromise decisions—it requires problem solving at the highest level of joint intellectual effort.

Faculty, students, and trustees need to achieve a higher plane of goals and of programs than the common denominator ordinarily arrived at by bargaining. The alternative is to organize participation on a basis that best promotes the overall purposes and functions of the institution and that accords as well as possible with sound behavioral theory and good management practices. This is the group participative model. It derives from the concept of consensus.

Let me repeat, for their bearing on the immediate issue, a few generalizations. In a college, the really important matters of education and research occur in individual and personal relationships. The products of teaching and research are clearly intangible; a college converts tangible resources into intangible results. Effectiveness in reaching these intangible goals, then, must be the primary guide to action—not efficiency in the use of funds. Decisions in education are best made where the professional effort must be made. Society is the benefactor of this professional and highly decentralized decision-making approach.

In the group participative model, participation of the parties occurs in relation to their investment in the situation and to their ability to make positive contributions. The model involves an organizational structure that interweaves the groups and subgroups to facilitate appropriate participation in the decision-making process. Both students and faculty must have some voice in policy decisions through streamlined representative methods. Thorstein Veblen, John Kenneth Galbraith, and others have argued that the faculty should govern. But giving the faculty control simply passes the dominant voice to another interest group. Faculty must have a large measure of participation, I agree; but in universities where they have governed, tradition and academic prestige and departmental self-interests have impeded progress of the kind I am advocating. The conservative attitudes of faculty bodies is well demonstrated by a resolution that was passed by the faculty of the University of Paris over five hundred years ago. It read: "The university should be told that the faculty wishes to keep its statutes as it has done, and would that other faculties do the same."[3] One is reminded, too, of the long struggle, never fully successful, of the faculty at Harvard to regain control over that institution.

It is neither advisable nor possible in a public college to ignore the interest of the public. Both Wilhelm von Humboldt and Abraham Flexner were in error in assuming that the German university could be insulated from the state—under the Nazis the state decimated the uni-

[3] Quoted in Eric Ashby, "The Case for Ivory Towers," in *Higher Education in Tomorrow's World,* ed. Algo D. Henderson (Ann Arbor: University of Michigan, 1968), p. 9.

versities. The public interest is germane; it needs to be represented in governance under a plan that permits the conflicting interests to be resolved. The corporate structure is sufficiently flexible to permit the academic, student, and public interests all to be represented on the governing board. Such participation provides the intercommunication that is so badly needed. The only real security for the academic program lies, I believe, in the acceptance of goals and roles by all three of these interests.

But such a conclusion does not resolve the problem of securing genuine representation. People must feel that their views are being considered—a universal problem in democratic societies. It is hardly feasible, even in a college, for everyone to decide everything. It does not seem wise to decide issues by "votes in the street," as advocated by some militant students; this is, in fact, a way for an articulate, aggressive minority to gain an influence that is out of proportion to its members. A solution is not easy, but representation of primary groups in the high decision-making council is feasible and more desirable than any other existing plan. In planning for change, sufficient group discussion must be fostered to develop understanding of points of view by all representatives. In this way confidence can be created in the governance system, leading to full acceptance of it.

The usual means of depicting the organization of an institution is a chart that shows a job-pyramided structure. There are two major objections to such a picture: One is that it entrenches the impression of authoritarian decision making, accompanied by downward communication through directives; the other is that it fails to take account of several other dimensions of decision making, including the sociometric pattern, the influence of informal communication, and the existence of expert, referent, and other forms of power. The actual pattern of decision making is shown better by several overlay charts, each of which describes one of these dimensions. The group participative plan, however, suggests the use of interrelated circles to picture the organization. The circles represent the governing board, the university council, the president, the administrative staff, the faculty, and the students. Interrelated, they denote interaction, two-way communication, and consensus. For policy and program formation, these characteristics of decision making are most appropriate. The execution of decisions and subdivisions of labor can then be more accurately portrayed by the job-pyramided structure.

The public interest demands that—in the governance of systems of institutions—a distinction be made between issues of a political nature and those of an educational cast. Questions about who should be encouraged to go to college, what broad programs of higher education should be provided by the state, where institutions are needed, the functions of individual institutions within the public system, what portion of the state income should be devoted to higher education, and how the appropriations of public funds should be distributed are issues of public policy and, in this sense, political. Heretofore, they have been resolved through cumulative actions by individual institutions and through decisions by governors and legislatures. In view of the growing complexity of the problems of the state as well as of those of higher education, uncoordinated approaches are no longer sufficient. Comprehensive planning is essential. Governors and legislators need advice, based upon data and professional analyses, as bases for decisions about public policy in higher education.

Let me be perfectly clear: The educational issues are the familiar ones relating to what is to be studied or researched and how, and how an environment conducive to freedom of thought, discussion, and reporting is to be maintained. A distinction between the public policy kind of issue and the educational one can best be maintained if the operational function is clearly left to the individual institution, and if the function of planning and coordination, as defined above, is given to the statewide board.

These new state boards are growing rapidly in power and, following the Parkinson model, will seek accretions of power. In Great Britain, the University Grants Committee has had considerable freedom of action, but it is under increasing pressure—especially from the Public Accounts Committee of Parliament—to submit to direction from the ministry. The use of state executive authority in the operation of institutions of higher learning stems from the notion that higher education is a department of government. Consequently, it is urgent in this formative stage to determine the true roles of the state boards of higher education, lest we unthinkingly establish fifty ministries of higher education in the United States.[4]

Part of the problem of control arising from college–state relationships is caused by differing perceptions about these relationships.

[4] Algo D. Henderson, "State Planning and Coordination of Public and Private Higher Education," *Educational Record*, Vol. 47 (Fall, 1966), pp. 504–5, 507.

Briefly posed, there are two theories that are basically antithetical. One is that the implementation of programs of higher education is as much the role of the executive arm of government as is the administration of highways or the maintaining of law and order. The opposite theory holds that the university is an autonomous institution, governing itself as do the professions generally—establishing codes of behavior and disciplining those members who do not maintain the agreed upon professional standards. Colleges do this kind of thing through professional societies and voluntary accrediting associations. One view of this second theory is that institutions of higher education constitute, in effect, a fourth arm of government, resembling the other three arms (legislative, executive, and judicial) in the need for sustenance and the determination of overall public policy, but differing in that the function of higher education is to examine all knowledge, modes of social organization, and behavior. More, it must be free to examine critically even government itself. To carry out this role, institutions of higher education must be free of domination by the political party in power.

Faculty and student bodies generally subscribe to the second theory; governors and legislators subscribe to the first. With the growing size, complexity, and demand for funds by universities and systems of colleges and universities, the trend has been going rapidly in the direction of more and more executive influence, with control by the governor and state agencies. Demonstrations, especially violent ones, by students have caused public opinion to swing more definitely into support of this view. But the movement toward stronger controls from the governor's office is not in the long-run interest of the public.

The distinction in functions between the planning–coordinating board and the operating–institutional boards can best be preserved through appropriate stipulations in the constitution of the state. If this is done, neither the legislature, the governor, nor a coordinating board would have the power to counter constitutional provisions. The University of Michigan has had constitutional standing since 1850. The original impetus arose because of attempts of clergy to control the institution, but many court decisions have assured the university protection against political interference as well.[5] If one can judge by the emi-

[5] Fred W. Hicks, "The Constitutional Autonomy of the University of Michigan and Its Significance in the Development of a State University" (unpublished doctoral dissertation, Center for the Study of Higher Education, University of Michigan, 1963), p. 36.

nence of this and other universities which enjoy such protection, constitutional status is highly desirable. The full nature of the collaborative relationships between such universities and their respective state coordinating boards has yet to be worked out; doubtless some conflict will occur. It is, however, in the interest of all institutions to cooperate so that the legislature and the governor, acting upon the advice and recommendation of the state board, can make the best possible public policy decisions.

The corporate setup for colleges probably will not be abandoned because it has too many advantages, both from the states' and from the institutions' points of view. If this is so, the institutions must operate with a board of control with primary power and authority. There is no reason, however, why the boards must overwhelmingly represent one segment of society, passing over women, the young, and persons from a variety of occupational and civic interests; and there is no reason why it must be wholly a lay board. A democratic society that is flexible, elastic, and capable of evolving requires trustees to be intelligent about, but not subservient to, the established mores and conventions of the folk culture and the power structure in society. The university is the primary means of discovering the knowledge basic to dynamic evolution and of preparing persons to undertake creative roles. Environmental pressures cannot be wholly ignored, for a hostile environment does not provide a congenial atmosphere in which to work or the funds with which to operate. But the free development of ideas must also be encouraged and protected. It is in the best interests of society, in the long run, to have the superculture prevail on the college campus. The state, however, has an interest in higher education and must determine public policy relating to it. The complexities of issues and finance now require that the governor and legislature be advised by a planning–coordinating board for higher education. The solution to control in higher education lies in fashioning a model of organization that engages all interested and concerned parties in the processes of communication and decision making.

CHAPTER 22

GOVERNING
BOARDS

The most serious of the many polarizations that are occurring in colleges and universities is that between the governing board and the people who compose the institution, the faculty and students. Differing viewpoints about goals, operating methods, and academic freedom—to mention the more serious ones—have long existed under the American system of college governance; but under the impact of rapidly accelerating demands for funds and for change polarization has intensified. This situation is not good for the institution and it is not in the long-run interest of the nation and our society. When conflict occurs, as it has in many institutions, it becomes a major threat to the security and tenure of the president. Several of the ablest educators in the United States have resigned

257

recently as the result of such conflicts. Reform of the governing board is a must.

In a college there are many parties of interest—the public, the state, the faculty, the students, and the administrators. A theory of organization is needed through which these interests can be united around objectives that advance the interests of humanity. I have suggested such a theory in the previous chapter and now examine more fully the role—indeed, the several facets of the role—of the governing board in this theory.

A college or a university may be founded only in accordance with the law, the usual instrument of establishment being the corporation.[1] As organizations in the public interest and as creatures of the state, colleges and universities are subject to a degree of supervision by the state. At the minimum level, the purpose of this supervision is to see that the institutions' responsibilities under the charter are fulfilled and that the law is not transgressed.

Colleges, then, are corporations. A corporation is a collection of individuals united by authority of law into one body under a special name. Certain obvious advantages inhere in this corporate form of organization. The device permits a group of persons to act as a single party in the eyes of the law; the corporation may make contracts. It has limited liability; members of its board (in the absence of fraud or misdealings) are not individually liable for the debts of the corporation. It has continuing life, irrespective of changing personnel; it may remain as a legal entity within the term of life stipulated by the charter, or as determined by law until the charter is cancelled. The corporation is a very convenient legal device used to weld together the many elements that compose a complex institution and secure operative viability.

The charter of a corporation is given to a group of individuals who have petitioned for it, or who have been appointed by a governor, or who otherwise have come into existence as a group. The charter creates the board, and the board thus becomes the corporation and exercises the powers of the corporation. The board operates as a unit by majority or other vote, as determined by its charter and bylaws. Individual members have no authority to act for the corporation or to endeavor to direct its affairs, unless the board as a whole has given

---

[1] As an illustration, see "General Corporation Act," *Compiled Laws of the State of Michigan,* 1948, and *Supplements,* 450.1-450.696; especially 450.117; 450.124-450.127; 450.170-450.177.

specific authorization for this purpose. This limitation on the authority of a board member, a trustee, is often not understood by college trustees, and especially by those who are ex officio members by reason of the political offices they hold. The whole legal structure is usually not understood by faculty and students, nor indeed by the public. The charter ordinarily gives the board complete power within the limits of its express purposes and the implied authority. Charters sometimes mention specific officers, the faculty, alumni, boards of visitors, and so forth, with some indication of duties and responsibilities. Legally, all such provisions are delegations of the authority vested in the board itself, for the state can have only one central body directly responsible to it.

Board members of colleges and universities are commonly called trustees—literally because they are involved in trust relationships. Among the trust responsibilities of the body are those of managing the institution in the public interest, accounting to official bodies and to the public for actions taken and funds used, carrying out the ethical responsibilities involved in the education of youth, holding title to and administering endowment funds, and executing other specific trusts. In part, these responsibilities are the same for any director or trustee of any nonprofit or charitable organization: no individual may secure any personal financial advantage or benefit. In part, too, they represent the duties of a trustee under a legal trust: title is given to one party but the beneficial interest lies in others. The holder of the title is a trustee and he is responsible under the law for administering the trust faithfully in accordance with its conditions. A college receives many trust funds to administer. Members of boards whose experience has been limited to the boards of business corporations or who do not understand the legal theory of trusts sometimes fail in their responsibilities as trustees of an educational institution because they do not comprehend the nature of the trust.

Board members are selected in many ways. In independent institutions, it has been the custom for the board to be self-perpetuating —that is, to have the power to elect new members to fill vacancies. In church-sponsored colleges, the appropriate church body names the trustees or controls their appointment by specifying qualifications. Among public institutions, practices vary—election by the public, appointment by the governor, selection by the houses of the legislature, or a combination of these. Overall, it has become rather common for charters to be amended to permit alumni to select some portion of the trustees, an instance of an interest group securing representation on the board.

The question of whether the faculty should be represented on the board has often arisen. A few colleges and universities have included faculty—Cornell is the outstanding example—and apparently with good results. In many foreign universities a faculty council is the board or dominates it through majority membership. The American practice is the opposite. But generally speaking, foreign universities have not demonstrated results superior to the American plan; in some countries these institutions are really controlled by a national ministry of education.

It can be argued that the primary work of an educational institution is the operation of an educational program; therefore, those who know most about the job—the professors—should be represented on the board. Many faculty have thus contended. Their principal concern usually is to protect academic freedom, about which they have a better understanding and feel more zealous than do lay trustees. They may, however, influence the board in other desirable ways because of their expertness of knowledge and because they must implement many of the decisions. On the other hand, a faculty dominated board can become highly introverted and lead the institution down the most conservative of academic paths until it becomes remote from the real world of affairs. (In mid-nineteenth century, the Oxford and Cambridge faculties had to be awakened from their self-complacency by the professional societies in Britain.[2])

The opposing contentions cite the advantages of having members who are personally free from involvement, who can look at the institution and its problems objectively and disinterestedly. The infusion of faculty into the board, it is said, can lead to muddy waters in administrative responsibility. If the lay members represent a variety of occupations, civic interests, and personal backgrounds, as they should, they can bring fresh perspective to education. Some boards have solved the problem of including professional educators by electing distinguished members from other faculties. The balance of argu-

[2] W. H. G. Armytage, *Civic Universities* (London: Ernest Benn Ltd., 1955).

ments favors having some educators on the board, whether from the inside or outside or both.[3]

Charters sometimes make special provision allocating to the faculty the responsibility for the educational program and for making and enforcing rules and regulations pertaining to the students, but this responsibility is always subject to the express or implied delegation of authority from the trustees.[4]

As the president of Antioch College, I found great merit in providing informal exchanges between faculty members and trustees, and in an earlier book I discussed the matter in connection with that college. Let me quote one passage from that book:

> Theoretically the trustees are the representatives of the public; by controlling policies and finances they insure that the institution is fulfilling its social duties and proceeding on a sound educational path. Actually this is what the Antioch trustees do. Not having to spend their two day session in minute discussion of college investments and administrative detail, they can find time to consider the real questions of the institution's role in society and its larger social usefulness. . . . These men and women provide an excellent sounding board not only for the present program of the college but for contemplated changes and additions. And, finally they represent to the college a cross section of public opinion concerning how far and how fast we can advisedly go in the direction of educational change. Antioch trustees are eager to get acquainted with both faculty and students and to find out how those inside the institution feel and think. The trustees meet regularly with the administrative council: they stay in faculty homes; they meet groups of the faculty informally for discussion; and joint faculty–trustee dinners are arranged. A feature of almost every meeting of the board of trustees is a report from the community manager or from a student group, usually followed by an informal discussion and question period. Thus the trustees can form first hand judgments about the Antioch personnel who are behind the policies and can function as part of the group.[5]

[3] For recommendations from the teachers' viewpoint see the reports of Committee T, American Association of University Professors, for various years.

[4] For examples of such charters, see Edward C. Elliott and M. M. Chambers, *Charters and Basic Laws of Selected American Universities and Colleges* (New York: Carnegie Foundation for the Advancement of Teaching, 1934); Charter of George Washington University, pp. 197–98; or Charter of the University of California, pp. 64–78, Art. I, III, V.

[5] Algo D. Henderson and Dorothy Hall, *Antioch College: Its Design*

The composition of most governing boards becomes skewed in favor of the upper socioeconomic segments of society. This situation leads to criticisms of the American practice of using exclusively lay boards and of the composition of lay boards. It has been said that trustees do not understand higher education and that many members are not even well-educated. The criticism continues along several lines: Membership is biased strongly in favor of businessmen, lawyers, persons of wealth, and older people; the boards, whose dealings are with problems that affect young people, have members who are too old and conservative when, instead, genuinely progressive leadership is required; large segments of the public—notably women, labor, and the lower socioeconomic classes—are not represented.

Thorstein Veblen, a voluble critic, stated the more extreme view of the faculty: "Plato's classic scheme of folly, which would have the philosophers take over the management of affairs, has been turned on its head; the men of affairs have taken over the direction of the pursuit of knowledge."[6] Veblen advocated that the professional job be left in the hands of the profession. His view has been shared widely by faculty. The Veblen–faculty criticism has a degree of consistency with that of certain students. The students of the Free Speech Movement at the University of California in 1964 and 1965 voiced criticisms of the establishment along the following line of reasoning:

> Most of the Regents, FSM leaders argued, are not qualified "academically" to govern a university; moreover, they are not non-political, as the Constitution requires. Indeed, the FSM suggested, it is naive to believe that this is possible. Regents have their own views of proper social policy, and their interests are intimately bound up with those views. Since most of the Regents are associated with large and successful commercial, industrial, or financial corporations, the FSM leaders reasoned, it is to be expected that they will strongly favor preservation of the status quo, will opt for stability and for little change of existing "power-relations" in society. The FSM charged the Regents with pursuing such interests by systematic attempts to suppress student political action for social change.[7]

for Liberal Education (New York: Harper & Row, Publishers, 1946), pp. 210–11.

   [6] Thorstein Veblen, The Higher Learning in America (New York: Sagamore Press, 1957), p. 57.

   [7] Terry Lunsford, The "Free Speech" Crisis at Berkeley, 1964–65:

This charge by students seems to add a dimension to the age old argument about academic freedom. Faculty who voice or publish criticisms of existing social behavior and structure invariably invoke the principles of academic freedom to protect their position. The purpose of academic freedom is to assure freedom in the search for truth. Some students apparently feel that there should be complete freedom in speech and social action. The issue of freedom goes beyond this discussion, but the Berkeley controversy sheds light on the problem of maintaining the essential function of a university, which includes inquiry into controversial issues, concern with finding solutions to the unresolved issues of the day, and a search for the good life.

A prime responsibility of the governing board is to protect the institution from the wrath of groups that would destroy the institution's function. The board must guard zealously the privilege of objective search and responsible advocacy regarding change in our society; it must support the administration and faculty in any endeavor to direct the motivations and energies of students of high intellectual ability and strong social sensibility into constructive educational channels.[8] At the same time, it must support the administration in avoiding impairment of freedom because of actions of individuals—faculty and students— whose minds are controlled by external groups or whose agitation is not the fruit of intellectual inquiry. The dividing line is sometimes hard to identify, but it is better to err in the direction of freedom than to stifle speech and action. Members of governing boards have a high duty to society to acquire for themselves a thorough understanding of the essential nature of an institution of higher learning. The very existence of the problem implies the great care that must be exercised in selecting board members. It suggests that members should be open-minded on controversial issues and objective in making inquiry.

In a nationwide survey of board members, Rodney Hartnett

Some Issues for Social and Legal Research (Berkeley: Center for Research and Development in Higher Education and Center for the Study of Law and Society. University of California, 1965), p. 126, mimeographed.

[8] There is much evidence that students who are articulate about the ills of society and who engage in social action are high in intellectual potential. See Paul Heist, "Intellect and Commitment: The Faces of Discontent" (Berkeley: Center for the Study of Higher Education, University of California, 1965), mimeographed; also his chapter "Uneasy Youth: Four Sketches" in Paul Heist (ed.), *The Creative College Student* (San Francisco: Jossey-Bass, 1968).

recently found evidence of much maldistribution in representation among trustees. His findings include the information that

> In general, trustees are male, in their fifties (though, nationally more than a third are over sixty), white (fewer than two percent in our sample are Negro), well-educated, and financially well-off (more than half have annual incomes exceeding $30,000). They occupy prestige occupations, frequently in medicine, law and education, but more often as business executives (in the total sample over 35 percent are executives of manufacturing, merchandising or investment firms and at private universities nearly 50 percent hold such positions). As a group, then, they personify "success" in the usual American sense of that word.
>
> Most are Protestants, with only four percent being Jewish and 17 percent Catholic, the majority of the latter serving on boards of Catholic institutions.[9]

These data confirm those published by Beck in 1947. At that time business and professional people held 71 per cent of the posts. The clergy, who a century ago controlled privately financed American higher education, in 1947 occupied only 6.6 per cent of the positions, and three-fifths of them were Catholic priests. Only 3.4 per cent were women.[10] Data collected in 1965 by Troy Duster showed that the median age of trustees is sixty and the median income between $50,000 and $75,000 per year. In his sample of 306 trustees, there were ten professors, eight clergymen, one Negro, and one labor official.[11]

People with these qualifications have many contributions (besides money)' to make to our colleges and universities. The question arises, without suggesting criticism of any individuals, whether the boards should not be more representative than they are. Would there not be value in giving larger representation to younger men and women who are closer in age to students and whose viewpoints would be less inhibited by acquired interests that they are accustomed to protecting?

[9] Rodney T. Hartnett, *College and University Trustees: Their Backgrounds, Roles, and Educational Attitudes* (Princeton, New Jersey: Educational Testing Service, 1969), pp. 19–20. A resurvey conducted by Hartnett, dated 12/30/1969 indicates that many institutions are revising the membership of their boards in line with my recommendations in this chapter.

[10] Hubert Park Beck, *Men Who Control Our Universities* (New York: King's Crown Press, 1947), pp. 130–33, 168.

[11] Data collected by Troy Duster, Center for Research and Development in Higher Education, University of California, Berkeley, 1965.

Women constitute more than 40 per cent of enrollments. Are women sufficiently represented on the boards? Blacks and men from organized labor are on the boards of only a handful of institutions; should these groups not be more widely represented? Such questions are pertinent.

Hubert Beck suggested a number of reforms: Fix a definite retirement age (with, perhaps, honorary trusteeship following); revise the method of cooptation so that the in-group does not always recruit from among its own type; use a principle of broad representation, for example, draw in—from the public—representatives of business, the professions, agriculture, and labor, and—from the universities themselves—faculty, alumni, and students; make the term of office at least four years and possibly six or eight.[12] All of these suggestions have merit. But before any of these approaches to the problem of representation can have any genuine impact, we must foster a change in the attitudes of the American people and especially of the in-group.

The data from Beck and Hartnett confirm an impression that board members too often are selected for their ability to make gifts to the institution. Much as the money is needed, this policy seems unwise. In the first place, it does not always produce the desired results. But second, and of greater importance, it puts into the hands of persons chosen on a single criterion the governance of institutions in which there is a substantial public interest. Our colleges and universities deserve to be governed by persons who have been selected on grounds other than sheer expediency. Legally, the board of trustees has the full authority and responsibility for the institution; there is no way in which it can avoid its charge. Customarily in higher education, however, a board delegates large areas of authority. The institution employs faculty members who have professional competence, and to them the board and president entrust the educational program—a practice that was started even before lay boards came into existence.

K. F. Burgess, a trustee of Northwestern University, defined three basic duties of trustees: to select a president and to have a hand in selecting other officers who might logically be in line to succeed the president; to declare the principal objectives and policies of the institution (with the president and other officers); and to preserve and invest the assets of the institution.[13]

[12] Beck, p. 147.
[13] K. F. Burgess, "The Trustee Function in Today's Universities and

Raymond M. Hughes, a distinguished university president, divided the responsibilities of the board into two categories, those that are specific and those that pertain to policies. As specific, he listed the responsibility to "hold all property, authorize the budget and budget changes, fix policies, appoint the president, and serve as a court of final appeal in all matters." The responsibility for policy formation, Hughes believed, should encompass the size of the institution, the general admission requirements, the campus and the buildings, the scope of the work, the policies affecting the faculty, the library, the chapel, scholarships, student activities, athletics, the fraternities and sororities, the residence halls, the placement of students and graduates, and alumni relations. To draw a distinction between the responsibilities of the board and of the faculty, he said,

> The faculty, under the board, teaches all students, determines all curricula and courses to be offered and classes to be taught, and assigns classes to teachers, determines grades, who shall graduate and who shall receive degrees, both in course and honorary.[14]

Most authorities agree that the selection—and sometimes the dismissal—of the president of the institution is the single most important responsibility of the trustees. This statement in no way implies that the trustees should not consult with the faculty and other parties concerning nominees for the position. A highly desirable procedure is to have parallel committees, frequent consultations, and final agreement on the choice. The faculty must recognize, however, that the final legal responsibility lies with the board. The board's duty to declare the principal objectives and policies of the institution derives from the charter. The basic objectives and policies are formulated at the time of the initiation of the institution; thereafter the board will ordinarily consult through the president with the faculty on these matters. Policies need frequent review and reconsideration if the institution is to attain fully its objectives in education and research. The prevailing structure of boards is awkward for faculty–board consultations, and their manner of holding meetings is a further barrier to communication. It is

Colleges," *Association of American Colleges Bulletin* (October, 1958), pp. 399–407.
    [14] Raymond M. Hughes, *A Manual for Trustees of Colleges and Universities* (Ames, Iowa: Iowa State College Press, 1951), p. 11.

easy to overlook the consultative step in the process of making decisions. This situation illustrates once again the desirability of fusing the interests of the several parties in a single board.

Inasmuch as the board holds title to the property of the institution, it feels keen responsibility for its preservation and management.[15] Money and people are two principal ingredients in the conduct of any operation. Governing boards must be kept fully informed by the president about the acquisition and status of funds and about the employment of key personnel. An important vehicle through which to plan, implement, and control a college or university is by controlling the use of funds—the budget. Usually the board requires that the budget be submitted for its inspection and approval. Although the board does not participate in the formulation of the budget, it discusses the guidelines for its preparation. In general:

> it can and should ensure that the budgetary operation has been conducted in a sound fashion, that it adequately reflects the aims of the institution, that economy is being practiced, and that there is balance and good sense in the whole process. Without second-guessing the president on specific items, the board may exercise a powerful long-range influence on budgets by throwing the weight of its opinion and judgment in one direction or another.[16]

A president is unwise not to seek the approval of his board on appointments to top-level administrative posts, especially those of provost, vice president, or dean. Boards sometimes claim the prerogative of identifying and appointing these officers. Such actions are inconsistent with the policy of acting through a single executive officer, the president; and if the president yields his own prerogative of recommendation, he is in for future trouble. Traditionally, boards have approved faculty appointments by voting a list, proposed by the president, which has been arrived at in collaboration with appropriate segments of the faculty. Under this plan, if a member of the board has any objection to an appointment the case can be discussed by the presi-

---

[15] For a more detailed discussion of the responsibilities of trustees, see Morton A. Rauh, *The Trusteeship of Colleges and Universities* (New York: McGraw-Hill Book Company, 1969). See also the report of the self-analysis made by the Board of Trustees of Columbia University, *The Role of the Trustees of Columbia University* (William S. Paley, chairman), 1957.

[16] "The Role of the College and University Trustee," (New York: Carnegie Foundation for the Advancement of Teaching, 1961), p. 11.

dent with the board. Board approval of appointments can be justified on two grounds: the courts have held that a board may not abdicate the responsibilities that are specifically given to it; and the president needs the understanding support of the board for the policies affecting faculty appointment and tenure.

During their one- or two-day meetings, boards usually are deluged with materials that require formal approval. One of these items might be a request to approve from fifty to two hundred faculty appointments, with most of the information about each person presented in a one-page "Who's Who" memo. Formal approval, based upon confidence in the recommending officers, is about all that can reasonably be expected.

Some boards have endeavored to open the way for more productive use of their time in considering basic policy and long-range planning. This approach is illustrated by an action at the University of Chicago. A trustee of Chicago, Laird Bell, expressed fresh views about functions of the governing board and described the attempt made at Chicago to delegate more complete authority to the president. He stated:

> Logically the trustees as the controlling body have the right—and in fact the duty—to determine what *kind* of education shall be offered. As custodians of the property and funds they are bound to see that they are devoted to the purposes for which they were given. They are free (subject to terms of their charter and endowments of course) to determine whether the institution shall be a liberal arts college, a technical school, a professional school or teachers college, whether new projects shall be undertaken, new schools or institutes created, existing ones liquidated, and so on. They also can and should have much influence on what might be called the tone of the institution. But once overall policy is decided it *ought* to be true that the educational experts should determine how the policy is to be implemented. Curricula, personnel, promotions, tenure and the like should be prescribed by the experts.[17]

The view expressed by Bell, a trustee, is similar to a position taken by Clark Kerr during his presidency of the University of California. At a meeting of the Board of Regents of the University of Califor-

[17] Laird Bell, "From the Trustees Corner," *AAUP Bulletin* (October, 1956), p. 354.

nia on June 18, 1965, Kerr made recommendations for reorganizing some of the procedures of government.

> He stated that his proposals assume that The Regents may be willing to reverse their historical approach to their responsibilities and delegate to the administration responsibility for all matters not specifically reserved for action by the Board. He pointed out that his proposals do not contemplate that the Regents would relinquish their traditional authority over and responsibility for the affairs of the University, but, rather, that they would devote their time to matters involving major policy decisions, major appointments, review of performance, etc.[18]

To illustrate the functioning of the board at Chicago, Bell described how the trustees passed motions giving the president authority to make all appointments to staff and faculty subject to departmental approval and to referral to the board of cases likely to involve public criticism. As a further illustration, he described the duality of responsibility of the chancellor (president) and the council of the university senate regarding the educational program: ordinarily they arrive at agreement, but in the event of a deadlock the matter is carried to the trustees for a decision. This role for the board seems to concur with Hughes' idea of using the body as a court of appeals.

Assuming that Burgess has defined aptly the basic functions of the governing board, and that Hughes has shed light on the functions as they are usually carried out, Bell and Kerr have offered constructive suggestions for performing the functions in a manner that makes optimum use of members' wisdom and energies. The ability to operate with the degree of delegation of authority that the views of Bell and Kerr implied will depend, of course, upon the mutuality of confidence that exists between the board and its executive officer. Because the functions of trustees of a college or university differ from those of directors of business corporations—their trust responsibilities, the authority delegated to faculty for academic matters, the intangible nature of the products of teaching and of research—new members should be given an orientation to their role. Probably this should be done by the president and the chairman.

At a number of public institutions, there has been discussion

[18] Minutes of the Regents of the University of California, June 18, 1965, pp. 1–2, as quoted in Lunsford, p. 132.

in recent years about whether board meetings should be open to the public, including representatives of the press, faculty, and students. The contention goes: The institution uses public funds, renders public services, and engages in educational activities of great importance to taxpayers, parents, faculty, and students; these matters should be debated in public, and the public should get its news direct from the scene of action rather than from news stories prepared by the institution. Further, some faculty and student groups contend they should have the privilege of addressing the board on matters of educational and environmental concern. On the other hand, it is argued: The board members are representatives of the public, the lay board existing for this very purpose; the president should be the spokesman about all internal matters; the presence of outside parties not directly responsible for decisions inhibits the agenda and the discussion; and the meetings can be conducted more efficiently when only board members are present and participating. In any event, it is said, the institution normally does publicize the principal actions taken at board meetings, and it publishes annual reports detailing both achievements and finances. The pressures for open meetings have gradually caused more public institutions to open their board meetings. In some states the law has been revised to require that meetings be open, although the privilege of holding executive sessions has been retained.

I contend that each college or university, generally each campus, must have its own operating board. The trend is in the opposite direction—to place many colleges under a single board and chancellor or president. Reflection reveals the deficiencies in this plan: Standardization for the several campuses results, shutting off innovation that relates to particular communities and educational goals; decisions are made with insufficient study and discussion and often seem arbitrary. More, if the majority of the members have a special bias—relating to academic freedom, for example—all of the institutions are immediately affected. When the board is politically appointed, the appointing authority has a simple chain of communication through which to exert political influence. It is impossible on such a board to have representation in accord with the theory of organization that seems to be best for colleges. I find it difficult to state arguments in favor of operational control through a single board and officer, because any such argument would have to relate squarely to control, placing it in hands that are remote from the problems and from the historic role of universities.

Yet I do not agree wholly with those who contend that the lay board system is archaic and should be abolished. There is a public interest, and there is a trust role that requires its own type of competence. The system, however, must be reformed. Our major universities cannot function well or in the best long-run interests of society if they are governed like business enterprises. None of our institutions of higher education can function well with absentee "owners." In a period of rapid change—and this means the foreseeable future— final decisions on policies and programs cannot be left wholly in the hands of persons who view as their major function the protection of taxpayers. Decisions about change must also be made expeditiously and not frustrated by bureaucratic involvement.

We need two reforms: a mode of selection of governing board members that assures a composition of interests which are both academic and related to public policy; and a mode of operation that assures delegation of authority to on-campus groups, with postaction reporting on the manner in which responsibilities undertaken have been discharged. The group participative model of governance, described in Chapter Twenty-One, has high potentiality for use.

CHAPTER *23*

COOPERATION AND
COLLABORATION

ₘₘₘₘₘₘₘₘₘₘₘₘₘₘₘₘₘₘₘₘ

Cooperation and collaboration among colleges and universities are not new ideas, as is apparent from reflecting on the history of Oxford and Cambridge, on moves to affiliate professional schools with universities, and on the responsibilities of our oldest planning–coordinating agency—the University of the State of New York. Today, however, there is a surge of fresh interest.[1] There is a new movement, and the cases number in the hundreds.[2]

Why is there this mushrooming of interest? Light can be shed

[1] Lawrence C. Howard (ed.), *Interinstitutional Cooperation in Higher Education* (Milwaukee: Institute of Human Relations, University of Wisconsin, 1967).

[2] Raymond S. Moore, *Consortiums in American Higher Education, 1965–66* (Washington, D.C.: U.S. Office of Education, Publication No. OE-50055).

272

on the question by referring to the statements of purposes of some of the newly organized efforts. The Associated Colleges of the Midwest state their purpose very simply: "The purpose of the Associated Colleges of the Midwest is to contribute to the educational effectiveness and operating efficiency of the member colleges."[3] The Committee on Institutional Cooperation (operated by the Big Ten universities and the University of Chicago) spells out three reasons for their effort:

> The goal of the CIC is to improve educational and public services while minimizing costs by: (1) encouraging cooperative efforts among the eleven institutions, (2) identifying specialized areas of teaching and research in which cooperative arrangements may be desirable, and (3) initiating cooperative activities in instruction and research, particularly in graduate areas, among the institutions.[4]

Of similar import but still more detailed in statement is the preamble to the bylaws of the Mid-America State Universities Association:

> Being mindful of the increased costs of higher education in all of its phases, including but not limited to the ever-increasing requirements for expensive equipment to properly conduct research programs, the competition with other segments of society for competent staff members, and the explosive interest in student enrollments, the state universities of Mid-America have entered into this agreement to achieve the following goals: (1) to promote the improvement of specialized facilities and programs at the several institutions and to prevent wasteful duplication in order that each university may achieve a high degree of excellence in all of its programs, (2) to make the specialized or unique educational programs of these universities available at resident fee levels to students on a regional basis, (3) to promote the cooperative use of unusual research facilities among the member universities, and (4) to *cooperate* wherever possible in providing a unified voice in bringing major research and advanced educational facilities and programs to the region.[5]

The new movement, however, is much broader than these illustrations indicate. Interdependence among colleges and universities is growing in many ways, and the various forms of cooperation can be

[3] Communication to the author from the Association, Chicago, Ill.
[4] Communication to the author from the Association, West Lafayette, Indiana.
[5] Communication to the author from the Association.

described more fully by categorizing the objectives to be achieved. They include, as one of the older forms, the fostering of a creed or the accomplishing of a mission. Examples abound among the colleges that are affiliated with churches; their aim is to provide higher education as a service of a religious body and to incorporate in the instruction and in the environment the religious and moral values of the church. A second type of cooperation has as its purpose obtaining financial support. Fund-raising groups of colleges, such as the college foundations that exist in nearly every state and the United Negro College Fund, are examples. Their aim is to attract wider public support for the group of member colleges than would be possible if each college worked alone. Third is a plan for the coordination of educational programs, resources and public services. I have already given examples: This type of consortium is based upon geographic location or similarity of goals, and it is growing rapidly. The aim is to provide a unifying organization that generates ideas for collaboration, assists in perfecting agreements among the institutions, and takes initiative in securing additional funds with which to carry out joint projects. A fourth type is one to foster the development of new or less favored institutions. Examples are the nurturing of a new institution by an older one and giving assistance to an institution to improve its quality or scope of services. The aim is to enlarge public services in higher education. Both the federal government and several philanthropic foundations have given assistance to developing colleges by arranging for the collaboration of other, well-established colleges. Fifth is organization to achieve political objectives. Examples are state planning–coordinating systems and interstate compacts for planning and coordination. The aim is to determine, at a high political level, public policy relating to the nature, composition, availability and support of higher education. Historically, colleges in America have been competitive rather than cooperative, and so there must be underlying conditions in our society that are stimulating this new activity. A reflection upon the aims, as defined here, will make some of these conditions obvious. But for further clarification I discuss certain of them in greater detail.

The diversity of institutions and programs has been a characteristic of American post-high school education. The report of the President's Committee on Education Beyond the High School gave much emphasis to the subject of diversity; and the report pleaded for recognition of continuing diversification.[6] Diversification will continue to increase for reasons relating to the continuing fragmentation of knowledge, the expanding number of differing occupations and professions, the upgrading of occupations, and the growing complexity of problems with which American society is concerned.

A few of the recent types of diversification illustrate the need. One of these is the development of two-year colleges, including technical institutes. Among the programs are those for numerous occupations for which two years of college provide reasonable preparation. One of the most interesting educational developments in the United States has been the introduction of this new level of occupational training that lies between the trade–vocational programs of the high school and the professional schools of the universities.

If we look back half a century or so, we realize that many new types of colleges have been introduced into our educational system. This elaboration of curriculum and division into specialized schools continues. Examples of new types of colleges include the New York State School of Industrial and Labor Relations at Cornell University, the Graduate School of Public and International Affairs at Pittsburgh, Monteith College at Wayne State University, Harvey Mudd College at Claremont, California, the Fashion Institute in New York, and the Air Force Institute of Technology at Wright-Patterson Field. Another innovation is the ethnic studies college initiated recently at a few universities.

Certain types of schools heretofore not included within higher education have been pressing for recognition as colleges. For example, the Bible schools in the United States have set up their own organization for the purpose of accrediting the schools as four-year colleges. These institutions, in turn, are bringing pressure to bear upon other accrediting agencies to recognize them as regular colleges. Business colleges (bookkeeping and secretarial schools), some of which have become nonprofit, have recently organized their own self-accrediting association; some of the members now want accreditation as colleges. We no longer have a simple structure composed of liberal arts colleges and professional schools at the post-high school level. Numerous two-year colleges and other schools with specialized programs are being admitted to the family of institutions in higher education.

[6] President's Committee on Education Beyond the High School, *Second Report to the President* (Washington, D.C.: Government Printing Office, 1957).

It is a matter of ordinary common sense that a particular college cannot and should not do everything for everybody. If a particular college must limit itself to a more homogeneous set of objectives and group of students, then clearly it is catering to limited needs. The needs of the student, on the other hand, are not so confined and extend beyond what the institution in which he is enrolled can provide. This presents an opportunity for interinstitutional services. Indeed, the need for the services and products of colleges and universities is so great that these institutions must complement and supplement one another rather than compete without regard to the welfare of all.

This principle was adopted by and became basic to the recommendations of the legislative commission that studied higher education in New York State in 1946–48.[7] The commission's study was comprehensive, and all colleges and universities in the state participated. The findings showed clearly that the critical needs rested at two points: one was at the freshman and sophomore level of college; the other was at the opposite extreme in medical education. On the other hand, at that time it appeared that New York State had among the private universities a sufficient number of high quality programs in the upper class levels and among the graduate and professional schools. The legislation, including that forming the new State University of New York, was directed at supplementing and complementing the existing facilities of the other colleges and universities, both public and private. In the intervening years much progress has been made in solving the two critical problems mentioned, but in the meantime others have arisen. With the passage of time, it has become clear that the state must also complement the private universities at the advanced levels by providing additional graduate and professional schools. Private philanthropy alone is not able to provide sufficiently for the more advanced programs in New York.

Conditions are now ripe for an era of cooperation between private institutions and public ones. The number of students seeking college today is sufficient to utilize much more fully than ever before all of the available facilities. Under the circumstances, severe competition would be wasteful if not disastrous.

When colleges, especially private institutions, seek philanthropic funds, they cannot depend as they formerly did on the gifts of one or a

[7] Temporary Commission on Need for a State University, Report, Legislative Document No. 30 (Albany: State Education Department, 1948).

few individuals. Federal policy on taxes has changed; the income tax now siphons off the disposable income of persons of wealth. The growth of incomes in the lower socioeconomic brackets has caused a dispersion of wealth. These changes in the national scene necessitate the tapping of a wider base of disposable income than formerly. Still another factor is the ability, through cooperative endeavors, to secure larger grants from corporations and foundations. In order to solve their financial problems to better advantage, the colleges have resorted to collaboration in raising funds from certain sources. College presidents join in solicitation much as they would in working for a community chest. For the business at hand, they have subordinated their rivalries, and they have found that it pays to do so.

The same reasoning applies when public funds are sought. The American public does not as yet place a sufficiently high value on higher education, but the potential for financial support is there because most parents want their children to go to college. The national income is large, but convenience and luxury goods and services compete with education for shares of the income. College and university officials need to collaborate much more fully than they have to date in educating the public about the values of higher education.

When colleges discover that they have a common desire to offer a program of benefit to their students and realize that combined efforts can conserve energies and resources or attract fresh sources, they often collaborate in organizing and operating the program. For instance, the Great Lakes Colleges Association offers programs abroad in several countries on four continents. A member college takes administrative charge of a particular program, but the operation is supported by all of the colleges and is open to students from all. The administration must be coordinated, and the Great Lakes Colleges Association has a president and staff for this purpose. Thus twelve colleges, banding together, voluntarily subordinate their own programs in order to operate a program for all.

Similar cooperative systems are beginning to evolve as a result of technological advances in storing and retrieving information. The computer is enabling data banks and central depository libraries to be established. Through computer connections, materials are instantly available to member institutions. Developments in the use of computers may profoundly influence the interlibrary services of colleges and universities. Indeed, instructional and library materials are becoming so vast and so proliferated, so expensive to maintain and house, that computerized collaborations are a must for the future.[8]

It may be argued that the public is too indifferent to higher education as a whole. If so, colleges are in need of better promotion with the public. Perhaps groups of colleges, rather than individual ones, should be publicized and promoted. By organizing for this and other purposes, the colleges of a region or those with similar programs can bring before the whole community, including parents and high school graduates, knowledge of the resources in higher education that are immediately at hand. The Kansas City Regional Council for Higher Education, although this is only one of its activities, is an example. All the colleges in such a grouping benefit, and the results can exceed those secured through intensive competition.

Let me turn for a moment to a discussion of public systems in higher education, a subject that is pursued more fully in the next chapter. When it becomes public policy in a state to provide opportunity to all youth to attend college, the means are usually found in geographically decentralized public colleges. At the immediate post-high school level, these are public community colleges. Complementing them are four-year public colleges and universities, also placed in strategic locations throughout the state. These colleges become a system because they form a geographic pattern that comprises the whole of the state. Together with the more complex universities, these colleges become part of a larger system of public higher education served by a planning–coordinating board. The function of this board is to develop a master plan for higher education in the state and to advise the governor and legislature about the best utilization of available resources. In matters of geographic area, tax base, commuting policy, scope or length of the program, and educational role, the individual college is subjected to constrictions within which it must develop its own policy and administer its own program. With these several illustrations in mind, two conclusions are justified: Cooperative attitudes and policies are to some extent displacing the highly competitive ones; and administrative attitudes and practices within each institution must be revised to take account of losses of autonomy and of fresh opportunities for joint endeavors.

[8] C. R. Carpenter, "Toward a Developed Technology of Instruction—1980," in *Campus 1980,* ed. Alvin C. Eurich (New York: Delacorte Press, 1968), pp. 236–53.

Trends toward cooperation and collaboration are having much impact upon administration. When functioning within a master plan for a state, the public college or university must do its own planning within this frame of reference. Its broad role is identified by a body that is higher in authority. However, accompanying this constraint is the positive encouragement given to the institution to develop its role as fully as possible. Longer-run planning is facilitated under the master plan because of the sanction given by the state, which later must provide the funds.

Cooperative arrangements imply that decision making is based on data available for the purpose. Colleges and universities have been notorious for acting without good information and secretively hoarding existing data. Under the changed relationship, much additional information must be collected, analyzed, and made available for decision making.

If interinstitutional cooperation is to be effective, ideas and efforts must be shared. The implementation of joint programs means that prerogatives need to be surrendered, concessions made, and certain resources shared. The frame of reference becomes the welfare of the whole group. Methods require time devoted to interinstitutional committee work. Formulas, often involving many compromises from original positions, must be found for carrying the responsibilities and participating in the fruits of the venture. There is, of course, an offsetting stimulation arising from the interactions.

Education is much affected by new methods of transmitting knowledge. These include new techniques of educating by television, the computer, and programmed instruction. Such innovations open the way for the use of the educational resources of one institution by others. A kinescope, a programmed syllabus, or a computer data bank can each be made accessible to an indefinite number of students in an indefinite number of colleges. Administrators must keep alert to and informed about these developments. They can prove to be of special value in enriching the teaching, in expediting research, and in reducing costs.

If it is assumed that a jointly sponsored project requires a director, this person will need to have a superior officer or committee to whom to report. On the other hand, his loyalty should relate to the whole group of colleges. The style of leadership in interinstitutional relationships cannot be authoritarian—nor can it function at the extreme of permissiveness. Negotiation is a necessary technique to secure agreements, but power confrontations would spoil the climate and lead to dissolution of the relationship. The administrators must be mutually supportive.

The advantages of consortia and of systems concepts and planning are obvious. One highly beneficial plan has been the interstate compact known as the Southern Regional Education Board. Through this agency, the several southern states, by jointly planning and financing programs, have been able to provide more adequately for education in such areas as medicine and veterinary medicine than they could have by dissipating their efforts state by state. They have also developed many programs for stimulating change and sharing the resources of the colleges of the region. Collaboration in planning results in clearer definitions of functional roles, each role being supportive of the whole. This principle becomes clear if one looks within a major university and sees there a dozen faculties, each carrying out its role, all together constituting a rounded offering in education and research. The principle can apply to relations among institutions. The problem confronting the institutions in a consortium or a system is to learn how to work together to achieve the desired objectives. Inhibitions and habits of action, a residue from past competitive practices, must be overcome. In a positive vein, the efforts must flow from a high degree of commitment to the declared purposes.[9]

The social press today is toward cooperation and collaboration, resulting in part from the need to use the available resources wisely. But it is also a consequence of the increasing complexity of society. Individualistic competition is becoming less effective in achieving goals. Cooperative planning and collaborative actions in meeting the needs of society are new dimensions in college operations.

[9] Ernest L. Boyer, "Interinstitutional Cooperation and the Exchange of Instructional Materials," in *In Search of Leaders* (Current Issues in Higher Education), ed. G. Kerry Smith (Washington, D.C.: American Association for Higher Education, 1967), pp. 281–85.

CHAPTER 24

COORDINATING
COMMISSIONS

꫞꫞꫞꫞꫞꫞꫞꫞꫞꫞꫞꫞꫞꫞꫞꫞꫞

In nearly all of the states, coordinating commissions for higher education have recently been established. The role of such commissions is still in the formative stage. With this thought in mind, I should like to analyze some of the problems arising from statewide controls. My thesis is that statewide planning and coordination are necessary today, but permanently established commissions have some limitations. They cannot be expected to do the whole job of long-run planning. Furthermore, it is a serious mistake to convert them into operating boards for higher education.

The bandwagon mood about compulsory planning and coordination of higher education causes noncritical observers to assume that a state board always provides itself with reliable data, always makes wise decisions, refrains from enlarging its power, and continues to be

281

noble and professional in its actions after the initial period of missionary zeal has passed. These assumptions, like mirages, never become realities. Let me recite some New York history to illustrate the point— The New York experience shows how a longstanding board can fail to keep alert to the public interest and how a power conscious government can suck institutions of higher learning into its vortex.

The Board of Regents in New York historically favored the development of private higher education. Initially, it received a directive to this end from the state. In 1784, as I have mentioned in Chapter Twenty-One, the state decided not to absorb King's (Columbia) College as a state college, but instead to create the University of the State of New York as a public agency, to stimulate the development of private colleges, and to supervise them in the public interest. The issue of a state university was raised several times again, and actions were taken that seemed valid at the time. One of these occasions resulted in the establishment of Cornell University, a private institution with several affiliated state colleges, whose programs are recognized as among the most outstanding in the nation. In 1912, discussion of the issue resulted in the initiation of a state scholarship program, the first of its kind and today clearly the best in the country.

In meeting another need that became evident during World War II, the Regents upgraded six vocational schools to college level technical institutes and recommended a program of twenty new institutes, to be geographically dispersed and to have diversified specializations of programs. Unfortunately, only five new institutes were authorized by the legislature. These eleven programs are of high quality and originality, and today they serve as models to the country's public community colleges, so many of which have been making stumbling efforts to establish technician training programs.

To the credit of the Regents, the initiation of state systems of colleges devoted to two objectives of major public interest—the training of teachers and the development of natural resources—should also be mentioned. Over the years, the development of New York's private colleges and universities has been superior; examples of their achievements are their excellent graduate and medical schools.

But here a general observation should be made. A public body, as well as a university, becomes satisfied with things as they are, and fails to grasp the implications of changes in social conditions and demands. T. R. McConnell has made this point about the University

Grants Commission in Britain[1]; it happened also to the New York Regents. The problem in both cases was the chronic one: the failure to be alert to changing concepts and needs. Both systems had been elite oriented, and times changed.

The new view of the mission of higher education in postwar United States was fully and forcefully advocated in the report of the President's Commission on Higher Education in 1948.[2] But a great clamor of opposition to the recommendations arose, much of it coming from educators, especially from certain presidents of major private universities. And among those who had blinders on their eyes were the Regents of New York, the state's public planning and coordinating board.

And that leads to another point: When a problem has become acute, it ordinarily takes a fresh study by a newly constituted body to define the issues, gather objective data, and make recommendations that challenge the status quo. The President's Commission made such a study and the study has had a nationwide impact. New York legislators, whose ears were closer to the ground than were those of the Regents, could hear the swelling demand for colleges and could sense the new feelings about discriminatory practices, and they therefore proposed a study in New York. It was made by the Temporary Commission on Need for a State University. That commission, which also reported in 1948, made recommendations that resulted in three items of legislation: the State University of New York Act, the Public Community Colleges Act, and the Education Practices Act.[3]

In late 1947, after two years of data collection and analysis, the commission was virtually ready to recommend the creation of a special board, subordinate to the Regents, which would devote itself to studying, planning, and coordinating higher education in the state, and would initiate a dynamic policy on public higher education. Some of the recommendations were for a statewide system of public com-

[1] T. R. McConnell, "The University and the State, A Comparative Study," in *Campus and Capitol: Higher Education and the State,* ed. John Minter (Boulder, Colorado: Western Interstate Commission for Higher Education, 1966).

[2] President's Commission on Higher Education, *Report* (Washington, D.C.: Government Printing Office, 1947).

[3] Temporary Commission on Need for a State University, *Report,* Legislative Documents Nos. 30, 31, 32, 33, 34 (Albany, New York: State Education Department, 1948).

munity colleges, new undergraduate state colleges, the possible development of a single campus university, and the establishment of state schools of medicine and dentistry. The rationale was twofold: The Regents were too involved with elementary and secondary education (where they had done a superior job) to give sufficient attention to higher education, so they needed to have a special commission to assist them; and the public was demanding a revised public policy for more active promotion of public higher education.

At this final moment in the life of the Temporary Commission, the Governor of New York intervened to change the nature and the status of the proposed board. Wanting political credit for establishing a state university, he changed the board into primarily an operating body. Although he observed certain legal prerogatives of the Regents in supervising all operating institutions, he reduced the relationship with the Regents to nominal proportions and moved the new board into the Executive Office. This move had several effects. It enmeshed the university within the departments of government, making it subject to civil service, the purchasing department, the architectural office, finance, and so forth. The operations of the numerous colleges were centralized in the state capitol, enhancing the tendency to make decisions there. The staff was loaded with operations and their planning activities, other than for the existing state colleges, were inhibited. And the usefulness of the board as a planning, coordinating agency of influence with private colleges and universities and municipal colleges was destroyed because the State University had now become a rival institution.

This political move also distorted the public community college movement. The Temporary Commission had recommended that these colleges be organized as a partnership between the local community and the state, with the majority of the board members chosen in the local community. The state board was to develop a master plan that envisaged districts encompassing the entire state, and to approve programs that would meet diversified needs. Its leverage in supervision was its administration of state aid, which was to be distributed only as the conditions of the state plan were fulfilled. The Board of Trustees of the State University of New York, however, virtually incorporated the Community Colleges as units within the university. This distortion caused local initiative and responsibility to be diminished in favor of control through the executive office of the state. Thus was created a cumbersome administrative structure that ignored the wisdom of British and American experience about institutional autonomy and that violated good principles of localized decision making in administration. To embed a university within the executive structure of the government is precisely the way not to operate it.

Fortunately, the State University has begun to extricate itself from the tentacles of the state offices—further studies such as the one by Henry Heald, Marion Folsom, and John Gardner (1960) have had an impact in getting the legislation revised.[4] Subsequent to the Heald report, which helped to reorient the state, the planning and implementation for the State University has made much more rapid progress. The plan to develop four of the campuses into major universities is timely and commendable. It remains to be seen, however, whether the university, with its centralized decision making, can achieve operating viability.

Yet the New York Regents have continued to issue plans for higher education, often in apparent duplication of and confusion with those offered by the Trustees of the State University. The justification for the Regents' activity is obvious: because of the background of history, during which private colleges and universities were given strong encouragement by the state, overall planning for higher education in the state must include the private institutions. The future relationship of the City University of New York to the state system has yet to be resolved. In all, statewide planning must encompass state, municipal, local, and private institutions, and this type of comprehensive planning cannot be done acceptably by the State University of New York. By its nature, it is inhibited from planning except for the state system. The Regents must continue with the larger planning and coordinating job.

State research, planning, and coordination of higher education is one thing; the centralized operation of public institutions is something very different. Before returning to the main theme, I should like to make a few comments on centralized operations. A college or university functions best within an environment that affords it an optimum degree of freedom. This is true because each faculty member is a professional man, and each student is an individual learner. Both

---

[4] Committee on Higher Education (Henry T. Heald, Chairman), *Meeting the Increasing Demand for Higher Education in New York State* (Albany, New York: State Education Department, 1960).

faculty and students are exploring for knowledge. Each person rises to his highest potential as he becomes self-directing and creative. Further, it is in the interests of society that institutions of higher learning—especially those engaged in substantial research—remain sufficiently apart from political and other pressures toward conformity that they can make critical judgments about and bring fresh perspectives to bear upon our accepted modes of functioning in society. It is false economy to use size and complexity of organizational fabric as tests of high achievement. The inevitable result is to introduce rigidities that tend to reduce the quality of the product and, indeed, the effectiveness of operation. It is interesting to observe that the University of California is moving to decentralize the operations of its several campuses in a manner consistent with the recommendations of the Byrne Committee,[5] for the purpose of diminishing constricting influences on the academic program.

What we really want from our institutions are fresh ideas and productive human beings. The contributions of colleges and universities to society greatly exceed the cost of their operations. This being so, we can well afford to be patient with some of their inefficiencies as they try to resolve the many intangibles and imponderables involved in achieving effectiveness in student learning and in faculty research. Let me emphasize again that effectiveness in reaching goals—rather than efficiency in using funds—is the predominant criterion for appraising a college. This effectiveness is best obtained through optimum utilization of the talents of professional men. Hence permissiveness, rather than authoritarianism, should be characteristic of the administrative structure. Coordination of operations on a broad basis may be wise and necessary; but coordination through the centralized approval of operational decisions is inefficient and duplicative, and it induces tendencies toward conformity and mediocrity.

Now I want to deal briefly with two additional issues. First, I believe that we need a great diversity of types, sponsorships, and geographic locations of institutions beyond the high school. I have contended that educational institutions seek conformity through emulation of the more distinguished schools; this situation results from the aspirations of faculty, most of whom are narrowly trained in their specializa-

[5] J. C. Byrne, Report on the University of California and Recommendations to the Special Committee of the University of California (Los Angeles: Regents of the University of California, May, 1965).

tions and do not take time to debate the comprehensive mission of higher education and the role of their particular colleges. Other educators have argued that centralized planning can also result in stereotypes and mediocrity among institutions. The universities in Italy, for example, are required to use uniform course syllabi, the reasoning being that this assures the government that all institutions will have equally good standards. San Francisco State College, in my opinion, has suffered a trauma (which began under John Summerskill's presidency in 1967) because of the terribly complex decision-making structure that characterizes the state college system in California. The constricting influences on innovation that result are unbelievable. In many countries, too, the central agency in education has had a fixation about segregating teacher education for the universities. This view, previously imposed on New York State, delayed for many years the logical and needed development of the state teachers colleges into multipurpose institutions. I think that one must conclude that, if we are to maintain diversity among institutions, we must keep open the channels of communication and allow influence from diverse sources in our society—including both recommendations from the pinnacle and innovations that arise through local initiative.

The second issue relates to finances. One argument for compulsory coordination on a statewide basis that seems to be persuasive with many persons (especially legislators)' arises from the problem of distributing equitably the limited tax revenues of the state. This is an important point, but it overlooks a more basic issue. The first concern of society should not be with distributing limited funds, but rather with assuring adequacy of funds for the things on which it places a high value. The question is: What value do we attach to the work of colleges and universities? In spite of the growing demands by youth for more education, the American public does not, as yet, fully accept the view that higher education is a wise investment for society. The portion of the gross national product that is devoted to higher education is very tiny when compared with the expenditures for luxuries, for highways, and for national defense. When we have sufficient urge to explore space or to aid foreign nations, we find the money to appropriate for the purpose. The distribution of appropriated funds should be a secondary concern, significant only in meeting needs in accord with their relative urgency and merit.

Once funds have been appropriated to an institution, that institution, accountable through its own operating board, must be permitted discretion in the use of them. Those universities that have had constitutional protection in this respect—Michigan, Minnesota, California, for example—have become distinguished. Private colleges of excellence also have this kind of freedom; at least there is a strong correlation between freedom to use funds as professional wisdom dictates and the academic results attained. On the other side, one can identify many colleges whose records are mediocre and which are hamstrung by control devices.

The line-item budget imposed by a state or city constitutes just this type of handicap. Inflexibility in operation arises because of the necessity to obtain bureaucratic approval of changes in expenditures. For example, in the state college system in California, it is necessary for a member college to seek the approval of the State Department of Finance on three kinds of variations from the approved line items: changes in functional use, the use of savings in salaries, and expenditures that will be reimbursed (nonstate funds). Thus, the college is literally frozen into a budget, the planning for which had to be made eighteen months in advance. The result is that important decisions on education, such as an innovation, are made by a clerk in the state finance office. And since the governor likes to effect savings in operations, requests are routinely declined. So the college is stymied, even though the legislature had initially appropriated more funds than the institution is permitted to use. These control devices, appropriate for the construction of highways, simply do not make sense when applied to higher education. To use them is to substitute the brain of a bureaucrat or a politician for the wisdom of professional men. The losers are our youth, the users of research findings, and society.

Thus far, my analysis has been directed largely toward pointing out the hazards of turning over to the administrative hierarchy of the state functions that heretofore have been performed—and in the opinion of some authorities performed well—by the institutions themselves. Here I have been concerned primarily with the internal functions of designing a program, developing learning experiences, employing a professional staff, and so forth. But we should also recognize the achievements made through voluntary collaboration among institutions: accrediting associations, professional societies, joint ventures in programs, concerted efforts to raise funds from private sources, and cooperative arrangements in making budget presentations to the legislature. Voluntary planning and coordination within a state has had its successes, as the case of Indiana so clearly demonstrates. The examples of colleges, both public and private, that are collaborating in programs voluntarily number in the hundreds.

I am also concerned with the manner in which bureaucratic agencies strive to enlarge their powers. In many states the original authorization for the state board has been amended. In some instances this has been done for the purpose of authorizing vertical coordination of programs in addition to horizontal coordination of geographically decentralized facilities. In New Mexico the original plan of budgetary coordination may have been too narrowly conceived. On the other hand, the present Texas law has its alarming aspects; there, a revision appears to give to the State Commission the power to reach within particular institutions and delete courses or remove departments. The intent of the provision was good—to eliminate unnecessary duplications—but provincials and superpatriots must be laughing up their sleeves at the golden opportunity thus offered to them. If the implied interference ensues, the cost to society of undermining the academic integrity of a university must be weighed against the cost of maintaining a few supposed duplications. The revisions in authority seem always to enlarge the power of the board; and once power has been gained, it is difficult to reclaim it.

Lest I leave the wrong impression, however, I shall now repeat my positive belief in state planning and coordination. I disagree with those who contend that colleges and universities, on their own, have done a sufficient job. Their individual self-interest prevents their full collaboration in statewide planning and coordination. But having been a state officer for planning and coordination (in New York), I am also realistic about what the state can and must achieve. No sufficient solution to the problem of planning and coordinating higher education at the state level has, as yet, been found. This is not surprising, considering the number of centuries during which universities have developed their autonomy in operations and their freedom in research and teaching. Both voluntary and political experiments to secure comprehensive planning and coordination need further trial and more intensive efforts to find viable methods. Thus, I plead for flexibility in attitudes and for pragmatic efforts to find solutions.

The essential dilemma is this: to find a means through which sufficient coordinated planning can be effected to meet the needs in education beyond the high school—and in doing so, to resolve the financial problems involved, and at the same time to avoid the creation or evolution of a centralized operating bureaucracy, integrally embedded within the administrative structure of the state. One crucial matter involved is: How can institutional problems of location, type, scope of program, and size, as well as of the financing of higher education, be recognized and treated as political issues without submerging teaching and research in politics and cumbersome administrative structures?

In its larger sense, provision by the state for higher education is a political issue. But the issue needs definition. It is a question of determining the overall needs of society for higher education and the ways of providing sufficiently for institutions so that they can meet those needs. The needs have two dimensions: the provision and distribution of facilities to ensure equality of opportunity in education, and the mobilization of resources behind programs where the demand is not large and the need for special facilities and high quality is great.

Perspective on the nature of the issue can be obtained by looking at the federal scene. The President's Commission of 1948 (under President Truman) made a study to help determine what the national public policy should be. The subsequent Republican Administration (under President Eisenhower) made its own restudy in 1957 and, to the surprise of many persons, predicted college enrollments considerably in excess of the 1948 estimates. (Interestingly enough, both the 1948 and 1957 estimates are now being exceeded.) It takes time to make adjustments in public policy. In this instance, responsibility for some of the delay in implementing the recommendations of these commissions must be attributed to the colleges and universities because of their differences of opinion about federal involvement. But an issue so ticklish and so important as that of the relations between private and public education requires public debate and repeated conferences aimed at producing viable solutions. These seem now to be materializing. In any event, the President and the Congress have recently taken significant steps toward putting much needed federal resources into higher education. Prefatory to this action, educators have been able to advance proposals that have been harmonious, and the public has had time to reflect upon and to come to accept a larger degree of responsibility at the national level.

These events portray well the political process at work. In finding an answer to the issue of the nature and scope of federal support for higher education, colleges and universities, voluntary associations of institutions, political parties, and agencies of government have all been involved. The same process applies at the state level. Although this process uses precious time when emergencies are at hand, the eventual solutions are not injurious to morale or to programs, and they attract support that is both constructive and lasting.

The heart of the matter at the state level has been that the legislatures and the governors, under pressure from all segments of society, have simply not had the time to give intelligent attention to each of the problems that has faced them. In higher education they have been confronted with many competing and sometimes conflicting demands, all of which require increasingly larger appropriations. Their attention has been directed to the needs of particular institutions rather than to the needs of the state as a whole. In most states they have not, heretofore, had an agency to which they could turn for objective data and advice. It is no wonder that both the legislature and the colleges have felt badly frustrated.

The state agency that is needed, then, is one that will advise the governor and the legislature in the performance of their responsibilities. The agency must have leadership of a professional type and staff sufficient to do its job. The staff must report to and work with a public planning and coordinating commission or board. The advantage of a board is that it can assess on a statewide basis the need for legislation and for appropriations, using data collected and analyzed by its staff and tempering its judgments through hearings. This preliminary planning can result in recommendations of great value to the governor and the legislature.

Such a board and staff should advance plans for the long-run development of higher education. For one thing, the states need to get away from giving their exclusive attention to annual or biennial appropriations. Higher education has been in a state of crisis because the future has not been sufficiently anticipated. For another thing, the state must coordinate the establishment of institutions. For example, if it is decided as a matter of public policy that the districts of public community colleges should eventually include the whole state, the authorization for a particular district should conform to the larger pattern; or, if a state decides that it wants programs of high quality at the advanced professional and graduate level, it must assure that the available resources are not dissipated through being used to support an oversupply of such programs. Of course such a board and staff, in the long run, can not resolve all of the crises in education. The experience in New York State, the experience with the University Grants Commission, and the experience with ministries of education so indicate. Occasional *ad hoc* commissions of the New York, Truman, Eisenhower, and Robbins (British)[6] type will still be needed.

Let us say yes to state planning and coordination of higher education. But in the long-run public interest, let us also prescribe carefully the responsibility and authority of the agency that is created. It should be advisory, focusing its interest on the initiation of legislation and on the determination of appropriations. It should be supervisory to the extent necessary to implement legislatively authorized plans and appropriations. But such a board must be prohibited from operating any programs of education or any institutions. It must be prohibited from controlling operations by indirect means, such as by requiring pre-audits or line-item budgets. Its primary role must be research and development in higher education.

If these conditions prevail, private colleges and universities can participate with confidence in the planning and coordinating efforts. Public institutions can do so as well and can join together, with the board, in preparing the governor and the legislature for their task in making decisions about public policy in higher education.

[6] Committee on Higher Education (Lord Robbins, Chairman), *Higher Education Report* (London: Her Majesty's Stationery Office, 1963).

TOWARD
INNOVATION

ᛞᛞᛞᛞᛞᛞᛞᛞᛞᛞᛞᛞᛞᛞᛞᛞ

America has benefited enormously
from its industrialization, which was based upon advanced technology.
Much of this progress has been due to the research in universities and
to the education of youth. Innovations in education—notably the
establishment of the land-grant colleges—have contributed enormously
to the productivity of the nation. The colleges and universities can be
proud of their record and the public should be aware of their debt to
these institutions.

Now we are in a period of change, and the colleges must again
innovate. As technology becomes more sophisticated, our society
becomes less able to distribute the benefits equitably. The more knowledge in science increases, the less the masses of the people benefit.
Sophistication in science has led to space exploration, atomic bombs,

and communication satellites, rather than to the eradication of poverty, hunger, and racial prejudices. Industrialization, spurred by competitive enterprise, has also led to dissipation and pollution of our natural resources. We Americans have become engrossed with materialism, which has warped our sense of values; yet, the disadvantages of blacks and other racial minorities lie heavily on our consciences. Youth are concerned with these social ills, concerned with the task of reorientation to human values. They believe that the colleges should define fresh objectives and devise new methods directed toward social change. I agree. But I do not endorse the disruption and violence practiced by the militant fringe. If persisted in, these methods will lead to suppression and totalitarianism. The alternative is the evolutionary approach, which is the democratic way. Because I do not believe that it is necessary to tear down before one can rebuild, I have suggested changes that can be made in a constructive manner.

The problem of values must be attacked in the liberal arts colleges. The concept of liberal education has been changed several times —at successive periods it has included the trivium and quadrivium, the Greek and Latin classics, the elective system, general education, and emphasis on the academic disciplines, to mention several variations. The problem now lies in the inadequacies of European culture in meeting the needs of a society based upon a plurality of cultures. White supremacy, for example, is now a matter of history. It is intolerable as a value in America and in the world today. The glorification of war, the pursuit of materialism, the belief in the infallibility of Christian dogma are other examples from our heritage that should be reexamined. Some Western values should be conserved—for example, respect for the worth and dignity of the individual. But liberal education must investigate all of human experience, whether Western or other, to find the best way to guide our lives. It is not enough to create peripheral institutes that study other cultures. We have those. Black and other ethnic studies serve purposes of discovering identity, infusing knowledge of the respective cultures, and adding to our store of knowledge. They, too, are inadequate solutions for the long run. We are one people in spite of differences in origins. The task lies in creating a synthesis of cultural knowledge through which we can educate.

To achieve this result, it will be necessary to reorganize the faculty. The emphasis needs to be shifted from refining knowledge in the disciplines to developing the good life in a comprehensive way.

This shift means also a change in the reward system for faculty services. The liberal arts colleges, especially those institutions with doctoral programs, are seriously handicapped by the manner in which the faculty erect walls between disciplines. Liberal education becomes the prisoner of the graduate faculty, who are devoted to advanced study and research. This focus of attention means that the unity of liberal thought and culture is minimized and specialization is maximized. In addition, students lose contact with the creative teacher-scholars. If we could start again, I question whether we would organize undergraduate colleges by departments. Academic specialization should be a characteristic of the doctoral program, not of undergraduate study. But even here, research problems today do not fit comfortably into administratively devised pigeonholes. The creation at major universities of centers and institutes—often many dozens of them—reveals the interdisciplinary character of research. Graduate and professional schools should reorganize their curricula to permit flexibility in study by their students and in research by the professors. Undergraduate education should emphasize broad divisions of knowledge, rather than narrow ones.

The cluster college, an aim of which is to divide the liberal arts faculty into small, integrated teaching units, shows promise as a reform. Under this plan it is also necessary to separate the graduate function from the undergraduate one. The faculty needs to compose one unit—focused on liberal learning—for the cluster college and a different unit—based upon disciplines and professional knowledge—for their research and advanced teaching. This reorganization of faculty should permit the inclusion of appropriate faculty from the professional schools in the graduate operation. Graduate schools have been dominated by the faculty in the arts and sciences. But doctoral programs in such areas as engineering, business administration, and education have grown large and should be represented in the decision-making.

The public community college needs refinement of its role in serving post-high school youth and the needs of its community. It has special usefulness in combining cultural and vocational objectives. It can implement the egalitarian ideal by serving the needs of people of many differing interests, ages, and stages of learning. The community college can also contribute greatly to the cultural development of our urban centers, an urgent need.

296 THE INNOVATIVE SPIRIT

The two-year college, however, cannot meet all of the needs of the urban center or the metropolitan region. Yet I do not favor extending the junior college curriculum and function vertically. To do so would distort the role of the college, for the faculty would then devote their energies to the more prestigious (in their terms of reference) specializations and to emulating the senior institutions. There is needed and there is room for additional institutions at the senior level to devote themselves to urban problems and services. This should be a function of regionally located colleges whose major roles are education and public service rather than research. The number of universities needed to emphasize research and to offer doctoral programs is not large; and it is a dissipation of the resources available for these advanced programs to spread them among too many institutions. California, for example, needs a half dozen well-financed, -equipped, and -staffed major campuses; it does not need two or three dozen. Each of the regional state colleges should devote itself to its community at the undergraduate and masters levels. Before this goal can be achieved, the faculties must redefine their goals, and the institutions must revise the incentives they place before the teachers. Since I am not optimistic about making rapid progress on this front, I have offered suggestions for the organization of new urban-focused colleges—suggestions for a curriculum based upon studies of the community, occupational training, and the study-and-work plan, and for plant design.

One of the great disparities among people is in the benefits they derive from our affluence in medical services. Advances in medical knowledge have been significant, but the benefits flow to those who are able to pay well for the professional services. The poor get very little. The medical schools have contributed to the maldistribution by needlessly limiting enrollments, by favoring applicants with scientific interests, by emphasizing research and specialization, and by motivating students toward the fee-for-service system of medical practice. We are in a crisis, the solution to which is a reorganization of health services. Medical schools need to change by revising their admissions policies, the ratio of students to faculty, and the environment of the schools. More, much more of the energies of the faculty should be devoted to teaching; to accomplish this change the incentives need to be changed. A few schools have initiated innovations that deserve emulation by others. Among the promising innovations are some that provide new categories of health personnel—for example, nurse pediatrics practitioners. The costs of medical education can and should be reduced, mainly by abandoning the obsolete shibboleths about the faculty-student ratio.

Engineering schools have been graduating good technicians and technologists, but the engineers of the future must be concerned with the impacts of technology on people. Engineers have contributed heavily to the exploitation of natural resources and to pollution. As exploitation policies are succeeded by conservation, and conservation by resource management, an engineer of different ethical outlook and theoretical background is required. He must recognize that the social interest is dominant, overriding the interests of private enterprise. Engineers must also be concerned with systems, which requires a comprehensive education integrating a number of disciplines.

I have used medical and engineering education as examples of professional schools that have been affected heavily by technological change. There are others, such as agriculture, architecture, business administration, and dentistry. Each school has new challenges arising from the social crisis, whether to assist blacks to become better educated, to influence professional ethics, or to learn to use the computer fully. Graduates of these professional schools help solve problems, and each profession has a reasonably clear role. But many social ills today are complex and require a team effort for solution. A team is often composed of persons from several specialties within a profession or from each of several professions. Team efforts require training for this purpose.

The computer is revolutionizing the solving of these comprehensive problems because of its ability to compose many variables. An illustration is the attack on the complex problems of congested population areas; here sustenance, health, education, and transportation are interrelated. Analysis made by teams of experts, using the computer, is the only method that achieves results. Students can be prepared for this work through the study of simulation games and systems problems. The game is essential also in preparing persons to become managers of complex enterprises, institutions, and government, for the game can simulate large and varied operations over a period of years.

We are subjected to so much indoctrination—in education as well as through television, newspapers, and political pronouncements—about private enterprise that it becomes a threat to the security of an institution, its faculty, and students to voice any criticism of the practices of private enterprise. But the United States has emerged from its pioneering, exploitive stage. As the social consequences of actions loom ever larger, resolution must be found by reconciling the interests and freedom of the individual with those of the community of people. The problem is to retain the advantages of enterprise and freedom. On our highways we can see that discipline and concern for others are necessary to maintain freedom for the individual driver. So it must be in a system of private enterprise. We must therefore educate not toward materialistic goals and undiscriminating support of free enterprise but rather toward good human relations and social welfare. This change is partly a matter of orientation in ethics, but it also requires training in the dynamics of group processes.

To get perspective on controversial issues, we need to recall the furor that was aroused when the colleges began to teach evolution. The colleges had been very much under the control of religious institutions and the clergy. Religious dogma was accepted and was passed to the young through required courses, daily prayer, and chapel. When Thomas Huxley lectured at Johns Hopkins in 1876, there was an outburst of public denunciation of the college. Not only did he discuss the theory of evolution but the meeting was not opened with prayer. The college was clearly blasphemous. Today we know better. It is the business of colleges to examine all questions, controversial and otherwise. It is in the public interest that they do so.

Another problem, however, exists because of the relative newness of the social sciences, which are just beginning to evolve useful theory. The findings of science were once objected to strenuously, especially by the faculties devoted to the classics and to religious study. Science was accepted at Oxford and Cambridge only after the learned societies forced the issue. It entered Harvard and Yale by the back door; but the land-grant universities based their research and curricula on the new sciences and technology. Now technology, with its vast financial support, has left the humanities in the shadow. This imbalance should be corrected, especially in the search for values. But the social sciences are now in the frying pan of public opinion, and here additional effort must be made. The greater the controversy, the more the need to expedite the search for solutions. The reform in ethical outlook cannot be achieved merely by adding a course in ethics. It must be based upon the systematic inclusion of relevant knowledge from the social sciences.

I advocate the generous use of problem-solving as a means of learning. I refer not only to problems that have known solutions but also to problems that require analysis and an evaluation of proposed solutions. In medicine, for example, knowledge has increased so much and often is so specialized that it is no longer possible to fill a prospective doctor with medical knowledge and to turn him out as a finished practitioner. He must be trained as a problem solver because, in the future, his ability to diagnose cases and to search for solutions will determine his competence. He must continue as a student, and the medical school (through a continuing education program) must assist him. Another example of problem-solving in education is the use of the urban situation as the frame for learning in new urban-related colleges. Black students, for instance, are deeply concerned about the black ghetto and are motivated to change it. They can see the relevance of study to their lives and to the development of their communities. This motivation can be highly effective in learning. Coupled with the study-and-work plan, the study of the community can draw upon the disciplines for theory and practice. The social problem of the urban center is so serious as to make departures from traditional education a must.

The change in student status is revolutionary, for the paternalism of the nineteenth century is dead. The students of today are much more mature, both in age and in attitude, than they were before. They are conscious of their power and motivated to participate in decision-making. The implication is that Mickey Mouse student governments have become ineffective. Representatives of the students must be brought into the mainstream of college government. The regulation of morals by rules is also no longer feasible. In addition, due process for students is essential and is now protected by the courts. But as rules are dropped, personal counseling takes on new significance.

In college government, I draw a distinction between policy-program formation and administrative implementation. Administrators generally have tried to do both by creating an oligarchy of presidents and vice-presidents who run the institution. This change is not wholly their fault because governing boards, and indeed governors, press them to do this. The size of institutions also creates the opportunity and sometimes the necessity for autocratic decisions. However, in the long run, the best education takes place when the men trained for the purpose—the professors—and the direct consumers of the education—the students—have an important voice in determining policy and program. I say voice because I think that the academic administrators also have a highly important contribution to make.

Hence, I advocate the replacement of the business-inherited form of college government with a new model—the group participative plan. A university differs radically from a business enterprise, and this difference has not been sufficiently taken into account. For example, in education, tangible resources are used but to obtain intangible results. Effectiveness in student learning or in researching a hypothesis is the controlling criterion, not the efficient use of money or the production of a profit. The group participative plan, which I have described for its inclusion of all interested parties—students, faculty, administrators, and trustees—meets the need.

Thus it is time for a change in college government, and the change must begin with the governing board. The corporate form is useful, but the composition of the board can be revised. Nearly all boards are composed of older men who are WASPs, affluent, and strongly oriented toward business and the status quo. They perform as absentee owners and protectors of the taxpayers. Under the group participative theory, the boards would be revised to include representatives from various segments of the public and also educators and consumers of education.

Another change that is needed is in the presidency. Presidents have become managers and have lost their role as educational leaders. The men of the past whom we perceive as strong leaders—Charles Eliot, Daniel Gilman, Henry Tappan, William Rainey Harper, and Benjamin Wheeler, to mention a few—had a very different style of leadership. They wrote vigorously about education, they lectured on public issues, they presided over their faculties, and they communicated with students. The increasing size of institutions is partly responsible for the change. But the point is that the functions should not be lost. Our colleges badly need educational leadership. Here again, the distinction made above is highly important. If presidents caused their staff to implement decisions, they could reorder their activities to stress the policy-program function. And here they could work with faculty and students, not in town meetings, which would not be practicable, but through representative councils. To effect a change in orientation and training a number of universities have initiated new programs to train college administrators. As of now, these programs have grown

rapidly and contain questionable practices. Hence I have offered proposals for a reassessment of aims and for strengthening these programs.

Formerly colleges, both private and public, were individual
to their own hill top and carried on without reference, other than
friendly emulation, to other colleges. In a way, this situation is natural
to education because education occurs between teacher and student.
However, the demand for higher education and for money with which
to operate has become so vast as to necessitate a change. A state must
think of the colleges that it authorizes and supports as a system. Both
private and public colleges now find advantages in cooperation and in
collaboration. By a system I mean a group of institutions that are
planned together, are coordinated in development and are each given
a functional role. For these purposes, nearly every state now has a
commission on higher education. The state boards are needed but are
also dangerous because of their tendency to operate the system. The
urge to administer is often encouraged by the governor because he desires political control and credit. Such operation, however, is fatal to
the educational process as we perceive it. The role of the state, both
the commission which recommends and the legislative and executive
branches which determine public policy, is precisely that of determining
overall policy. The individual institutions must be left free to educate.
On their part they must resolve to perform their defined role and not
to try to substitute a role they desire because of their place in the pecking order. Unless the role of the planning-coordinating commission is
both carefully defined and limited, we shall develop in the United
States fifty ministries of higher education. The performance of ministries in those countries where they try to run the universities is not
sufficiently impressive that we should emulate the system. The movement for collaboration among colleges is dynamic, and there are now
literally hundreds of examples. I have offered a categorization of institutional problems which consortium relationships can help solve.

The colleges and universities have tended to be defensive about
their programs and policies rather than open to ideas for change. The
times require change. The solutions to problems must be found in
action, even if it involves departures from tradition. The situation calls
for an innovative spirit.

INDEX

304

BURGESS, K. F., 265, 269
Business administration, education in, 124, 125, 126, 156
Business colleges, 275
BYRNE, J. C., 268n

C

CADBURY, W. E., JR., 74n
California Master Plan, 54
California Polytechnic College, 100
California, University of, 154, 241, 268, 285, 288; at Berkeley, 91, 182, 262; at Davis, 126; at Los Angeles, 127, 128, 156, 157, 175; at Santa Cruz, 83, 84
California, University of, Master Plan for Engineering at, 149
CAMPBELL, R. F., 224n
CARMAN, H. J., 74n
Carnegie-Mellon University, 122, 123, 128
CARPENTER, C. R., 278n
Case study, 124, 154
Case Western Reserve University, 120, 128, 134, 136
CHAMBERS, M. M., 185n, 261n
Change, social, 36–40, 42, 44–45, 49–50
CHASE, E. T., 146
Chicago, University of, 78, 79–80, 121, 125, 130n, 174, 195, 208, 241, 268, 269, 273
Chile, University of, 48
Chulalongkorn, University of, 111
Cincinnati, University of, 19–20
CLARK, B., 66n
COGGESHALL, L. T., 130, 132
Colleges: administration of, 214, 230, 235–236, 279, 299; administrators of, 216–219, 221, *see also* President, college; change and, 36–38, 42, 188, 220–221, 223; conflict in, 203–205, 221; control of, 245; as corporations, 245–247, 258; image of, 200; origins of, 245–247; role of, 183, 205, 215, 234; trustees and, 247–248, 256. *See also* Universities
Colleges: cluster, 84–85, 285; community, 55, 61–72, 235, 276, 284–285, 295; land-grant, 96, 111,

235, 293; liberal arts, 73–86, 294; state, 56–57; urban, 87–102, 235, 296
Colorado, University of, 90, 123, 141, 142
Columbia, University of, 53, 78, 79, 81, 175, 219, 241, 246, 267n, 282
Commissions, coordinating, for higher education, 281, 289; administration and, 288–289; change and, 282; finances and, 287–288; politics and, 290–292; role of, 281, 283; studies by, 283–287
Commission, Temporary, on the Need for a State University (New York, 1948), 276, 283–285
Committee on Higher Education (Robbins), 292
Committee on Institutional Cooperation, 73
Commonwealth Fund, the, 141
CONANT, J., 79
Cooperative Urban Extension Center (Buffalo), 95–96
COPE, O., 133n, 135
Cornell University, 260, 275, 282
CROMWELL, L., 156n
Curricula, 9–10, 68–71, 78–84, 100, 118–121, 123–124, 136–140, 155–157, 164–165, 175, 277–279

D

Dartmouth College, 246
Data processing, 122–123
Degrees, academic, 89, 123, 159
Delhi, University of, 111
Denver, University of, 127
DEWEY, J., 14, 75, 169
DIMOCK, M. E., 225
DODDS, H. W., 216
DOI, J. I., 112n
Doshisha University, 105
DRESSEL, P. L., 83n
Duke University, 121, 123, 135, 142
DUSTER, T., 264

E

ECKERT, R. E., 207n
Ecumenism, 45–46
Education, 22–23, 45, 62–63, 96, 112n; change in, 4–5, 19, 27–35, 62; de-

ficiencies of, 13–14, 19; experience, practical, in, 12, 17–18, 24; general, see General education; role of, 9, 16, 56–57
Education Practices Act, 283
Educational Facilities Laboratory, 101
ELIOT, C., 222, 300
ELLIOTT, E. C., 261n
Emory University, 127
Endicott House, Summer Study on Medical Education at, 133
Engineering, education in, 18, 19–20, 30, 148–159, 175, 297
ESKOW, S., 72n
Ethnic studies, 94. See also Black studies
Experience, practical, 13, 15–19

F

Faculty, 91–92, 161; academic freedom and, 205–206; administration and, 203, 213; change and, 44–45, 122, 180–181, 208–209, 242, 294; criticisms of, 50–51; ethics of, 195; evaluation of, 206–208; incentives for, 191–196; loyalty and, 201, 203; morale of, 219; motivations of, 75, 190–191, 196, 197–199; professional societies for, 196, 201, 202; qualifications of, 71–72; role of, 200–202, 228; salary of, 193–195, 198–199
Fair Education Practices Act (1948), 127
Fashion Institute of Technology, 88, 275
Federal City College, 94
FELDMAN, K. A., 166n
FLEXNER, A., 252
Flexner Report, 130
Florida State University, 241
Folk schools, Danish, 96
Ford Foundation, 175
FORD, L. C., 141n
Freedom, academic, 43, 46, 205–206, 263
Free Speech Movement, 182, 262

G

GAFF, J. G., 84n
GALBRAITH, J. K., 252

Gallup poll, 131
GEE, H. H., 145
General Education, 75, 77–81, 93, 99, 110–111, 162–163, 175
Generation gap, 14–15
GERARD, R. W., 133–134, 135–136, 137–138
Germany, universities in, 252–253
GILMAN, D., 222, 300
GINSBERG, B., 174n
GORDON, T. J., 27n, 150
Great Lakes Colleges Association, 277
GREENE, T. M., 95
GREGG, R. T., 224n
GUTHRIE, E. R., 207

H

HALL, D., 42n, 82n, 261n
HAMILTON, C. V., 54n, 93n
HARPER, W. R., 222, 300
HARRELL, G. T., 116
HARRIS, N. C., 70n
HARRIS, R., 131n
HARTNETT, R. T., 263–264, 265
Harvard University, 78, 79, 127, 156, 246, 252
Harvey Mudd College, 275
HAWDEN, C. T. M., 95n
HAWKES, H. E., 219
HAYES, A. M., 174n
HECKMAN, D. M., 241n
HEISS, A. M., 83n
HEIST, P., 118n, 263n
HELMER, O., 27n, 150
HENDERSON, A. D., 13n, 42n, 45n, 75n, 76n, 82n, 206n, 207n, 233n, 261n
HICKS, F. W., 255n
HILBERRY, C., 86n
Home economics, 32
Hong Kong, Chinese University of, 106
Hong Kong, University of, 105
HOULE, C. O., 133
HOWARD, L. C., 272n
HUBBARD, W. N., JR., 131, 140n
HUGHES, R. M., 266, 269
HUMBOLDT, W. von, 252
HUTCHINS, R. M., 19, 80, 208, 209n
HUXLEY, T., 298
Hydro-Electric Power Commission, 42